THE
CHÂTEAU
Forever Home

T0349951

Also by Dick and Angel Strawbridge

A Year at the Château
Living the Château Dream

THE
CHÂTEAU
Forever Home

Dick and Angel Strawbridge

SEVEN DIALS

First published in Great Britain in 2023 by Seven Dials
This paperback edition published in 2024 by Seven Dials,
an imprint of The Orion Publishing Group Ltd
Carmelite House, 50 Victoria Embankment
London EC4Y 0DZ

An Hachette UK Company

1 3 5 7 9 10 8 6 4 2

ISBN (Mass Market Paperback) 978 1 3996 0316 4
ISBN (eBook) 978 1 3996 0317 1
ISBN (Audio) 978 1 3996 0318 8

Typeset by Input Data Services Ltd, Bridgwater, Somerset

Printed in Great Britain by Clays Ltd, Elcograf S.p.A.

www.orionbooks.co.uk

To Arthur and Dorothy,

Once upon a time we escaped to a château. You were just babies then and we said to you both 'I wish this moment could last forever' but somehow every moment since has been just as magical.

Thank you for being you. We are so proud of your passion, love and fearless imagination.

We love you 'infinity plus one'.

Your gushy Mummy and Daddy.

XXX

Contents

Preface

From the bottom of our hearts, thank you for coming along on our family journey and, of course, for buying the book! Many of you have supported us from the early days and, whilst we have travelled far, it's fair to say it has also been a sprint. It's easy to forget that it was only eight years ago, in 2015, that we moved to the Pays de la Loire in France with our two children, Arthur and Dorothy, and 'dared to do it'.

Our dream was to create a multi-generational family home that in time could sustain itself and allow us all to be together. That same year, my mum and dad, Jenny and Steve, joined us and together we began our adventure in our beautiful, run-down 150-year-old château. Back then, we dreamt of turning the château into our forever family home, whilst also creating a business that could support us and allow us to continue renovations. But never in our wildest dreams could we have envisioned where this journey of a lifetime would take us.

Angela and I are meant for each other, and it's only because in 2010 we found each other, and we are a strong team, that we could change our lives and move to France. As a couple, we had already built our lives and businesses in England, but when we decided our future, we went all in, with every penny we had, to create our new life. In parallel with continuous renovations, we have built a business and done our utmost to provide our children – now nine and ten years of age – with a loving environment to allow them to thrive and have a balanced start in life. My mum has a saying that 'the harder you work, the luckier you get'. We know we are very lucky people. Maybe it's because over the years, living at the château has been a lot of hard work, and at times it's been bloody exhausting.

Like many, our journey over the past few years has been unexpected and challenging, but amidst the adversity, we have always been positive. In this book, we look forward to sharing how some very personal dreams of ours were achieved.

We are always looking to our family's future, especially Arthur and Dorothy's. Every decision is made with them in mind and, even during the most frenetic times, we see every adventure we have, every little discovery, every task we complete as an investment in our forever home or a memory to be captured.

We feel incredibly excited for the future and with so many foundations laid, we know it's just the beginning of endless new adventures, which we look forward to sharing with you. Just in case you haven't worked this out, when you see writing in bold, that's me, Angel, telling a story.

And when it looks like this, that's me, Dick.

New Rhythms

Arthur was first to wake up. He came running into our room sleepy eyed and cheeky faced. 'Pinch and a punch for the first day of the month!' Before we could say 'white rabbit' he ran off.

Sunday 1st January 2023 was our eighth New Year's Day here in our forever home. The feeling of happiness, contentment and knowledge of the foundations we have laid for our children and future generations we felt that morning meant we had done what we set out to achieve. As I offered Dick a coffee he said, 'Yes please, beautiful. Who has told you they love you today?' I smiled and knew that he felt that too.

We sat on our bed and chatted. I asked Dick if this New Year's Day felt different and he said it did. We had no real deadlines this year or urgency to renovate. Whilst we most certainly still had projects to finish, and to start, after eight years of non-stop renovations, the château was looking rather lovely. With many of the rooms now fully restored and decorated, our roof and render refurbishment completed, plus our windows underway and even a few coppers left over, we felt light as a feather. We joked about retirement and then giggled even harder because this year was looking rather full with weddings and guests booked. With that, Arthur and Dorothy came running in to see what the laughter was about and then the four of us sat together and planned our day.

Angela, Arthur, Dorothy and I saw in 2023 together. New Year's Eve had been spent observing our Strawbridge tradition of looking through all the photos on our various devices and reliving the highlights of what had been a very full year. The château had reopened for business; we'd completed major works and we had concluded the ninth and final series of our family journey *Escape to the Château*. The finale party was just so full of joy and fun, and having said all our goodbyes to loved ones, we tidied up and snuggled down for a peaceful Christmas.

Tomorrow was a bank holiday, we had one more day of the holidays before Arthur and Dorothy had to go back to school, and as the first day of the year was a Sunday, we were having a doubly relaxing start. We decided to have our favourite slow family brunch before we completed the ceremony of packing school bags and pencil cases for a new term.

We all ventured downstairs to collect Petale who was waiting for us, tail wagging and eyes exuding excitement. Now the family were all together, we could continue our favourite morning routine that we only get to do all together on days like this when there is more time. In the cloakroom, everyone was slowly putting on their jackets and scarves, still a little dozy and very much in a 'non-school day pace'. It was sunny but nippy, the type of weather that catches your first breath. As we walked across the gravel, we could see the white of our breath and the children's cheeks were starting to get rosy.

First on our list were the geese. We had five originally but now there were just four – during the Covid lockdown one of our neighbours did us a favour and then in passing mentioned he was struggling to find a goose, so Dick swapped kindness for a goose. On this crisp January morning, the children set about their tasks. Today was a divide and conquer kind of day.

Dorothy opened the wooden 'Frankenstein' gate that we had all grown to love. Considering our little girl was only four when we got the geese, and was literally terrified by their squawks, I felt proud to see that she was growing into a real country girl. At the same time, Arthur was collecting the feed from the woodshed. The bin for the geese food is very tall, but so is our boy now. In fact, he's become so tall that he was able to kiss my forehead one morning over the holidays and I thought, 'Oh it's happening, he is overtaking me!' As the geese said their loud goodbyes, we walked around the side of our outbuildings, past the old piggery.

As we passed, we talked about how this was going to be Dick's first project of the year – to turn the piggery into his art studio. I remember this made me glow. Firstly, how wonderful to do a project with no real time pressures. And secondly, about time my husband did something for himself (a concept he truly struggles with)! Dick has worked tirelessly for years, always putting the family and business first, and whilst I know retirement is not in his nature, the thought of him pottering over here, painting, writing or even fixing up an old car, was a vision of the future I loved to have.

Last on our list of morning duties was the chickens. As we

walked up to their rainbow-painted shed they made lots of noise and they were literally pushing their way out as Arthur opened the hatch. He collected a couple of eggs, which I took control of, and then we all pottered back to the château, picking some fresh mint along the way.

It was nearly 09.00hrs by the time we got back into the château, and it had been fresh enough to blow away any cobwebs. We'd decided to pop into the village and bought some fresh baguettes and some sourdough to toast – this is Angela's favourite as it reminds her of crumpets (though it doesn't look like a crumpet, or, to be honest, taste like a crumpet, but it makes my girl happy, so . . .). On the way home, we shared a buttery croissant – our *boulanger* makes the best – and we all giggled as Angela/Mummy said she would allow crumbs in the car as it was the first day of the year, but I could see her twitch!

We decided to have breakfast in the new winter garden. However, the winter sun was slow to rise and barely added any heat as the weak rays were filtered by the leafless trees, so I popped on the heater and light, whilst Arthur made some of his world-famous guacamole, which is a brunch favourite with us.

We have certain rituals that all come from us living in France and observing the French choice to work less and spend more quality time with family. This, combined with our desire to suck the marrow out of the bones of our new life, means we always do a sanity check on our plans to see that we have taken time to breathe. For us brunch is one such ritual, and we were really excited about doing it more often as we lived more and worked less.

A couple of important points. Firstly, brunch is not just a big breakfast, or indeed a second breakfast, as made fashionable by hobbits. Having 'brunch' allows you to wander far from the breakfast menu; in France that is very important, as breakfast is light. Breaking your fast with a croissant does mean that you are ready for a midday meal by midday, but it is very continental. The second important point is that it has to be eaten early enough so as not to be confused with lunch; this is always made clearer if you have something 'breakfasty' on the table.

. . . .

ARTHUR'S GUACAMOLE

Ingredients

2 ripe avocados (good luck with that! We tend to buy those ready to eat and wait for them to be perfect before we use them rather than buying them and expecting them to be right)
Juice of half a lemon(ish)
Fleur de sel (this is the best of the best when it comes to salt – it is a salt that forms as a thin, delicate crust on the surface of seawater as it evaporates. It has been collected since ancient times and the name comes from the flower-like patterns of crystals in the salt crust. It tastes very special!)

Method

The success of this dish comes from how you make it. The flesh of the avocado is put into a bowl and roughly mashed with a fork. Some lemon is added, as is a sprinkle of salt. You mix it and taste.

If the balance is not perfect, you add some lemon and/or salt. You mix it and taste.

If the balance is not perfect, you add some lemon and/or salt. You mix it and taste . . .

You get the point?

*Take care to leave some texture in your guacamole as you don't
want baby food-type goo. It's great on hot, buttered toast,
especially crumpetty sourdough, with some fresh ground pepper.*

....

At this stage, I have to admit that Angela and I are not always
harmonious in the kitchen. We have both done lots of catering and
we both have firm ideas. At breakfast time, all the activity takes
place in the 'service kitchen' just off the dining room. Arthur and
Dorothy have cooked us breakfast and consider themselves experienced, so we basically have all four of us, who are individually
capable of making brunch, working together. The kitchen is actually quite small but we're well organised in there, with a comprehensive '*batterie de cuisine*', but it does involve a lot of moving past
each other. We were in no rush but hunger adds an impetus.

Our menu:

*Coddled eggs – plain, with smoked salmon and a splash of truffle
salt*
*Boudin noir – a French blood sausage cooked crispy but soft in the
middle*
Hot buttered toast
Arthur's guacamole
*Salad – roquette and mache (mache is lamb's lettuce which is
hardy and available everywhere in France and throughout the
year)*

**When Dick and Arthur are in the service kitchen, Dorothy and I
try to give them space. We become the hosts and set the table, get
the drinks and take things in when 'service' is called. We normally
have orange juice with brunch but on extra special days like
this I'll make a smoothie. Dorothy can pretty much do these by**

herself now, but I am still close enough, keeping a sneaky eye. We have tried hundreds of combinations but our favourite is orange juice, frozen strawberries (which we picked from our garden last summer), mango and frozen pineapple (not from the garden sadly) and a couple of bananas. It's the winning combo and adds a real fruitiness to the first breakfast of the year.

Within a few minutes of the table being laid, I called out 'service' and we all carried something through to our new winter garden. The heat had been on long enough to take the edge off the chill, which meant we were all wearing jumpers, except Angela who, since the day we moved to the château, has believed dressing up warm is to put socks on.

At the start of every meal we make a toast. It's our moment in time, before we all tuck in, to remind us that we are together and that every time we get to share something it should be cherished. We do and we did. 'To family.' 'To the first day of the year.' 'To health and happiness.' 'To Petale having babies!' We all toasted at the same time, chuckled at Dorothy's toast and got stuck in.

Relaxing, eating together, snuggling on the sofas in the salon watching a film, tending the chickens and geese, walking around the walled garden . . . it doesn't matter what we do as a family, we try to always remember it's special. It was only yesterday that it took all our attention to keep Arthur and Dorothy safe and amused; now they love doing things for us and with us. Like lots of parents, I'm sure, Angela and I used to regularly say that we'd like time to freeze as the children were at a perfect age and our family was so happy. Interestingly, experience has told us that every stage is a perfect stage and we have to keep loving every moment . . .

The rest of the afternoon was chilled. I'm a sucker for sorting out the children's stationery. Arthur is relaxed and not very interested; he would rather help Dick put air into all the tyres and play Lego. Dorothy, however, is competing with me for the stationery geek championship title, and I'm fine with that. We put *Home Alone* on, the first one, as it's the best, and then sharpened two cases worth of pencils. For many, this is a chore but for Dorothy and me, it's rather satisfying. Every now and again she would check with Arthur to make sure he was happy with his pencils and every time he would say, 'Oh yes' or 'Great job'. Our children's hearts are so big and so gentle, and in this moment I could not help thinking, 'You could be anything you set your sights on.' And for Dick and me, as long as it came with a big dollop of happiness, we would not care.

The sun sets around 5pm in January and as we looked outside, the day had just slipped by beautifully. It was dark and we started to prepare supper. First I poured us both a glass of Saint-Émilion, which we had opened the night before. Dick gave me a look and asked how it felt being the lady of the manor! I laughed and said, 'Fabulous, darling, but quite full on.' I think we were both feeling nostalgic. This really felt like the start of a new era, and a new beginning.

This was the first day of the rest of our lives and it was too good to be true. We had worked silly hours to get here but we had survived lockdown and rebuilt our business and our home. We could see the future . . . and forever looked good.

PART ONE

CHAPTER ONE

Finding Balance

It was early June 2018 and Dick and I were sitting on the steps of the château having an aperitif. I'd made Dick a pastis. He is very particular about how he likes it served. I usually fill the glass around a quarter full and then add very cold water. We chatted about how this year really had started with an almighty bang. Despite the never-ending soggy weather conditions earlier in the year, we had managed to finish and launch our new glamping domes, 'Château Under the Stars', and had our first glampers, Byron and Scarlette. Their visit had ended with a proposal down by the orangery and an acceptance (always good!). Now we were in the midst of our third wedding season (if you count Richard and Charlotte's wedding back in 2016 as 'wedding season number one').

Late spring at our forever home is glorious. The wisteria is divine, the meadow starts to flower, the temperature is just right and it's truly such a joy to be in the great outdoors. Even the pollarded trees have started to look like trees again, rather than stumps. At the château, we are always guided by nature's seasons. Dick is a true 'season' guru, he understands every nuance of the word and its meaning. He understands what needs to happen when and why, and how nature always leads every step of the way. From pollarding (an official swear word in this household) to planting, sap rising to the sun rising and falling. Being a city girl, I had always been slightly removed from nature's cycle; for me, seasons changing meant swapping over my wardrobe twice a year. But Dick's connection to the great outdoors is not only endearing, it's fascinating, and his passion to share his knowledge with Arthur and Dorothy makes my heart melt. He is an encyclopaedia of information and every day, as a family, we grow and learn.

However, the word 'season' has started to take on a new meaning for us here at the château. For five months of the year, our general life balance shifts gear in order to focus on the hospitality side of our business. Naturally, this means lots of weekends are spent hosting. We share our home, our knowledge, our skills and our family, with others. And in return, this allows us to continue renovating the château and taming the land. Our hosting season runs from 1 May to 30 September, to be precise, and once it starts it is like rolling a ball down the hill – our pace constantly quickening to ensure we keep up as, even on those days when we feel tired or our feet are hurting, once we're in the season that ball keeps rolling. With nine three-day weddings, three 'Food Lovers' Weekends', four 'Fun and Festive Days', five 'Garden Days', multiple Château Under the Stars bookings and countless wedding tastings still to host, the remaining part of the 'season' was going to be very busy.

Our plans for the year may have been manic but the château has seen years come and go, and there was a feeling that everything should be taken in context. From 1868 to 1874, during the six years the château was being built, the whole area would have been a hive of activity with artisans working side by side, and indeed above, and below, each other. At one time, the only manifestation of the vision would have been the architect's original drawings that now hang in our salon. That always puts our endeavours into perspective.

We know that the stone and oak beams from the old fortress that had stood on this spot since the twelfth century were reused, so they must have been put to the side and new foundations dug to follow the shape of the new château. The task was immense and all done by hand. When we put in our sewerage system, we saw a foundation stone that was the size of a small family car. So when the plans had all been agreed by the count and countess, and it was time for someone to take apart the remnants of the fort, the team must have taken the equivalent of a collective deep breath and said 'let's do this'. With that in mind, it was with a similar determination that we launched into our busiest year ever . . .

To be fair, we weren't just heading into our busiest year ever, we were launching into a new phase of our life here in France. We had the physical infrastructure in place and the team to run our business. What we needed to do was keep pushing forward on the restorations that the château needed, and just keep making everything better so it met our requirements and long-term, forever, needs.

The château, the walled garden, the outbuildings and the land were all going to be part of our future and we needed to make sure our master plan came to fruition. We were going to ensure that our family had the best multi-generational home possible. Starting with the oldest . . .

We'd sorted out the granny flat within the coach house and Jenny and Steve were comfortable, but it was always our intention that the building, which is massive, would be spacious for the family 'elders'. That meant a sociable kitchen, space to dine inside and out, bedroom suites and all mod cons. It may be Angela's parents', Jenny and Steve's, now but we see it as the probable home for Angela and me, when the then elderly elders move back to the more manageable granny flat and Arthur and/or Dorothy take over the château with their families. We have the flexibility to look even further ahead and if we are all still about when Arthur or Dorothy's children take over the responsibility for the château, fear not, we have a plan! Even longer term, we have planning permission for the outbuildings to be converted into houses should we, or any other members of our family – my sisters, or Angela's brother, or basically any relative who needs a home in the future – desire it. Château de la Motte Husson definitely has the potential to be our – and I mean all of our – forever home, so Angela and I always have the long game in mind. We did when we bought the château, though it was a bit hazy. However, once we established our business, every bit of reinvestment was aimed at making it easy for the next generations to be here.

Despite all the activities that we had going on in parallel, we always had areas of calm, such as the walled garden. Bit by bit it was evolving and we somehow managed to make it productive in terms of flowers and produce. There are some things that just taste so much better when they are home grown, and top of the list are strawberries and tomatoes (and potatoes, and peas, and figs, and in fact all soft fruits and . . .)

We had bought some strawberry plants and, as they do, they had multiplied. Each little offshoot was planted up and we had a very reasonable quantity of plants. Early April saw them flowering and by mid-May it was a race to get up the steps onto the walled garden to see who would have the pick of the day's lovely, sweet, positively fragrant strawberries.

The walled garden was becoming more and more part of our sanctuary. For Dick, having a moment to potter in his walled garden is his relaxation. I watch Dick watching the children, and they share his excitement and happiness for every blossom, flower and edible in the garden. The smell from the strawberry beds this year was aromatic and tangy. The aromas started before you even reached the beds, and on this particular day, the sun was shining and that intensified everything, including the smells and vibrancy of the greens and reds.

There's a saying, 'I'd rather be lucky than smart', and somehow we had the plants spread out sufficiently to allow everyone to be a winner, though Angela and I got so much pleasure from watching the children excitedly dashing around that we seldom had more than a token taste. These forays into the garden also allowed us to harvest some of the leaves from our salad bowl lettuce, and anything else that we could take back to the kitchen. There was usually something but never enough, so it was like a tease as to what the future would be like when the garden was truly productive.

By the time June arrives, nature has achieved amazing productivity and the landscape around the château is at its most vibrant. Spring sees the trees and bushes transforming from twigs, through the buds to their leaves in all different shades of green. With the longest days of the year, leaves are in their full glory and everywhere you look it feels like something is in bloom or growing as much as it possibly can.

* * *

MOVIE NIGHT

June was filled with Fun Days, Arthur and Dorothy's school spectacular and Mum's birthday, which we considered sacrosanct. Mum is such a hero to us, always supporting us and making us home-cooked meals, and just being there for us in every way we need, so we like to use any occasion we can as a way to say thank you and to spoil her.

With the grounds bursting with colour and happiness, we thought doing something outside would be perfect for her birthday. A few things then happened in succession that secured the way forward. First, Dad had finally got around to sorting out his collection of Cine8 footage from my childhood and had taken the step to have it transferred onto DVD. Then, on a trip to the local *vide grenier*, we had found an ancient cast-iron pot which Dick said would be perfect for cooking popcorn. *Et voila!* They were all the signs I needed: we decided to have an outdoor movie night for Mum's birthday.

First things first, we had to arrange for my older brother Paul to join us because we couldn't debut our childhood memories on the big screen without him. I got into hospitality because it was my passion, but I had wondered if hosting so many events would turn a family party into 'work'. But the answer is a definitive 'NO'. If hosting is in your blood, every event is a joy because you love doing it. It's like how chefs say they never tire of making people smile with food.

To make my plan work, we needed outside cinema seats, and with pennies being tight we were looking for robust materials that would stand the test of time. This gave me the perfect excuse to make some car-tyre chairs. I was excited. I had been looking at various designs and uses for this unbreakable material for yonks and this was my chance to play.

EXTERIOR CAR-TYRE SEATS

You will need

Car tyres (one per seat)
String or spray paint
Glue/glue gun (if using string)
Plywood
Foam
Dacron
Fabric for seat pads
Stapler and staples
Saw/jigsaw
Pencil

Method

Step 1: Making the seat top

First, cut a circle of plywood to fit on the top of the tyre. Use a layer of foam, followed by Dacron and finishing fabric to cover the circle and make a seat pad.

To do this, staple the foam on first. Then cover the foam with a piece of Dacron just a bit bigger than the foam, bringing it round the edges to the underside of the board. Staple the foam and Dacron in place and trim off any excess close to the staple line.

Finally, cover the seat pad with the fabric. Lay the fabric over the seat. Keep it nice and taut and put a staple in the centre front, back and each side – i.e. at the 12, 6, 3 and 9 o'clock positions to make sure the Dacron is covered. Once you're happy, fill in the gaps with extra staples and trim off any excess fabric.

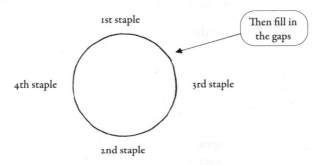

1st staple

Then fill in the gaps

4th staple

3rd staple

2nd staple

Tips

- Use the flat of your hand to smooth the fabric (not your fingers to pull). Smooth it in all directions to get it completely flat. If the fabric is stretchy, stretch with the flat of your hand to keep it taut before stapling

- Keep the staple gun pressed firmly on the wood when 'firing'

- Make sure the staples don't go all the way through the wood

- Put in lots of staples to prevent 'cat's teeth' – this is when the fabric pulls up away from the staples and goes bumpy

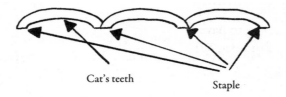

Cat's teeth

Staple

- Hammer in any staples that stand proud
- Make sure the scissors are sharp and cut cleanly
- Cut as close to the staples as you dare!

Step 2: Decorating the tyre

To decorate the seat, you can either spray the tyre or cover it with string.

If you decide to spray the tyre, take your time. It's best to do lots of thin layers rather than one thick layer of paint – this will allow you to get the best finish with no drips or runs.

To cover with string, start at the underside of the tyre and glue the end of the string in place to hold it firm. Use the glue gun to make a line of glue before pressing the rope onto it. Work in a circle around the tyre, gluing and pressing the string as you go, making rows. When the tyre is fully covered, cut the string and glue the end in place. It takes some time, so be patient, and keep the rope as taut as you can and as close to the row before to minimise gaps.

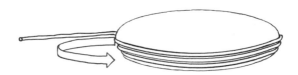

If you are going to have an evening al fresco you have to embrace all the opportunities. When Angela decided that we should have a 'home movie' night by the orangery to watch some of Steve's old Cine8 footage it seemed obligatory to have popcorn.

We had recently visited a *vide grenier* (a car boot sale – literally 'empty attic' in French) and I had picked up a cast-iron cauldron for pennies. I must have known we'd need it in the future. It could not have been simpler. Once I had spent two hours cleaning it and oiling it with vegetable oil, all we needed was a circle of stones, some logs from the log store and off we went. The fire would be a lovely focal point when the sun went down but, in addition, it was functional. So I popped the cauldron directly onto the coals and within a few moments the oil was smoking. In went a good glug of sunflower oil and a whole bag of corn. We gave it a quick stir and on went a make-do lid. Then it was a matter of waiting for a very few moments . . . The staccato firing of the corn reached a crescendo quite quickly and, as it started to die down, I took the cauldron off the heat.

It was early evening and everything was in place. I did my final check and went to get Mum, Dad, my brother Paul and Arthur and Dorothy. It was a balmy evening and peaceful too, except for the sound of nature. As I walked to collect everyone, I remember thinking that we were on the cusp of golden hour. When I arrived at Mum's, the excitement was tangible. My brother, who really is a big kid at heart, was ensuring that the energy levels were high (through the roof, in fact). So as soon as I said the words 'we are ready', Paul, Arthur and Dorothy ran out the door and we ended up chasing them over to the orangery.

There were two things that have stuck in my mind's eye from that moment. Firstly, Dorothy's *Frozen* dress. Dorothy had slightly outgrown Elsa but she still loved her light-blue outfit with layer upon layer of chiffon that twinkled when caught in the sun. The fact that Dorothy was wearing this dress meant today was officially a big deal. And secondly, Mum and Dad, all dolled up, walking arm in arm down the path to the orangery. After over fifty years together, they looked enchanting. Mum was smiling in a really gentle 'I'm so happy and content with my life' way and as they walked, savouring the moment, they would look at each every now and then and smile. That moment, that exchange of glances, stuck with me and I knew then this was going to be emotional.

There was no subtlety: I shovelled out half the popcorn and sprinkled lots of sugar over it and the remaining popcorn was sprinkled with salt and ladled out. Everyone was scrambling over the chairs to get settled. Then they tucked into the popcorn and loved it. It was probably the first time we had more popcorn than we could eat.

With everyone comfy and wolfing down popcorn like it was a race, Dick turned on the projector. Growing up, we had always joked that my dad had one arm and a Cine8 for the other. But clearly, he had a vision. He wanted to capture every moment, every smile, every memory, every nuance of us growing up. And it worked. The silence and flicker of the screen that only a Cine8 can give you was mesmerising.

The first scene was my grandma and grandad with my mum and dad and my brother Paul, all in a garden that was not familiar to me. Birthdays always make me feel nostalgic, but for me they are also a reminder that there is only a certain number of them in one's lifetime, so they must be enjoyed to the max. I saw the tears of happiness in Mum's eyes as she thought about Grandma and Grandad. To remember is to celebrate a loved one's life.

Then the silence was broken. 'Where are you?' said Arthur. 'Is that Mummy or Uncle Paul?' Dorothy asked. They had not even considered that forty or so years ago I was just a twinkle of the eye, a star in the sky! Everyone was engrossed in the home movie that Dad had spent decades curating. Great Nan, aunties, uncles, friends, neighbours, my brother, Jimmi – Arthur's godfather – and then, finally, me! I was born seven years after Paul and that was a lot of Cine8 footage, but there I was. Always smiling, always with a look of determination on my face. Our first bike rides, Christmases together, days at the seaside, flying kites. It was all there.

Those memories are precious and if I'm brutally honest I have very few fresh memories of life before the age of ten. Maybe subconsciously this was part of the reason we continued to film *Escape to the Château*, to capture beautiful memories to share with Arthur and Dorothy and with our grandchildren, and for them to share with their grandchildren, and so on . . .

Mum's movie night was a huge success and I could see the pride in Dad's eyes. And rightfully so. Watching Mum laugh and cry as we took a trip down memory lane was a precious memory in itself.

* * *

The summer was heating up and the meadow had started to turn golden. With that, the weddings got closer together. It was officially the school holidays and we now realised that's when most people want to get married! Eloise and Matt were due to be wed here in mid-July. They were a young, energetic and beautiful couple, on the inside and out, and their families were complete Francophiles. Eloise's style was boho and elegant, and her attention to detail was outstanding. It was going to be a huge wedding, way more than the eighty people we ordinarily host in the orangery, and so we adapted our plans to an alfresco wedding breakfast and prayed it wouldn't rain!

A hot topic for Dick and me was how we would handle the accommodation for the guests. And with Ann and Ian getting married the week after, and Lynne and Simon the week after that, and then another four between then and the end of the season, we decided to bite the bullet and go for it.

The last suite we intended to finish in the château was on the second floor. I'd named it the potagerie suite because of the most wonderful views to the south and east that overlooked the walled garden, *le potager*. As with all the suites, the bathroom needed the most infrastructure. Before we started our plumbing, before we'd even moved into the château, we had made a plan. This involved making decisions on where we were to put bathrooms and toilets in the future and a rough idea of the function of the rooms. I then had to come up with a design for our water, waste and electricity. 'No plan ever survives contact with the enemy' so we knew there would be some changes along the way, but we did have an idea of what went where and our priorities.

It feels like many moons ago that Dick and I sat down in our Southend flat to brainstorm how the château could pay for itself. Dick being the organised, incredible man that he is, had prepared nibbles of cheese, olives and wine, along with an A-board for our notes and ideas. It was October 2014 and Dorothy was zero. She was all snuggled into me and I remember thinking this is the start of us shaping our lives, a blank canvas. That feeling was incredible and so exciting!

With Dorothy hugging Angela, it really put into perspective that we needed the château to pay for itself so I did not have to travel and spend time away for work. We were realistic and knew in the early days this would be impossible, but it was our objective, and with that in mind we started to brainstorm. Weddings and special events, foody weekends, high-end bed and breakfast, hen parties . . . there were many on the list and we put a smiley face by the side of the ones we thought we'd enjoy as well as them being lucrative. Planning was key here, because on our next visit to the château our vision would determine just how many toilets we would need.

When we officially became the custodians of the house in January 2015 we walked around on a complete high. I wanted to discuss decoration, and we did to an extent, but Dick was insistent that the priority was working out how many toilets were needed to meet our goals. That planning from Mr Strawbridge was just about to be proven invaluable.

When we came to the bathroom that is now known as the potagerie suite bathroom, we had already decided that the honeymoon suite would have two toilets, our Strawbridge suite one, and the botanical suite and boudoir both one each. And so now it was finally time for the potagerie suite, the fifth and final suite, to be completed. The room had been used for storage and it had incredible oak-panelled cupboards which ran floor to ceiling. The light was golden in this room and I had felt sad we would have to take the cupboards out some day. But Dick always knows the right things to say to stop me worrying. 'If we ever get around to doing this suite, we will have made our business work,' he said, and in a heartbeat my anxiety melted.

The potagerie suite is a love story that grew from the seed of Dick's happiness in his walled garden. In late 2015, weeks after our wedding, Dick named it and since then the name has really resonated with me over the years. Every time I visited this room, I walked around it, looked at the light, looked out through the windows at Dick's walled garden, and thought about how I would decorate it to celebrate my husband's love of his garden.

As our business diversified, we were often showing people around the château and every time I entered this suite I would show guests the view and talk about the reasons it was so special. I wanted it to have heart and meaning, similar to how we all feel about the wallpaper museum. I knew that I wanted to find a way to showcase the walled garden, and have leeks, artichokes and sweet peas all featured. It needed to encompass what Dick feels when he is pottering in his garden. Then suddenly, one day, during a tour, it was all clear to me: I would design a wallpaper with all of these elements within it, which would gracefully become part of the fabric of the room.

To work on the design, I based myself in the honeymoon suite salon. It has a lovely wooden circular table, nice natural light and beautiful calmness. It was the perfect place to bring all my thoughts and doodles together. Sitting beside me was a piece of the original toile wallpaper that I had managed to get off in one piece when we were stripping the room. They say small things can be very satisfying, and years later I still smile about this. I've turned this strip into many gifts, cutting pieces up and framing them to share the history and happiness it brings.

Anyway, I digress. The design was really coming together but there were a couple of small touches missing. There needed to be a nod to the original wallpaper – because that was an explosion of reddish coloured flowers that was easy. But I was also set on weaving in some carrots. Where and how does one incorporate carrots into a wallpaper design? I looked around the honeymoon suite with its art deco flourishes waving at me and all of a sudden it seemed like the most natural thing in the world: art deco carrots. Anything triangle shaped can be placed into an art deco trio. When I sketched it out, it was perfect and fitted in beautifully with my V-shaped leeks. Boom!

I'll be the first to say I am no artist but I do know how to put a design together, and this one was quickly becoming the perfect homage to Dick.

As the summer progressed, August felt hot and we agreed that our château was located in the perfect part of France for us. Any more south and it would just be unmanageable in the summer. The weddings were getting more and more enjoyable and this was partly because we were getting systems in place for everything they required and partly because our team was really bonding. At the heart of this was a new employee called Quentin. On 12 December 2017 we'd received an email with the subject 'French boy looking for work':

Bonjour Dick and Angel,

My name is Quentin, I am a French guy who has been following your journey on TV from the beginning. I have been a big admirer of what you have done with the château and the events you are hosting. I have been living in Australia for the past year and I am now back in Laval for good.

I am writing this email to you today because I am looking for a job. Seeing all the work you have to put through when you are hosting weddings and other events, I was wondering if you needed extra help at the Château. I have been in hospitality for five years now and I really enjoy waiting on people. I speak English fluently and I have work in hospitality in Australia and Ireland. So if you need a waiter or simply an assistant don't hesitate to contact me. It would be a great pleasure to help you and I am sure that I can learn a lot working with you.

Please find attached my resumé.

Bonne journée,

Quentin

You never know how significant certain meetings are, but every now and then people come into contact because you need each other. We have been very lucky with this at the château. We have to be fussy because our work space is also our home and we are very protective of this. But Tina, Steve, Sacha and now Quentin seem to fit our family like a glove. Quentin was kind, efficient and hard-working. He had a brilliant energy and everyone, including our children, loved him from day one. If I'm being honest, we didn't realise we needed Quentin when we first received his email, but it was only a matter of weeks before we were all uttering: 'What was life like before Quentin?' It felt great to have such a strong team in place and during the summer holidays especially, we needed all the support we could get.

If we wanted to make our future secure, we knew we had to work hard for the summer. This meant, apart from a five-day break in late August, we never had more than a couple of days in between commitments. It was a busy season and everyone worked non-stop, so alongside the hard work we made sure to enjoy our surroundings, and every inch of our grounds, as often as we could.

There is something very special about owning trees. It's probably because you don't actually own them; it's your job to tend to them, unless of course you make the decision to cut them down. I'm not sure how many trees we have here but there are enough to allow us to say we have a couple of areas of woodland and trees bordering the moat. Some are more prominent or important than others and we have lost some over the time we have been here. They must make a deep impression as I can clearly remember going to the walled garden and looking around and thinking, 'This isn't quite right.' I just couldn't understand what was different but I realised it was 'lighter' than normal. I walked around for about ten minutes then headed off to walk around the outside of the walled garden. There I found a large birch and a large sycamore that formed part of the barrier around the walled garden, lying side by side rather than protecting our *potager*. (I love the fact that most walled gardens are designed to have trees around them, set back so they don't stop winter sun from getting into the plants, but close enough to force the majority of strong wind up and over the garden. We have trees set back from our walls on the sides not protected by buildings.)

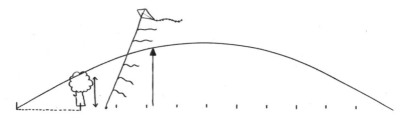

We have a few trees that we are especially fond of: the lone cedar in the meadow in front of the orangery, the huge horse chestnuts on the edge of the moat behind the château, and the family's favourite, and our biggest tree, the massive oak to the right of the driveway as you approach the château. This oak tree looks amazing but it is only when you approach it that you see exactly how big it is. There is the old adage that an oak grows for 200 years, lives for 200 years and then dies for 200 years. We wanted to try to work out what age our tree was and to determine what it must have seen in its life by our château. So off went the family with tape measure in hand.

Obviously, any guesstimation we made would have inherent inaccuracies but that didn't put us off. Research told us that an oak tree will increase in girth by approximately 2.5cm every year, and there we had found tables that allowed us to determine the diameter of the trunk and come up with an approximate age. Measuring approximately one metre-ish from ground level-ish, horizontally-ish, gave us a nine-metre-ish circumference. A quick calculation and we concluded our tree was 360 years old –and its birthday was on Wednesday!

We started talking to Arthur and Dorothy and explained that Louis XIV, that's Louis the Great, or the Sun King, was on the throne then. Both Angela and I were surprised that they had heard about him at school – full marks to the French education system! It was amazing to think that our tree was little when he built the Palace of Versailles. Such facts are great to know but, to be fair, most of our conversations revolved around the fact that Arthur thought it was wonderful that our old oak was 'tree hundred and tree' years old – obviously delivered in a wonderful Irish accent that did sound a tad American.

CHAPTER TWO

The Great Outdoors

Whilst our summer continued to keep us busy, it felt exciting, and I don't ever remember thinking we had bitten off too much. In fact, I think the family and the team were positively thriving. We had what I would describe as a happy balance – shock horror! In August, we had weddings for Emma and Simon, and Ben and Nicole, who was an incredible ballroom dancer. This was alongside other events, including welcoming guests to stay in our domes for Château Under the Stars, and the ongoing renovation to the potagerie suite as well as preparing for the new carpet on the double revolution staircase. So when we got a down moment we cherished it. In fact, we tried to make the most out of the simplest things. One evening, Dick suggested he might take Arthur camping. I smiled but also panicked. It would be interesting to see if Arthur was more in my 'camp' or Dick's when it came to staying in the great outdoors!

Being outdoors is like being in a huge adventure playground. Arthur and Dorothy are always happy pottering around when we have the opportunity. That said, we have a moat and sufficient space for them to get lost, so at five and four years of age they went nowhere without Mummy and/or Daddy being within easy reach. However, that did not curtail the ability to have proper adventures. As far as I was concerned, Arthur was old enough to endure a night in the wild. True, there were wild boar and owls hooting all manner of eerie sounds but we were men and decided to brave them all (to be very fair, at this point, it was nothing to do with us being 'men'; it was just that out of the four of us, it was only Arthur and I who loved the idea of camping! Angela had never been camping and had no desire to start, and Dorothy couldn't understand why we would want to be in a tent rather than our comfy beds . . .). Unperturbed by such negativity, we organised our provisions and some limited home comforts, then headed into the wild. It wasn't long before we found the perfect spot, even walking slowly we came to a lovely grassy clearing across the moat in a bit less than a minute, and just under 100 metres away from the château. You may think that wasn't far, but Mummy was freaking out as we placed the tent out of direct line of sight from the bedroom window, so we were truly cut off from civilisation. Setting up camp was fun, if a little chaotic. I was keen to get the tent up and the sleeping arrangements sorted so we could zip up the net door before lots of little insects invaded our inner sanctum. Arthur, on the other hand, wanted to set and light the fire so we could sort out the catering. We had cooked over an open fire before and loved the ritual of toasting marshmallows so he knew the treats we had in store. The compromise was Arthur collecting stones to demark the fire pit, whilst I sorted out beds and duvets (yes, duvets! Mummy had insisted!).

* * *

Dorothy and I had been banned. We were fine about this. In fact, we were going to have a girls' night and we decided to play dress-up and watch a movie. I was glad to see that Dick and Arthur made up camp far enough away, but also not too far ...

We had so much fun. Angela and Dorothy could hear us from the bedroom window but had been banned from coming out and making the tortuous journey to our encampment. Out in the wild, we had our meal, including campfire beans of course, and toasted marshmallows cooked on long twigs that I allowed Arthur to trim with my penknife. Then we got ready to settle down. We did call up to Mummy and Dorothy in the château to say 'goodnight', then we retired, zipped up our insect protection and cuddled up ...

I do not know what I was thinking with the beans, or how Arthur managed to process them so quickly, but as dusk started to settle, Arthur 'parped', and when I say 'parped', it was epic! I think the tent sides fluttered. We were in fits of laughter and thank goodness we only had the net door closed. After lots of duvet flapping, we settled down and talked about how comfy we were and all the adventures we were going to have.

Arthur was all but asleep when he said, 'I need a pee-pee.' To which I replied, 'Off you go.' Even in the near-dark I could see his surprise. I made the point that we were out in the wild, so all he had to do was to walk away from the tent a bit, have a pee and come back. I gave him a torch, let him put on my boots, as they were easy to slip on, and off he went. Arthur in his jimjams wearing my boots was a wonderful sight and he did pass comment it was one of the best pees he had ever had! When my big boy was finally fast asleep, I texted Angela that we were safe and happy, had a reasonable glass of Bushmills sitting by the fire embers and turned in for an early night. We both slept the sleep of the innocent and had a wonderful night. On awakening, it was a matter of pulling on some footwear and then we headed in to see the girls and to be fed a proper breakfast worthy of a couple of adventurers.

* * *

I never actually bought Angela flowers when we first started seeing each other. It was not a lack of romance, it was just that her business required her to have flowers available to decorate the spaces she used for functions, so she always had lots of spare blooms in her flat. It would have been 'coals to Newcastle', so instead I bought her vintage presents that I thought she would like. I love Angela for the fact she has kept everything I have ever bought her, even though some have never been worn or displayed, as I'm a bloke, so I regularly miss the mark!

Having failed to buy flowers for all those years, I had the opportunity to make up for it when we moved to the château. I felt planting anything from wild flowers to sweet-smelling roses or peonies, or masses of gladioli and sweet williams, allowed us to enjoy the colours and scent as they grew, and when they were transferred to the château their perfume filled the rooms.

We always joked about Dick not buying me flowers, especially as he is such a gentleman. It's an easy wind-up and he still twitches, but of course I understood why! Receiving a cutting garden was the epitome of romance; something you would read in a novel and dream about afterwards. Ten years ago you could never have convinced me that it could happen in real life, let alone to me. My cutting garden was a remarkable token and one that will continue to provide gifts well into the future (as long as you plant perennials!).

Dick dedicated a quarter of his walled garden to the cutting area. He meant business. To start, there were four 14m × 1m beds and all were in use. Dick always said, 'I'm not into flowers, I'm

into food,' but actually he is good at everything in the garden, including flowers, and initially he made all the choices to get it started, from a huge row of lavender to scabious, lupins, gladioli and a row of mixed wildflowers.

Earlier in the year, Dick took his love token a step further when he took Arthur and Dorothy to the meadow in front of the orangery and sowed literally millions of wildflower seeds. He had ordered a hessian bag full of wildflower surprises. I remember it not being cheap, but Dick reassured me, saying that once we populate this meadow it will self-pollinate for years to come. When everyone arrived back at the château they were exhausted (our meadow is quite substantial). I got them all a sweet lemon drink, which magically disappeared in seconds.

Arthur and Dorothy were very invested in the meadow and whenever we had a moment of calm (in between our moments of non-calm) we would all go and look to see if anything had popped up. We all got a kick out of the chance to be part of nature's magic in action. And over time, the meadow started to flourish, with blue cornflowers and yellow buttercups, bright-red poppies and delicate pink cosmos, ox-eye daisies and a prolific amount of wild carrot flowers, also known as Queen Anne's lace because the flower head resembles the delicate fabric.

On one of these walks, on a balmy morning, Arthur stopped and disappeared in the grass. A few minutes later, he emerged with his hands behind his back and a huge smile on his face. His eyes were twinkling. And then he revealed what was making them bright: a hand-picked mini bouquet of wildflowers. The placement of the flowers was remarkable. Unbeknownst to Arthur, he had nailed the arrangement; he was a natural. The placement and balance was extraordinary and, when he saw the delight on my face, he gave me the biggest hug. 'I must press these,' I said, 'so I can keep them forever.' And then we started to pick more flowers from the meadow for pressing. But it did not stop there because the wisteria looked enchanting, dangling like lilac drops of nectar from a gnarly tree, and I wondered if this would press too. It was the second round of the wisteria and I still couldn't get my head around the fact that it flowers twice! I had not tried to press such a large bloom before, but the petals were delicate, so I could not see any reason why it would not work.

We all headed back to the house and Dorothy and I went to my *trésorerie*, whilst Arthur and Dick went to make brunch. We were on an industrial-sized mission to press flowers. We have a number of cute wooden presses around the place, but our basket was overflowing and on this occasion none of these would have cut the mustard. For this I knew we needed something much bigger, so we made our own. The principle is very simple, and if you think back, old books with porous pages have been used for centuries to press flowers. All you need is to make a super-sized version of a book: porous paper and some pressure.

The children had a roll of drawing paper – it was 60cm wide and many metres in length. We laid out the first layer on the floor and carefully placed the flowers on it. This is the easy and fun part, but you must ensure that all the petals are placed nice and evenly, and any leaves are in a good direction, not folded over, and all stems look good. You then add another piece of porous paper and then some more flowers. This time we placed the wisteria. It was very delicate and precious and I had everything crossed that we could preserve this beautifulness. We continued by adding another piece of paper and more flowers and repeating until the paper ran out (of course ensuring our final layer was the paper to protect the copious number of books we then laid on top!).

It must have been three or four weeks later that the big unveiling took place. I can't quite remember the order of ceremony, but I do have Dorothy's amazing reaction imprinted in my mind. It was like nature had done a magic trick for her. The blooms were delicate, slightly fainter in colour, but perfect. It was fascinating taking each piece of paper off. In each layer, there were a couple of unusable flowers, but also dozens of perfect stems, and that's where the excitement lies, because once the paper goes down and the pressure mounts, you never know quite what those little flowers will do!

Angela and Dorothy were so proud of their pressed flowers and came down to show us and thank us too. It had been a family affair. I'll take credit for the idea and some of the early work. Arthur and Dorothy also planted and picked, and with Angela then having the idea to stick them onto the wall of the turret, none of it could have happened without all of us – teamwork at its best! If I'm honest, handling dried flowers is my idea of hell, but that afternoon we started a book of pressed flowers from the château which we looked forward to adding to and growing.

The potagerie suite was really coming together as well. Most of the grubby jobs had been completed: doors and floors had been sanded, holes filled, electrics and plumbing completed (no mean feat). Getting to this stage took weeks of work but still it looked like a building site. But as Dick has often told me, it's all in the preparation, and after that, everything started to come together much more quickly.

One of my finest moments of DIYing at the château was connecting up the bathroom in the potagerie suite, as the final connection of the waste pipes and the hot and cold pipes were onto pipes we had laid on the very first day that Lee, Kyle and I started putting in plumbing days after we arrived in France and before we moved in. I smiled a lot and I'm not sure people understood why, but I was quite smug – it's great when a plan comes together!

That said, I didn't quite understand all the decisions made on the potagerie suite bathroom . . . a copper bath? It just doesn't make sense. Copper is a great conductor of heat so the water gets cooler quicker than it would in a cast-iron bath. I did make my point to Angela as copper baths are not cheap either; however, her arguments won the day as it looked good and it was going to be lighter to carry up the stairs, which was the clinching factor. Each of the other suites had cast-iron baths, two of which Angela had refurbished, and they all weighed well upwards of 100kg and were a bugger to manoeuvre up and around the staircases. Getting the copper bath up proved to be a doddle but I did still complain a bit so it didn't seem like too easy a victory for my girl!

For the bathroom I manage to source emerald-green zellige-esque tiles. They were 20cm by 6.5cm. Zellige tiles originated in Morocco and are made from a special blend of clay that makes every tile irregular in tone when glazed and fired, resulting in oodles of unique character. Our tiles were 'inspired' by zellige tiles, so whilst they were not cheap, they were a lot more affordable than the originals. We placed these tiles vertically on the wall where the oak storage cupboards used to be so that they framed the copper bath and matching shower, which I had managed to convince Dick we needed. The copper sink sat opposite on an antique wood and marble kitchen cupboard. Drilling the holes in this was apparently very stressful but it looked stunning and also only cost 60 euros. As Dick was complaining about the holes he had to drill, I kept reminding him of his saying: 'Buy once, cry once.' I'm sure I caught a glimmer of a smile at that point.

Many years before, I had picked up a seventies emerald velour fold-away chair. It was odd looking and back then I couldn't decide if I actually liked it or not, but it came with a footrest,

Summer of 2018.

Family time.

Dorothy's first birthday celebration.

Brittany, 2018.

The potagerie suite.

The coach house

Our boot room.

which sold it to me, together with the fear that I may regret not buying it. When I placed this onto a hessian rug with gold threading through it, I could imagine no other chair fitting more perfectly in this suite. The salmon paint which adorned the walls tied everything together and hinted at our very subtle Moroccan theme. A couple of small tables and plants later and this was now officially my favourite bathroom in the house (please do not tell the others).

The master chamber was also glowing. This room was blessed with a magical golden-hour tone throughout the day, and my heart skipped a beat when I saw it lighting up the warm tones of the wallpaper for the first time. Complementing the wallpaper was a matt sky-blue paint, a dark wood rattan bed and a matching desk that sat boldly in front of it. It was really striking. The final touch was a sconce that mirrored the design of the wallpaper and that was all that was needed as decoration on the walls (I *may* have bought the sconce one evening thinking it was a light, but lucky accidents happen and it certainly looked better as a sconce). I laid down two rugs: a rectangular one called 'Arabian flower', which had all the tones of the room and created a 'seating zone', and a circular orange heron one, which overlapped with the first to connect it with the 'bed zone'. The lovely lights that I had found with beautiful frosted flowers were literally made for this suite and finished it off perfectly.

Last but not least was the turret, which was filled with the pressed flowers that were sown and grown by Arthur, Dorothy and Dick. These were stuck onto the walls that had been painted with my favourite lustre paint. Sticking them on was a total nightmare job and required patience and lots of hand-washing! I used a high-tack aerosol glue and sprayed the areas of the wall the flowers would be delicately placed onto. The stems stuck easily to the wall but there was no way of stopping your fingers from getting sticky.

This was a suite made with love, for my love. You felt that as soon as you entered and it made me think: our château was built as a love token for the count and his new wife Dorothy, who had a lot to say about the design. There must be countless stories and love tokens hidden in these walls. As the present custodians, we can never know all of these. Maybe they were private or maybe they've simply been lost over time, but we love a love story and truly believe only good can come from sharing and celebrating this. So with that in mind I wrote a note about what the room signifies to us and slipped it behind the mirror. Who knows who will find it. Maybe our children, maybe their children. Maybe it won't be found for hundreds of years. Moments like this always help to remind me that we are just custodians and we must live for every moment we have here. I called Dick in and we looked around the suite again together, smiling, laughing and chatting. As we walked out holding hands, Dick looked back and muttered, 'That bloody bath.'

* * *

If we stopped and thought about the year so far it could make you dizzy. Saying that, for both our ages, we were keeping up and what a summer it had been. With just two weddings, a couple of garden days, a food lovers' weekend, a viewing and a tasting left, we felt we had broken the back of the year, and it had all gone smoothly so far. The weddings had been magnificent; our guests had been kind-hearted and respectful, and the whole team loved what they were doing. People were connecting, laughing and having a great time, and even though some mornings it was hard to move, we always woke up with a smile thinking about how things were going.

In the middle of August we had a five-day break planned. We hadn't explored France enough and knew the beaches in Brittany were meant to be very special, so we booked an Airbnb in a place called Dinard.

Running up to our holiday we had also been in chats with a guest called Stuart who had stayed at the domes with his lovely wife. His company made stair rods and, on a tour around the house, he said he could recreate the original stair rods and also put us in touch with a man who could fit the perfect replacement carpet. Now, we were not really ready for this to be done, in fact it wasn't even on our list yet, but we've always thought that when you find someone who is literally the person you need for that job you have to grab the bull by both horns and say, 'Thank you, where do we sign?' Stuart's business associate was a man called Paul Bloom. He fitted high-end carpets and specialised in stairs. He was a busy man but had a slot the week we were away on holiday. It was all happening rather fast, but the thought of the double revolution staircase having a carpet with new but original-shaped rods was too good to say no to and it also meant we would have them in place for the final weddings of the season.

A new carpet! I'd had 'sorting the stairs' on a 'to do, but not for a while' list, but I was in complete agreement with Angela: when you meet someone who you immediately know can do the job and do it well, why hesitate? We had discovered grand stairways have carpets up the middle rather than the full width to allow the servants to walk up and down on the wooden edges so they would not wear out the expensive carpet, so, for us, our new carpet needed to match the traditional logic and maybe one day we'd have people walking up and down the edges?

Obviously I had no say in the colour or style, but I was wondering about how difficult it would be to lay and what underlay was needed when I discovered that Paul had a team capable of laying it whilst we were away, so actually, I would not even have to carry it up the stairs – a result or what? That made our short break to the seaside even more of a treat as we'd be coming back to something new and exciting.

I'd never heard of Dinard but Angela had done the research and it was exactly what we needed to recharge the batteries. It's a beautiful little seaside town with some lovely restaurants. Our apartment was only a couple of hundred metres from an idyllic beach, with beachside cafés and even rows of bell-shaped beach tents that were only about 13 euros a day, so we could have shade and play in the sand for hours. We could leave our beach stuff in our tent and walk 30 metres for an aperitif and a bite to eat.

Most cafés and restaurants have children's meals that include a main course, a drink and a dessert for about 10 euros, and, as they know you're ordering for children, the service is quick. We ordered Arthur and Dorothy a diabolo (lemonade and grenadine syrup) and a pizza bambino (ham and mushroom) the first time we went to our nearest little café that had wonderful service and became our local, but the children always get to taste what we order, so they both had some of our *moules frites*. Dorothy became a mussel eating monster that holiday. It was possible to order mussels and chips on the children's menu, but it wasn't long before Dorothy realised she wanted a proper bowl so we had to bite the bullet and get her her own adult meal, or only get a few from the dish we had ordered.

Our family holidays are simple: sandcastles, bodyboarding, eating *moules frites* and collapsing back at our apartment watching a movie. This break may have only been five days but I could see everyone quickly switch into wibbly wobbly holiday mode.

Having had lots of fun, and proven that Canute could never have stopped the sea as we failed to save our castles with the fair princesses in them every time the tide came in, we headed the couple of hours home. Angela didn't mess around when we got through the gates; she was off. On opening the front door, the sight of our stairs with the beautiful new carpet on them was stunning. I have no doubt that she was imagining brides gliding down on the arm of the person giving them away, ready to go out and meet their guests ... it just finished off the view as you entered the château and made it even more majestic. I knew it was good, as Angela just didn't stop smiling.

As I opened the door, I did a little fist punch (I was on my own so no one could see, because that would have been embarrassing). The family followed behind, very excited to have a carpet in the house. For me, it was honouring the original staircase and giving it back the beauty and elegance it once had. I had chosen a plain burgundy 100 per cent wool flatweave carpet with brass stair runners. Apparently it wasn't easy getting the carpet as it was out of fashion, but that felt like even more of a sign that it was the perfect choice.

Our next wedding really had the red carpet laid out for them. Christine and Neil were gorgeous inside and out, and I was trying to stop myself from being overly excited about the carpet in front of them. But alas, I could not really help it. Luckily, Christine saw the humour. She was also genuinely excited to be the first bride to walk down the newly covered stairs and Charlotte, Dick's eldest daughter, was here taking photos to capture the moment. Quite soon after Christine and Neil booked their wedding with us, Neil was offered a job of a lifetime in Portland, Oregon, so their wedding was the first time they had been with many of their family and friends for over a year. This made it all extra emotional. It was whimsical and beautiful, and Christine and Neil looked spectacular on our stairs!

The following morning, Dick and I woke early to get our bride

and groom breakfast. Our feet hurt but we knew we must be doing something right because the château was oozing joy (and hangovers). We had one more wedding to do this year and that felt fantastic. We knew the team would be feeling sad when the season was over, but the year was still far from finished and we had lots of plans to keep everyone busy.

Jenny and Steve were very happy in their 'apartment' but the plan had always been for them to live in the whole coach house, not just part of it, so it was time to start making their home 'grander'. The heart of a home is the kitchen and Jenny loves cooking so it was time for phase two of '*l'écurie*', which was not a trivial task. We had to turn what was basically a very large 'garage' with a store above it into a modern, open kitchen diner. That involved demolishing part of the ceiling to create a mezzanine to give a real feeling of space, digging out tons of soil to create a patio area at the back of the building and connecting it to the walled garden, and then there was the trivial problem of bringing power, water and waste to Café Grandma.

The very first thing to be done was to tape up the doorway between what would eventually be a 'granny flat' and our building site. We cleared the ground behind the building, bought a backhoe attachment for our compact tractor and set 'Papi' Steve on the task of digging out the patio area. Unfortunately for us, the ground level in the walled garden is about a metre higher than floor level in the building, so to make a reasonably sized patio we had to move tons of earth. And of course, to put in drainage for the patio we had to go down deeper and lay a pipe under the new kitchen then across the front of the building to reach the moat. It was a good-sized job and took weeks of work. Access to the mezzanine level was up a rickety old set of stairs in the tack room next to what would be the kitchen, and when we 'dropped' half the ceiling it very soon became clear just how big the room would be – it was cavernous.

Mum was excited about having the kitchen of her dreams and spent hours sketching out what would go where. Dad helped by making scaled-down paper templates, (a centimetre-square in size) so Mum could play and move 'cabinets' around. That was adorable. There were a few things I knew Mum had her heart set on: firstly, an island; secondly, making sure it felt fresh, modern, light and airy; and finally, making it a sociable kitchen, as she's known to be both a feeder and a talker. I suppose it's part of coming from a large family, as my grandma was exactly the same.

In any kitchen there is a triangle that gets the most footfall – it's sink and work surface to cooker to fridge. I had managed to nego-tiate that the island would only have electricity on it, no water or waste, which was a result, and once the conduits were sunk in, and the trench for the drainage pipes dug, we could damp-proof, insu-late and concrete the floor. That's a pretty significant milestone as we had to be completely ready for when the concrete truck arrived, as it heralded a couple of hours in wellies levelling and smoothing. With the floor down and the layout finalised, it was possible to finish the utilities' first fix and to start plasterboarding. Jenny and Steve like to be warm in the winter and cool in the summer so insu-lation was a high priority. We studded out the walls, put electrics, plumbing and heating pipes (though we hadn't yet sorted what the heating system would be) within the studwork and added lots of insulation. All of a sudden, after weeks of work, you could see Café Grandma, but there was still lots to do.

The mezzanine level was to be a 'man cave' for Steve, which would allow him to keep lots of his personal belongings out of Jenny's kitchen and had the added bonus of being the warmest place in the house . . . warm air rises and so all the heat in Grandma's kitchen was destined to keep Papi warm. The only stumbling block we had was the question of what we could use as a balustrade that would be in keeping with the building. It was high up there so it had to be substantial and safe!

The original stables that were now Jenny and Steve's apartment had been horse stalls full of old logs when we first bought the château. And we had a recollection that there had been dividers that had allowed the horses to see their neighbours (neigh bours?) but not bite them. So we went off to the large barn in search of what had been used. It took a bit of rummaging but soon we found several lengths of 'railings' that were basically oak top and bottom with metal rods between them. They were heavy but some of the wood needed to be treated and the metal needed to be de-rusted, sanded and painted. We now had a plan. I ordered some five-inch square oak posts that we bolted to the beam to support our old stable partition that had turned into a new balustrade. We were busy in the room so I set Jenny and Steve up with sanders and fillers, paint and stain, and they were made responsible for the finish of this part of the mezzanine. I know Jenny was out of her comfort zone but they made a good team and you could tell they took a real pride in what they were doing.

Mum and Dad were really making headway with their forever kitchen design. They had chosen the cabinets and the marble and knew what was going where. It was very modern with clean lines and I was chuffed for them. At the same time, I also wanted a little jazz or magic dotted around the place, but it needed to be in keeping with the rest of the room and not too fussy.

Dad grew up in Mile End in the East End of London and his family home, where Nan was still living, was just off of Grove Road where there is a specialist light store that had always caught my

eye. The Neon Sign Store is so cool and I'm sure it's where my fascination for neon signs began. When I had my first collaborative store on Brick Lane, I enquired about getting one, but they were always outside my budget. To be fair, they are actually very well priced considering they are made by hand and it's a real artisan job. But I never quite had enough to buy one.

Because Mum is such a pleaser, during the busy times when she would cook, she would often make different meals by request. Dick and I told her off as it was too much work, but she ignored us and, anyway, we knew the kitchen was her happy place. But that's how Café Grandma got its name. Once it was confirmed that all bar one of the walls would be white, I knew the magic would be in the lighting, and so I finally got to fulfil my dream of commissioning a neon light. 'Café Grandma' in classic neon pink – it's fun, fresh and no fuss. Alongside it I decided on some art deco-inspired white globes that would add sophistication and elegance.

It was so lovely popping back to see Jeannette, Angela's nan, when we went to collect the neon sign. From Jeanette's flat, all we had to do was walk around the corner. The sign looked great, but all I could think was how the hell do we put that up?

CHAPTER THREE

Wellies and Walks

The pumpkins in the walled garden had been getting tantalisingly big. They were just waiting for us to say enough is enough and pick them. When I was growing up in Northern Ireland we celebrated Halloween because bonfire night seemed a very English thing to commemorate. Somehow my father always seemed to find some fireworks and all the neighbours would congregate for a very clandestine gathering as they were banned throughout the years of the Troubles. We'd bake potatoes in the embers of the fire, cook sausages on long sticks and play games. It was a very simple party and the weather was irrelevant. Come rain or extreme cold it would always go ahead. When I left home, Halloween took a back seat and we celebrated the failure of Guy Fawkes, so we decided to introduce the children to an old-fashioned bonfire night, complete with an effigy of Guy Fawkes to burn, sparklers, toffee apples and traditional games to play.

Preparation with the children is more than half the fun so off it was to the kitchen to make toffee apples or, as the French say – in a more romantic way, it has to be admitted – *pomme d'amour*. When I first heard the name *pomme d'amour*, which literally translates to 'apple of love', I struggled to see how the sweet, sticky fruit had links into the art of seduction, but then again, I used to be a crusty old army colonel so what do I know?

There is a wonderful pleasure in sharing firsts with your children and Arthur and Dorothy had no idea what was coming their way as we headed into the family kitchen.

....

POMME D'AMOUR ROUGE

Ingredients

6 red apples, stalks removed and wiped with a dry microfibre cloth
6 lollipop sticks or equivalent
500g white caster sugar
75ml water
1 tsp lemon juice
4 tbs golden syrup
A good dash of red food colouring

Method

Push your lollipop sticks well into the stalk ends of your apples.

Put the sugar into a heavy-bottomed pan along with the water and lemon juice. Heat but don't stir the pan as it can allow crystals to form on the sides which will spoil the texture of your toffee apple covering. Instead, to mix, lift the pan slightly and swirl it around gently. Then add the golden syrup. Swirl to mix.

*Continue to heat until it reaches the hard crack stage (150 °C).
You can test this by dropping a small amount into cold water
to see if it goes hard. Be prepared to do this a couple of times if
you have two children!*

Stir in the colouring and then it's time to dip your apples.

*Place the dipped apples on a piece of baking parchment. They
will be crunchy in a matter of moments.*

*We always have a couple of spare apples so no 'toffee' is wasted;
however, it's just a fact that the last one will never be covered
properly and that is officially the 'chef's perk'. In our case,
when I felt we didn't have enough for another apple I took two
halved, cored bits of apple, popped them in the pan then put
them on a plate for Arthur and Dorothy. I won't lie, it was
messy, but I'm sure you could make the argument that they had
at least one of their five a day.*

. . . .

We decided to have a family celebration with Grandma and Papi
Steve. Our bonfire was a reasonable size and consisted of wood-
worm infested bits of wood and anything combustible that we
knew we could never use again. In the middle, at the bottom, was
dry tinder and kindling, and on the top was Guy himself.

**The ugliest Guy Fawkes I ever did see! I have fond memories of
bonfire nights with Dad doing a BBQ and Mum doing jacket potatoes, the cats being scared and the family freezing and smiling. It
feels so much more of a trend to celebrate Halloween now, but
whilst the children were young enough, Dick and I wanted to show
them some old-fashioned fun along with some British history.**

To ensure the family were warm and the place felt cosy, my contribution included some homemade 'sock gloves' and jam-jar lights scattered about the table on homemade bamboo tripods.

....

SOCK GLOVES

You will need

Sewing machine and cotton
Scissors
A pair of socks
Fur fabric
Tape measure

Method

Step 1: Prepare your sock

Cut the sock just before the heel to give a straight piece with a rib top which will form the wrist grippy bit.

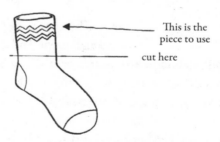

This is the piece to use

cut here

Cut a slit in the side of the sock to make a thumb hole and sew around the slit to stop it fraying.

Step 2: Add the fur fabric

Measure the width of the 'top' of the sock and cut a piece of fur fabric 6cm long and twice the width of the sock plus 2cm (the seam allowance should be 1cm at each end).

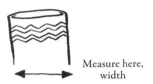

Measure here,
width

Sew the fur fabric into a circle with a 1cm seam along the 6cm edge. With wrong sides of the cut edge of the sock together with the right side of the fur, sew the two pieces together. Use a zigzag stitch on the sewing machine so the stitching will stretch when putting the gloves on.

With the right side of the sock outwards you will have a fur top around your fingers and the rib top of the sock around your wrist.

....

The evening was such a treat, all of us together again creating our own Strawbridge memories. Whilst we were waiting for the bonfire flames to take hold, we were treated to a truly majestic murmuration of starlings. In all my years in London I was not even aware of the spectacle, but during our first year at the château Dick had pointed out what looked like moving clouds that were transforming into the most amazing shapes, and he told me it was called a murmuration. I immediately loved that word. Dusk was near and we lit the bonfire while there was still enough light to allow a little cooking, prior to darkness taking over and us becoming reliant on flames and candlelight. Because of that, the timing was perfect.

As we stood together around the fire, hundreds of the birds gathered as if by some unseen signal and provided the most amazing ten minutes of aerodynamic displays. As we stood there in awe, I was asking myself: who directs the movement? How do they not collide? Do they know how amazing they look? Sometimes you realise that you don't have to understand, you just need to enjoy . . . And then, just as suddenly, as if a signal had been sent out, the birds all started peeling off and diving into the bamboo to roost. Within a few seconds there were no airborne birds left, so we turned our attention to the games while our sausages, western-style barbecue beans and hasselback baked potatoes cooked.

I was Dorothy and Arthur's age in the late 1960s and life was so much simpler in those days. That said, we did like a good party, so I delved back into my memory to drag up the games we used to play, which all had a couple of points in common: they required very little expenditure and they made people laugh. So with that in mind, the games began.

Angela looked at me when I produced a chopping board with a big, upturned bowl on it. With a flourish I removed the bowl to reveal a rather large pile of flour . . . I said nothing and everyone just carried on looking at me. Finally, Angela broke and gave me that quizzical shrug that speaks volumes. When I asked who wanted to go first, Arthur immediately volunteered, so I explained it was simple: there were Smarties in the flour and you're not allowed to use your hands, only your mouth, and the idea is to get as many as you can. I was not the nicest daddy ever as I didn't give any advice at all, not even 'don't breathe in through your nose . . .' I realise that some people use icing sugar so the whole experience is sweeter, but I'm old school and plain flour it was.

I laughed so hard I was worried that I might pee. Somehow Arthur had flour on his eyebrows, he had blown out and there was a flour cloud, and there was an ever growing build-up of floury goop on his lips. Every school child knows that flour and water make glue, and now you know flour and Arthur spit make glue too! I was so proud of his perseverance. He kept going until he had a couple of Smarties before seeing if anyone else wanted a go . . . The adults all looked at each other and no one was particularly keen to rummage in the now lumpy flour mess, but a man has to do what he has to do, so Daddy was next up.

I discovered that my moustache is a wonderful implement for excavation, though the Smarties didn't taste as nice as I seemed to remember. In the end, we all had a go, though Grandma did have to be stopped from using her fingers! By the time we had finished bobbing for apples (note to self: less water in the bowl for younger children) and trying to eat hanging apples, our grub was ready and boy did it taste good. It's amazing what a little hot cider and games by the bonfire does for your appetite.

The children curled up on our knees to eat and we bathed in the heat radiating from the fire. It felt good and it was a pity when it was time to carry our not-so-little babies to bed. Though they were too tired for their customary bedtime bath, they did have to have a serious wash before heading off to get their beauty sleep . . .

* * *

My dad loves a souvenir to remember family holidays by. Over the years, these have varied from massive sombreros from Mexico to illuminated life-size figures of Father Christmas that we had to bring home after a trip to Florida. More recently, with the possible (or definite) influence of my mum saying 'no' to his wild ideas, Dad has started collecting fridge magnets. So as we neared the completion of their kitchen, Arthur and Dorothy decided to make some homemade magnets for their new fridge.

FRIDGE MAGNETS

You will need
Old tins with undamaged lids
Resin, measuring jug, wooden spatula for mixing, plastic cup
Pictures
Scissors
Pencil
Small magnets
Hot glue gun and glue stick

Method

Step 1: Select your pictures

Take the lids off the tins, place them on the pictures you are using and draw around them. Cut out just inside the line, so they fit nicely inside the lids.

Step 2: Add the resin

Following the instructions as to ratios, measure out part A and B of the resin into a plastic cup and mix well.

Carefully pour the resin over the picture into the lid of the tin to form a thin layer. Allow to set overnight or longer if that's what the instructions say.

Step 3: Make them into magnets

When the resin has set, use the glue gun to stick a magnet onto the back of the lid.

Tips

- Stir the resin mix gently but thoroughly so as not to make bubbles and let it sit for a few minutes to allow any bubbles to rise to the top

- Tap the lid gently after pouring the resin to remove any air bubbles

- If there are a lot of bubbles, use a cook's torch or lighter wafted gently over the surface of the resin to help get them out

It was with great delight that my parents announced a last-minute holiday to get some winter sun. Who could blame them? They are retired, after all, and it also gave us the chance for a big push to get Café Grandma over the line. When I'm 'dressing' a room in the château it takes me time to potter and fiddle. I go back and forth as I work out what's missing, what's needed, what's not working. And I keep going until that day when I enter and it just looks and feels exactly how I envisioned it. I've always found it's harder being quite so blunt about what is and isn't working when other people are there; I'd much rather give them a grand reveal once it's all finished. So Mum and Dad's holiday gave us the perfect opportunity to do just that.

A stone flooring had been laid by our builder mate Steve and counters had been installed on a working holiday by their friend Ian. It was nearly there! Before they left, Mum had chosen a lime-green paint and I had ordered a solid wooden dining table, some velour chairs and a rug. We had numerous lights to go into place, including the neon sign, and, of course, we had to work out exactly where to place the 'made with love' fridge magnets.

Grandma's Café had progressed to the point Angela was dressing it and it was time for the sign to go up. Builder mate Steve and I were ready to go for it. It was delicate and Steve and I joked about Angela choosing somewhere difficult to work . . . and we were right! She came in, looked up at the two-storey high wall, pointed right up and said, 'In the middle, up there.' Sure as hell the sign ended up just beyond the reach of a tall person on a tall ladder, but it was the perfect place for it! Off we went and set up the internal scaffolding, then we got the power behind the stud walling to the correct place. Drilling the fixings in and attaching the sign was nerve wracking but we were slow and careful and when it was up, level and working we were more than a little happy!

The night before their return I had butterflies in my stomach, the ones where you are nervous and excited in equal measures. Café Grandma was looking very special, and seeing it with furniture in place, and finally the little touches of flowers and candles, made it feel homely. I had worried that such a large, white space might not feel warm, but it did, and with Dad's man-cave mezzanine above, now they both had a place of their own to play.

When they got home from their holiday, there was no 'spending a penny', despite the two-hour drive back from the airport, just in case it spoiled the surprise! As soon as they arrived, Arthur and Dorothy led them into their forever kitchen and their faces were a delight. They savoured every detail and walked around smiling and taking it all in, genuinely happy that it all worked together nicely. As they gave us a big hug I tried to redirect their eyes as they hadn't properly looked up yet . . . When Mum finally saw 'Café Grandma' up in lights on the wall she let out a squeal. It was exactly the reaction we had hoped for. Finally, the children gave them their magnets and totally stole the show.

* * *

When you live in the country, wellington boots are a fact of life, as are wet coats and umbrellas. There are two 'front' entrances to the château: the main grand door on the ground floor, which is actually up fourteen steps, and the entrance below those steps that goes into the *sous-sol*, the basement, which would have been the domain of the servants. If you've been out shopping and brought back provisions, or have been out working or walking and return soggy or messy, going into the château's high-status entrance hallway makes no sense. Instead, you enter via the stone floor of the basement. We had named this room the 'boot room' for obvious reasons. It was dark and very dirty with a wood store and some form of storage room on either side of the door and it felt cramped and always grubby. So it was time to transform our boot room from the dumping ground of the château into an orderly new home for our jackets and wellies.

As with every job, it always gets much worse before it gets better. We thought it best to get back to the skeleton of the room so we removed the unimpressive stores, dropped the damaged ceiling and had a look at our massive room. True, the floor where the stores had been was just rammed earth, and the floor joists by the entrance that supported the decorative tiles just inside the grand front door, directly above it, had to be replaced, but it was a lovely space that had five doors off it. The double doors directly in front take you up to ground floor. To the left is the door for the family kitchen and a door into the preserves cupboard that led through to what would have been the *laiterie*, where they made butter and cheeses. To the right are two doors into the cellars, one being for the high-end wines (this was obvious as there were grilles and locks there), and the other went into the room that used to have cider and vinegar barrels in it and was now my workshop.

When the château was cleared out, it was interesting how the attic and the *sous-soul* had the most remaining treasures. Old wooden barrels of all sizes, pots, ceramic cider mugs, urns, oodles of glass jars – some as old as the château itself and with the most exquisite detail. It gave an amazing insight into how the Baglionis lived, and from what we saw down there, homemade cuisine, preserving and plonk were a big deal. They clearly enjoyed entertaining and, judging by the remains in the attic, family time was important too. Looking through all the treasures, we felt even more connected to them.

The 'caves' excited me when we first saw them. They indicated just how decadent life could be at the château. In the 'high-end cellar' there was lots of racking for wines and spirits, and every time I saw it I daydreamed about when it would be filled. Some of the racks contained old, empty, handmade bottles. They felt fragile but they had survived and each one was slightly different. I loved taking some out and looking at them. Imagine how happy I was to find a gorgeous bottle that contained liquid! I could hear the warning bells ringing and I'm not in the habit of drinking liquid found in an old bottle, however ...

I took my treasure into the kitchen and carefully decanted the liquor into a clear glass jug. It was clear and my hydrometer told me it was about 45–50 per cent alcohol by volume. You can get an idea about the taste of alcohol without actually drinking it. So I poured a couple of drops onto the palm of my hand, rubbed my hands together and cupped them over my nose to breathe in the aromas. The bottle contained what could have been centuries old eau de vie, but apart from being slightly fruity I couldn't tell what the original base was made from. It was rebottled in a clean bottle and 'laid down'. Who knows, maybe someone braver or sillier will try it in a couple more decades!

Back in our soon-to-be 'boot room', we took a closer look at the bottom of the hall floor above us, which was made from nineteenth-century oak and chestnut. It was solid but to view it we had to move some of the very clever nineteenth century technology. Between the joists there were neat rows of oak battens wrapped in straw and clay, tightly packed together to provide insulation and sound-proofing. We treated every piece of wood we exposed, made repairs and renewed insulation with twenty-first-century rock wool. Soon we had the shell of a room with electricity and lighting. Even years into our project I still smile when I see a socket or turn on a light that wasn't there when we first started (that's all of them!).

At first, I wasn't sure what I could contribute to this room. I didn't even own a pair of wellies when Dick and I first met, and yet here I was chatting to my husband about what an entire room dedicated to boots would look like! We decorate a room to suit its use and this, the boot room, obviously served its purpose, but I wondered if it would be used differently if it wasn't always in such a state. It would actually be a handy place to do some service from, for our pre-wedding get togethers, and if done nicely we could even have the brides leave from this entrance, instantly changing the

path they would walk on their wedding day. All of a sudden, I felt needed!

As we talked more, a vision and a plan started to emerge. There was more refinement needed, starting with a ceiling and wall skimming from builder mate Steve, but it would pay dividends. We would use the stunning oak storage cupboards that we took out of the potagerie suite to make counters which faced each other on either side of the door that led to the inside stairs. We decided that the backs of these counters would need to be open in order for us to 'hide' our service drinks fridge and we agreed that this room should have a real country feel. As we started to shape what that could look like, Dick got more excited. 'I've had an idea for years for a really simple but efficient boot rack,' he told me. I had no idea what he meant but the creative excitement and twinkle in his eye was adorable.

We do not have plans to be self-sufficient at the château. It is such a lot of work and it becomes all consuming. However, we do love growing and rearing our own produce. When I visited Angela in London when we first met I used to take her up a couple of goose eggs from my smallholding and she loved them, so we had long talked about getting our own geese. In theory, we could fatten them for Christmas but we were only after the eggs. The laying season is relatively short; we could only expect eggs from mid-February to early May, but what a season. Breakfast is dominated by soft-boiled dippy eggs served in a glass as no egg cup is big enough, or massive coddled eggs. We have never really taken to scrambled goose eggs or omelettes made from them. And when you fry them they are simply odd, as the yolk sits up very high on a thin island of white, so to cook the yolk perfectly I feel that the white has to be overcooked.

We decided the château was ready to have six geese! A couple of very important points about keeping geese – they are quite scary and more than happy to chase you and even nip your bum or legs. You have to show them who's boss as you run away! On the positive side, they are very effective lawnmowers and guards.

The best place to keep the geese would be near the driveway so they could execute their guard duties effectively. Of course, we could have bought a shed and erected a pen, and we did have lots of electric fencing after having kept the pigs; however, the old ruined pigsty was in exactly the correct place so it was decided that we would see if it could be used as their shed. With the roof having fallen in some time in the distant past, and with trees growing out of it, the first problem was to get into it so I could open a door. Despite my advancing years I managed to get through the window quite nimbly and, after moving some debris to the side, the door was opened.

It was a lovely old building and I knew we would bring it back to life sometime in the future, but in the meantime, I cleared an area eight feet by six feet and built the geese a room with a roof and protection all around. Quentin and I organised an outside pen with fencing and it wasn't long before he was on the phone to one of his many relatives in the area sourcing geese. The next morning, the two of us headed off with a poultry crate in the boot of the car to collect six oriental geese. I had once collected some geese in a very plush Audi estate and the geese had placed their arses against the bars and squirted shit all over the carpeted boot area, so, funnily enough, this time the crate was on a tarpaulin . . .

My fondest memory of the geese coming home was Grandma and Dorothy trying to hide behind each other as the geese told them who was boss. It would be a while before our geese laid, but the guards were in place!

The boot room was really starting to take form. We had decided that we would have six lights and we had even agreed on their

position. Note, this is always an important and passionate decision as we have to balance the look, the functionality, and the route for the cables. The walls had been skimmed and I'd found the perfect sage-green paint for them. Some grey tiles had been purchased to fill the gap where the wood stores used to be. After this was sorted, I had my 'Angel' shopping list and there were four items I was actively looking for:

- Six lights to be mounted on the ceiling
- A radiator cover that we could dry wet wellies on
- A large entrance mat
- Some kind of seating

These were my priority items, but I would also start to gather other bits and pieces to give the room its defining character.

My first port of call was our attic, but I swiftly decided that our cast iron-daybeds wouldn't work, so I jumped in the car and headed towards La Gravelle Brocante, my favourite flea market, run by a rather lovely and eccentric husband and wife duo. We have happy memories of finds from this *brocante*, including a variety of ceramic sinks, baths, lights and glass Victorian domes, as well as some of my favourite *chaises du mariage* (decorative ornaments of chairs, usually about 40cm high under glass domes, that were traditional wedding presents). I'm not sure if the fact that they have so much 'treasure' is coincidence or luck, but I have always found something that fitted my requirements and every time I leave I am on a high, feeling like I've made the 'find' of a lifetime.

Today was no different, apart from being on my own because I needed to have the seats down in the back. As I turned the corner into the *brocante* following a thirty-minute scenic drive, I was greeted by two statuesque concrete lions, a number of cupids and a crazy amount of concrete chickens. The outside was host to pallets full of reclaimed tiles and slates, and around a third of this area was dedicated to cast iron. Gate after gate, many leant on each other like dominos. As I stood gazing around the cast-iron zone I started to question why I had come here. I'd never seen a great radiator cover here before, what was I thinking? Still, I walked slowly around and suddenly my eye was caught by a balcony railing. It was roughly the right size and I instantly knew that once Dick added a nice wooden top to it, boom, it would be perfect! It was heavy and awkward, so the owner helped me get it in the car, then off I went with another 'find' of a lifetime.

It might have been the unctuous, sage-green matt paint that adorned both ceiling and walls that made our new boot room look so nice, or perhaps the six symmetrically placed reproduction 1950s industrial pendant lights in a complementary forest green. To complement the panelled service counters, all the doors into the other rooms were stripped and waxed, and with that, the original panelled wood doors suddenly felt like a feature. The granite stone detail around the door also came into its own. For years, this area had had no attention, but now everything was polished and perfect.

For the final touch, Dick found some old shotguns and rifles at the same *brocante*. We felt they would look great on the walls, along with an old musket we had found in the attic and some of Dick's old 'split cane' fishing rods. I had never thought much about fishing rods, but these ones that had been made from bamboo split, glued and finished with such finesse, won me over, and soon we had designed a simple storage system that hung them from the roof. The same week, a surprise gift arrived in the post from John and Dan, one of the first ever couples to come on a food lovers' weekend. The deer-head 'trophy' with magnificent antlers were a complete coincidence but arrived with us at the perfect time and so quickly got added into the boot room mix with some old hunting prints that Dick had picked up years ago.

Of course, we also needed some seating for when people were taking their boots off. Dick said it had to be functional rather than comfy. I was stumped for a while and then started searching for anything that I felt could work. Then, late one evening, while Dick and I were sitting in bed working on our computers with a glass of port, I was browsing an online Paris-based *brocante* when I discovered a collection of old vintage cinema seats created by Fourel & Co, a Lyonnais company. I've seen many seats like these in my time but none quite as beautiful; everything from the wood and the red velour to the gold 'Lyon' embossed on the sides was stunning. And aside from the beauty, I also appreciated the idea that the seats folded up to allow the room to have that feeling of space.

I loved the fact that Angela was giving the boot room a very traditional feel. I don't worry about the colour palette Angela will use, but we did need work surfaces and some storage and that was going to have to be in keeping with the room, so no Swedish flat packs! Wherever possible we reuse something we have found or salvaged from the château. So for the panelling around the work surfaces we were really delighted to be able to use the lovely oak doors that had come off cupboards in the potagerie bathroom. The panelling was perfect and we had enough to do two separate areas. For the tops, I bought some oak planks which meant we would have a hard-wearing, solid work surface.

A boot room obviously needs somewhere to store boots. Our problem was we had lots of pairs of boots – tall ones, short ones and spares for friends who need to borrow a pair. I was delighted to try my design that allowed Dorothy's boots to sit alongside mine. It involved rows of hinged posts that could be out or flat. It is then up to you to make the posts fit your desired wellies. It worked and we have a wall big enough to host up to 15 pairs of boots. The best part is the boots are sole side up so they can dry out if necessary.

Dick's boot rack idea was genius, and for me, adding Arthur's first blue Hunter boots on there felt like we were really putting down our roots (or boots!). It was all taking shape but to add a little extra character, I managed to source four faux 'giraffe' feet to attach to the ceiling. They looked a little odd but were fun and anyone who had been in the dining room above had seen our faux giraffe neck and head, so the joke made sense. I never found the perfect entrance mat, but sometimes that leads to a better alternative. In every local DIY store in France they sell coir matting by the roll. The roll I bought was more than two metres wide, which meant I could cut it exactly to size, creating a magnificent entrance mat that was literally made for its environment! I finished this off with my 'château' stencil to create a bespoke 'château welcome' mat. Finally, Dick made some oak 'boot jacks'. The design was simple but this meant that no one would ever be struggling to take off their boots after a muddy walk. With the once-crumbling dumping area tidy, organised, full of character and with just the right amount of comfort, I couldn't wait for the family to start using it.

I was so, so pleased with our boot room. It is a countryman's dream, and I love the fact that the walls have old maps of the original fortress that was on this site before our château was built. I think it's fair to say the boot room is the busiest room in the house! It's the main thoroughfare in and out, so it finally got the attention it deserved.

As autumn turned to winter, the days were wet and the leaves continued to shed until the trees were bare. Our boot room had

quickly become a joy to come in and out of. It felt like it had been there forever and with many wedding tastings this year, in advance of next year's events, we were delighted that we could sit in the family kitchen and look out at this gorgeous room. As the countdown to the Christmas holiday approached and renovation for the year had been completed, Arthur and Dorothy's attention turned to the most magical time of the year.

The arrival of *marchés de Noël* are unquestionably the start of Christmas here in France, and over the years we have taken it upon ourselves to visit as many of these markets as possible! We have of course been to our local market but also those in towns and cities from Louverné to Laval, and Mayenne to Rennes. All have had their own magic, with different creative displays and lots of humour. Laval, our local city that is home to the department's *prefecture*, had Father Christmas's underpants hanging out one year! From memory, possibly not helped by the *vin chaud*, the markets all seem to take inspiration from the classic German markets with their wooden chalets selling colourful and artisan gifts, food and wines. But the magic comes from walking around and sharing the excitement of the families, the aroma of sweet chestnuts being cooked and being part of the bustle. The markets are full of smiling faces, it's a simple fact: Grinches and Scrooges don't go out of their way to absorb the fantastic festive atmosphere; they stay at home!

Arthur and Dorothy were the perfect age to go in search of *Père Noël* so we headed off to Angers, an historic old town just over an hour from us. We arrived late in the afternoon as it got dark and the market was wonderful. We were walking around absorbing all the sights, sounds and smells, when Arthur spotted *Père Noël* with a sack on his back. As we approached, Arthur just walked up to him and gave him a massive hug. Dorothy was a tad more reticent and hid behind me but our charismatic Santa coaxed her out and soon we were conversing in a mix of languages and all looking forward to Christmas. In France, many *Pères Noël* have their own suits and cultivate their white beards so they are at their best at the beginning of December, which is obviously their busy time . . .

We had a lovely evening and relished the *vin chaud* and the ubiquitous churros. To be fair, churros are not very French, but you find them at every single Christmas market and most *fêtes*, alongside the candyfloss and crepes. They are basically dough that is piped through a star-shaped nozzle into hot fat, cooked until golden and then rolled in lashings of sugar (usually cinnamon sugar at Christmas markets) and often served with a chocolatey hazelnut spread. I defy anyone to eat more than four or five but they are warm and sweet, and apparently the sugar sticks to your moustache!

We love the fact that Christmas doesn't really start in France until the beginning of December. But when it does start the month is busy. With the Christmas market getting us in the mood, we got all our decorations down from the attic and then the pressure was on to get the best tree possible. I think Dick was trying to share the responsibility when he suggested the whole family go on the search rather than him heading off on his own. I loved the idea and, with Arthur and Dorothy both having their own strong opinions now, I knew it was going to be lots of fun at a local Christmas tree farm. So off we went with a boot full of coats, wellies, orange rachet straps and, at my insistence, a change of clothes for the children, in search of the best tree we could find. When we first pulled off the road, I assumed we were lost, as it was just a muddy lane. I couldn't even see a Christmas tree.

Heading off to choose the best tree possible for the family by yourself can be a scary job with a lot of responsibility, but as a family adventure it is nothing but fun – after all, we'd all have to agree so there was joint culpability, and our local Christmas tree farm was bound to have something we liked. And, being ex-military, I had a fall-back plan – if not, we could pop into the supermarket on the way home.

We found the track to the farm. It was muddy but that's why 4×4s were invented. I pulled over and then it was time to get togged up with boots and coats. Behind the hedgerow were literally acres of trees of all sizes and types so we headed down what must have been the path in search of someone in charge. I loved the relaxed nature of everyone there – go for a walk, choose a tree and then come and get us. We'll cut it down, measure it, you pay and then it's yours.

We headed off and soon we had seen a couple of likely contenders but it was just too easy to lose your tree as you went off in search of an even better one. Soon I was tying my two hankies to Angela and Dorothy's favourites, a scarf around one for Arthur and a buff over the one I liked. But we hadn't finished, there were more to be seen. However, my lack of further fashion accessories meant that individuals had to move their marker to their favourite, favourite tree.

Soon we had four contenders and we each made our case, based on shape, size, bushiness and general beauty. I have to say I think my choice only won because Angela wasn't sure the one she had chosen would fit in our not small reception rooms! To be fair, it rivalled the 25-metre trees the people of Norway have given to Britain every year since 1947 in thanks for our assistance in the Second World War. So, leaving the family to guard the tree, I went off to get the chap with the chainsaw. We paid and the gallant farmer offered to help us carry it to the car, but I assured him the Strawbridges could do this. It was so much fun. We organised ourselves in height order: Dorothy, Arthur, Angela then me. Then we proceeded to put the tree on our shoulders. It was bloody heavy, though I noted my helpers didn't complain much, but that was probably to do with the fact that they were hanging from it rather than lifting it!

Somehow the family got our beautiful tree back to our car without it getting muddy, which is a lot more than can be said for Arthur and Dorothy. I think it was probably the lovely feel and the ooziness of the mud, as once Arthur had fallen over once he showed little desire to stay upright: at every opportunity he was on his hands and knees in the mud again. Sitting on the tailgate, the children were stripped down to their underwear and given fresh clothes as Dick chuntered and tied the tree to the roof of the car.

Having successfully got the tree into the château, I attached it to our clamp and hoisted it up. Then began the annual 'let's get the tree the right way around and perfectly vertical' challenge. It's actually quite relaxing. The tree is placed securely in its base and put roughly in position, I then lie on the floor with a couple of oak wedges I made years ago and rotate the tree clockwise and anticlockwise to get the best bit facing the room. Then I insert the necessary wedges to get it vertical – all the time taking direction from Angela and the children. Now that all sounds simple, doesn't it? But somehow, Angela varies her direction of rotation and her clocks seem to rotate the other way, I do some more chuntering and most often, the base ends up where it started. But once the tree is upright and stable, it's on with our wonderful fairy godmother, on with the lights, then off we go adding ornaments, all of which have a story and a known origin. I love this bit. Then, with Bing Crosby singing 'White Christmas', Angela and I have a glass of port, the children have apple juice 'champagne', there are nibbles and a couple of hours pass in the blink of an eye.

We usually have a couple of Christmas puddings sent to us by Dick's mum and sisters, but this year we had decided to make our own using the recipe Dick remembered making when he was Arthur and Dorothy's age. We all headed down to the family kitchen and Dick laid out the ingredients, bowls and scales. The recipe we followed was based on one from a cookbook that Dick's mum had been given when she first got married and the page bore the marks of much usage. We all measured, tasted and mixed, producing the most wonderful pudding dough. Then everyone took a turn at stirring and making a wish for Christmas. Dick started and the children watched as Daddy closed his eyes and solemnly stirred and wished. I had everything I could possibly need, but followed the ritual and closed my eyes, stirred and made my wish (which is probably the same as every mum's wish!). Arthur and Dorothy melted my heart as they copied us and their lips moved as they made their secret wish for Christmas.

Job done, the best part of the whole thing was the children licking the bowl clean. They had sultanas in their hair, dough in their ears and smiles wider than the kitchen. I'm not sure if the bowl licking was responsible parenting considering there was a gill of brandy added to our mix, but then again I'm also not sure what a gill is, so it couldn't have been that bad, could it?

Family time in the kitchen is to be savoured but is even more special near Christmas. Our Christmas pudding making took me back to my family fifty years earlier, and that's what Christmas is about after all. Our measurements may not have been 100 per cent accurate but it didn't matter. We made the most impressive Christmas puddings that we fed weekly with a bit more brandy all the way up to Christmas.

Decorating the château for Christmas is a moment in time that we look forward to all year round. Up until now, we have always used our own collection of goodies along with some home-made loveliness, like your classic toilet-roll angels. But as we started preparing for our fourth Christmas at the château, I could not shake off the feeling that I fancied something 'oversized', something a bit more statement. Cue my idea for football-sized Christmas baubles . . .

· ·

FOOTBALL-SIZED CHRISTMAS BAUBLES

You will need

Foam footballs
Spray glue
Spray paint (gold is my choice!)
Cable ties
Paper cups
Strong adhesive
Fabric
Scissors
Braid
Colourful rope to hang your decorations

Method

Step 1: Prepare your frill

Turn your paper cups upside down, spray them to the colour of your choice and allow to dry.

Once dry, snip around the edge every 1.5cm to create a frill. Your cuts should go approximately half way up the cup so it can be opened up.

Pierce two holes in the bottom of the cup and thread the cable tie through these, joining to form a loop, trimming any excess cable tie.

Fold the snipped edges out and use the tabs to glue the cup firmly to the foam football. Leave to dry so it is very secure.

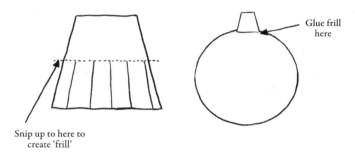

Snip up to here to create 'frill'

Glue frill here

Step 2: Decorate your football

Cut the fabric (see image below for the shape) into segments which fit top to bottom (NB: the length top to bottom is half the circumference of your ball – you don't need to do maths, just measure it with a piece of string) then use the spray glue to hold in place, repeat until you have covered the whole ball. The segments of fabric should look like those found on a globe. I used six per ball.

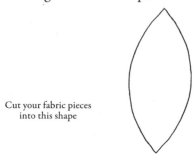

Cut your fabric pieces into this shape

Use the braid to define the segments and tidy up any gaps between the joints of fabric and around the top 'cup'.

Hang with the decorative rope. See picture section 2 for the finished results!

Tips

- Make sure the cup is really secure on the ball . . . you can't fix it easily if it comes off

- As an alternative, you could *découpage* with fabric or even paper and add trim, sequins, beads, etc. for that Christmassy feel

. . . .

In the summer, we had made *vin de noix* from our very own walnuts and we had been patiently waiting until Christmas to enjoy it. *Vin de noix* is the preferred aperitif of the Dordogne region, which is considerably south of us, but we had our grove of four walnut trees so we decided to go for it . . .

Just to be clear, we had been seriously unsuccessful harvesting them since we moved to the château. Every year, we'd glimpse our very cute red squirrels and every year, we'd see our walnut trees being productive with lots of nuts maturing well. Then, the day we'd go to harvest our bounty there were no walnuts to be seen. It's a bloody conspiracy! So rather than another year of 'squirrel-gate', we decided to harvest them before they were attractive to the squirrels.

Vin de noix, walnut wine, is made from the green, unripe walnuts that are picked between the *fête de la Saint-Jean* (the annual celebration of the birth of John the Baptist) on 24th June and Bastille Day, which is 14th July. There are hundreds of variations on the recipe but this is the one we used:

VIN DE NOIX

Ingredients

5l red wine
1l brandy (or you can use vodka)
Approx. 50 walnuts quartered (wear latex gloves as the juices
will stain your hands)
1kg sugar

Method

*Mix together in an eight-litre container and leave for six weeks,
mixing every week if you remember. Then strain, adjust the
sweetness if necessary, bottle and save until near Christmas*

Dick bottled our *vin de noix* in some of the stunning old handmade bottles we had inherited in the *cave*. I had also, much to Dick's surprise and delight, visited a local agricultural supplier, Gamm Vert, and bought some red wax in the bottling and preserving section. The wax is very attractive but also seals the corks so there is less chance for oxygen to get in and spoil the wine. I had seen it on our travels but only now put two and two together, so once Dick showed me our bottles of château *vin de noix*, we dipped the ends into melted wax to give them an authentic look and then returned them to the *cave* to wait.

I've always wanted to be able to bottle the feeling of being four or five years old on Christmas Day. It had been quite a marathon this year and even the night before, Dick and I had been up wrapping presents till the early hours getting organised for the big day. At 3.30am, an hour and a half after we went to bed, the fun began. Père Noël had been and Arthur and Dorothy could not believe it . . . they'd never even heard a thing! Both were jumping with excitement and before we even had time to negotiate for a little more sleep, paper was being torn apart and there were lots of excited screams. It always amazes us how Father Christmas just knows and gets it right. He even managed to keep up the tradition of putting a Toblerone in their sacks, which was something that I got when I was younger too. What a guy!

A number of presents later, both children were playing happily with their new Lego and Peppa Pig toys as Dick and I sat in bed, tired but smiling. Today was not a day to talk about our year, or plan, or even to think that much. Christmas Day was about soaking up each and every moment. It was about seeing if Père Noël had enjoyed the homemade mince pies we left for him, enjoying our annual ham, walking the grounds, playing games, working out how to use new toys, and just being. And, in every way, Christmas 2018 was perfect.

CHAPTER FOUR

A Year of Perfecting

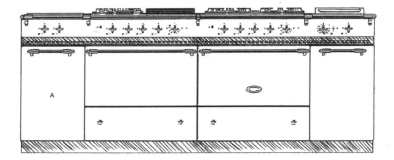

There is always a calmness on the first day of the year that is never felt on any other. I've often wondered if it's because so many people are feeling the same or maybe it's because there is less traffic, lots of people are in bed with sore heads or maybe it's just us in our bubble.

By the beginning of 2019, we were four years into our journey, and our bubble, which had always been afloat, felt light. At the heart of this was our family. The children were happy and content, they were doing well at school and as a unit we were incredibly strong. Their personalities were flourishing and they were understanding humour. They started to get their grandad's terrible jokes and, off the back of their new understanding, started to make up their own. We were in a different phase of their childhood, *petits enfants*, and it was a lot of fun.

My mum and dad were really settled and enjoying life too. There are a lot of things to get used to when you move to a new country; it's not for everyone, and whilst they had been content from the start, I could see a shift in how they were embracing France. Mum knew her favourite cuts of meat, she knew what to ask for at the fish counter, where she could get digestive biscuits from and she also had a huge cupboard of British tea. Life was looking rosy.

The first day of every year should always be filled with optimism, but 2019 was positively bursting. Twenty eighteen had been successful, and we had a full order book for our weddings and events and a fantastic foundation on which to build. What we now aspired to was efficiency. This year, we had sixteen weddings, a dozen tastings for future weddings, six food lovers' weekends, four garden days, four fun days, a fortieth birthday party for our friend, as well as Jenny and Steve's fiftieth wedding anniversary 'something'. We were bursting at the seams. We knew we had to work smarter and not harder. With a full order book and a successful year under our belt it was time to invest where we needed to and we didn't want to lose sight of quality family time. In addition to our quest to make the coach house more comfortable for Jenny and Steve, we were going to tackle the *sous-sol*, the heart of catering productivity . . .

When we had bought the château, the basement room in the north of the château was a 'cold' storage room, green with slime. It was damp and a portion of the room was taken over to form an outside, 'long-drop' toilet. For those of you who have not had the pleasure of using a long-drop loo, the clue is in the name . . . from where you sit, it's a long way down to where your poop finally lands. In our case, it was a couple of metres down to the water level of the moat, and there was a small tunnel connecting our poo pit to the moat proper so fish or whatever (!) could come and help with disposal. The crowning glory was that it was a double loo. That meant two people could sit side by side and chat as they abluted . . . how times have changed. We had no desire to reinstate this loo so we had taken down the internal wall partitioning this room and had put in a double-glazed door to give us outside access. We had put in some water and rudimentary electrics so it had become our utility room and a bit of a kitchen overspill area. However, we had big plans that involved a complete makeover for this room and the room next to it, which had been the *laiterie*, the dairy. We were going to have a proper commercial kitchen and bespoke utility area.

It was interesting drawing up the plans for the rooms as the kitchen was my domain but I'd always allowed Angela complete control of the aesthetics. Actually, we didn't argue that much as the functionality was my call and I knew Angela understood the need for a 'sterile' area, so I left it up to her to decide on the fittings. It is next door to our family kitchen, which is full of copper and wood and has a traditional Rayburn stove, as well as the island with its gas burners. But our commercial kitchen was to be completely different. To help keep things organised, we decided that the pantry that was off the family kitchen would have a second door put in it that would lead through to the commercial kitchen. That way both kitchens could share the dry goods and a wide selection of kitchen tools we keep in there. To make the pantry functional there was a quick trip to IKEA, providing us with simple but cavernous cupboards and work surfaces. We needed some power in there to make the most of the work surfaces, but by and large it was a simple space to turn into something very useful. White cupboards, on the ground and hanging off the walls, with slate-grey work surfaces, meant we had homes for condiments and spices, salts for curing, oil and vinegars, flour of every type, baking powders and yeast, cake decorations of every colour and type, flavourings and colourings, pulses and seeds, pasta and rice and even a cupboard for my mincers and sausage- and salami-making kit.

When we looked at all the kitchenalia on the work surfaces it was obvious how important cooking was to us, as we had amassed a collection of gadgets that allowed us to tackle nearly every job. We have always lived by the rule 'buy once, cry once'. In other words, try to buy the best you can afford. When one of the parents at the children's school told me her grandmother was 'too poor to buy cheap things', it really hit home . . .

On our surfaces, on top of the cupboards, and under work surfaces, we had a great array of toys: a vacuum sealer, slicers, Magimix, vintage Kenwood Chef, beaters, ice cream maker, sharpeners, stick blenders . . . it seemed a lot but I just couldn't think of any item we did not need or want to have.

For the commercial kitchen, we followed the same process for the renovations that we always did. First, empty and strip back anything that will not survive the next fifty years, then it is over to Dick for the utilities: water (hot and cold), waste, gas and electrics, as they always make a mess. This is followed by 'making good', which means more mess, then tiling and finally it is time to sort out all the bits that make it look good. One of our biggest challenges has always been buying what we need and getting it when we want it. That may sound simplistic but I don't know how many times I have found the perfect tile, cupboard or piece of furniture, only to be told it'll be available in six weeks, or maybe three months' time . . .

Dick and I were sitting in bed looking at commercial stoves and coming to terms with the fact we couldn't justify the cost or afford the La Cornue Château range. To fit that in our kitchen would probably cost significantly over £100,000, so we were searching for something good quality, in a similar design, that we could afford. I found the perfect alternative in a French brand called Lacanche but, as silly as it sounds, the cheapest and fastest delivery

was from a company in Dorset who had what appeared to be the cooker for us available as ex-display. With that big decision made and agreed I could now nail down the tiles, cupboards and colours.

I'd heard of Lacanche as a stove manufacturer but had never really researched them. I was pleasantly surprised as the write-ups were good and it was possible to have your choice of appliances linked together to make the perfect combination to suit your needs . . . I was the proverbial kiddie in the sweet shop. I obviously needed a bain marie, a gas oven and an electric oven (we'd tried to get our limited electricity at the château upgraded; however, it was always a problem, so to reduce our needs we had the second oven as gas), six gas burners, a gas simmer plate, a flat-top grill and, of course, a warming cupboard. This list was essential and, unbelievably, the ex-display model had everything.

It arrived just before we were ready to put it in. Jean Betram, our local heavy plant man, brought around his forklift, took it off the truck and delivered it behind the château within a couple of metres. A couple of days later, there was a lot of grunting and heaving and, dare I say, rude words as we used rollers and ropes to manhandle our massive range in through the back door. We never had any doubt that we could get it inside – after all, the Egyptians had built pyramids with similar equipment – but all of a sudden, the back step was higher than any of us had reckoned. We built a ramp and we levered, pushed and pulled to get it lined up with the double doors. It was all getting a bit frustrating when builder mate Steve and I said enough is enough and we told the youngsters (no one under forty, but still many years younger than us) to push when we yelled. It was like two weightlifters getting psyched up before the gold medal lift. I'm still not quite sure what we did or how a noise that must have sounded like 'now' was emitted, but the next thing we knew our stove was on rollers in our new kitchen.

There was still a lot of finishing to do in the new professional kitchen, but I loved seeing the smile on Dick's face as he stood by his sexy new stove and stared out of the doorway across the moat. He finally had the utility that would make catering this year's event, as well as all future ones, manageable and fun.

In the early months of 2019, we had a real winter and, for the first time since the year we moved into the château, we had snow! Arthur was just six and Dorothy four, so for the first time they got to truly enjoy the delights of building a snowman and trying to get Mummy and Daddy with snowballs. The joy in their little faces was amazing to see.

There was a real mad panic trying to find all the snow-friendly gloves, coats and shoes, and we could hardly control the pace at which Arthur and Dorothy launched themselves out of the boot room into the powdered snow. The grounds and the château looked like a scene from a Disney movie. Every twig, piece of grass and bump had been touched by the white crystals of snow, which had even made areas like our roof, windows and certain parts of the ground that were everyday reminders that there is still a lot of work to do look perfect.

After a snowball fight – which saw everyone's cheeks get very rosy, Dick getting very competitive, me reminding everyone that Dorothy was just four, and then Dorothy quite proudly getting her own back on Daddy and Arthur – we settled down to make a snowman. As children, we always marked our spot and loaded snow on top until it roughly looked round, then did the same again until we had a snowman. But this was us making a château snowman under Mr Strawbridge's supervision and, being as efficient as he is, there was a way to make a perfect snowball. It started with a tiny ball, which you roll along the snow so it collects the snow; then, in order to ensure you keep the ball shape, you change direction and so forth. Very clever, but then, we would expect nothing less from a process-driven gentleman. There were a couple of learning experiences along the way as well: plot your end position and don't start there as it can get heavy to carry if you end in the wrong place, and make sure you move in lots of different directions. We laughed so hard that at one time we were all resting on the body of the snowman. This one was to be Dick and we placed it at the start of the pathway to the orangery before adding a hat, a scarf, a carrot nose, some pine-cone eyes, some buttons and some straw for a moustache. It was very much a family effort and it looked brilliant.

The plan was to build the whole family in snow; however, by this time, everyone's hands were cold and the thought of a warm house and cuppa won. So it was decided that one snowman was exactly right and as we left, Arthur drew some boobs on the snowman, so it was a little bit Mummy too.

Later that day, when everyone had thawed out, we ventured over to see the geese. We had six geese and they seemed very happy and loud! We were all together but Dick suggested to Dorothy that she use the assistance of her 'brave mummy' to explore their beds. I'm not sure how I didn't cotton on to what was happening, but I didn't (that's the evolving country girl in me). But I'm glad I didn't as, after a little rummage, ensuring we missed the poo, Dorothy found her first goose egg and we both squealed with delight as she picked it up, gigantic in her little hands. Dick nodded and gave me the knowing look as I smiled inside at my innocence. Of course, we had to wait until we'd gathered four eggs before we could try them, but this just added to the anticipation.

The winter continued to be glorious. The snowdrop flowers covered the ground and we had many crispy walks out, crunching the iced grass and making mini snowballs from the frost. We hosted two food lovers' weekends, plus two birthday events, had a visit from our château friends Michael and Nathan and a sneaky out-of-season wedding for James and Liz, which was fantastic. We eventually got to eat our first dippy goose egg and, like all firsts, not only was it delicious, it was also heart-warming as we watched the children savour theirs. Dick got bees in his walled garden and life felt rich. We really were living our dream.

There are lots of ways of learning about France and of forming an opinion about the people, places and the cuisine. I had long been a fan of Julia Child, the American chef who brought French cooking to the masses in America, and her cookery shows never fail to make me smile or teach me something. The old black and white episodes that can be viewed on the internet have a naivety to them, and 'live' cooking leaves you nowhere to hide . . . Her half-hour on roasting a chicken was amazing and had me hooked. As a very early television chef, she was a real trailblazer and I found her book, *My Life in France*, inspiring, especially in the early years when she and her husband were exploring. When she decided to do the cordon bleu course she describes going shopping for her *batterie de cuisine* in one of Paris's oldest family-run kitchen shops, E. Dehillerin. It sounded like an Aladdin's cave, so when Arthur started showing an interest in cooking, and we had the chance for a boys' outing, we headed to Paris on the train for an overnight adventure.

We arrived, checked into our hotel and the city was ours to go and explore the culinary delights. I told Arthur he was completely in charge and could choose the restaurant and the type of food. We were in Paris and the choice was wonderful. It was early evening and there was no rush so we walked around and looked at what was on offer. I saw the moment Arthur had his brainwave. I think it was the smell of woodsmoke but he announced we were having pizza. I only

The Dolphin.

Mademoiselle Daisy's first adventure.

Modern family.

Dick's sixtieth birthday in Ireland.

Original wallpaper
found under the stairs.

Golden celebrations.

Fun and festivities, 2019

asked once if he was sure, and he was, so we walked past lots of little gems of restaurants to find the perfect Parisienne pizza. Which we did.

We had a ball. The place was busy and the atmosphere friendly. We ordered drinks and two large, thin-based pizzas. Arthur's was ham and mushroom and mine was a pizza alla napoletana with anchovies and olives. I say it had olives but I didn't actually get any as my seven-year-old ate them all, though he did offer me some of his mushrooms as compensation. The *pichet* of red wine I had to wash down my meal was smooth and young and, as always, Arthur was allowed to taste it, and confirmed that it was 'not terrible'.

Next morning, not long after it had opened, we were at the shop looking through the window, excited about what was on offer. The place was wonderful and not like any modern shop. There was kitchen equipment stacked on high shelves on either side of narrow aisles and everything looked precariously balanced. Arthur and I have been known to knock things over and this place was vulnerable to say the least.

We spent several hours walking around and amassed a pile that included a truly massive colander, a beech chopping board and a selection of stainless-steel utensils. I particularly loved going down to the cellar; it was so full of goodies and the selection of copper pans was to die for – the French have a pan for every purpose. Luckily, I had to carry what we bought so that limited our spending. However, we did leave with a Tatin pan, which was copper, lined with stainless steel, shaped like a frying pan and with two small brass handles that meant it fitted into the oven easily and was designed to turn your Tatin out easily – very clever. I also love the fact that it is of such quality that Arthur will be using it long after I am gone, and hopefully in the far future he will remember his outing to Paris with his daddy!

On getting home, we shared our adventure and, obviously, we had to use our new Tatin pan immediately in our new kitchen.

TARTE TATIN

Ingredients

A disc of all-butter puff pastry slightly 1cm larger than your pan,
pricked all over with a fork
6 dessert apples, peeled, cored and quartered
100g golden caster sugar
100g unsalted butter, diced and chilled

Method

Preheat the oven to 180°C/160°C fan.

*Spread the sugar evenly over the bottom of your pan and heat
over a medium heat until it reaches the amber caramel stage.
Take it off the heat and whisk in the butter.*

*Whilst it is still bubbling, add in your apple segments. Place
on a gentle heat and stir delicately until they are coated. Then
carefully arrange them neatly in the pan.*

*Take off the heat and lay the puff pastry on top, tucking in the
edges. Place in the oven and cook for 30 minutes.*

When we removed the tart from the oven the small brass handles
suddenly came into their own as it was truly simple to place a plate
on the top of the pan and invert it. You have to flip it whilst the tart
is hot so the caramel is still soft. Angela and I spoiled ourselves with
a rich custard-based cinnamon ice cream to go with our warm tart,
whilst the children had vanilla and loved it.

Apple pie holds a special place in my heart. This was always Mum's thing and because her dad, Don, my grandad, loved it so much, she made it every time we saw them. The taste of sweet apples with ice cream will always be full of nostalgia for me, so when Arthur and Dick put their own signature twist on it in our home, it reminded me that we were creating our own history, flavours and traditions. It tasted delightful and seeing Arthur's pride made my heart turn as soft as the ice cream!

* * *

To complete the downstairs renovation, our utility room was next on the list and was to occupy the old _laiterie_. We needed a wipe-down clean room large enough to handwash all the vintage china and turn around laundry in an efficient manner. None of this sounds glamorous but if this room was done right it would ease the pressure of everything else.

Angela and I walked around the room that was called our 'wedding room'. It may have started life at the château as the dairy, but now it was packed to bursting and really needed a good sort out! It had become the place to 'dump' anything china and generally to do with weddings that didn't have a designated place elsewhere. When we finally got it sorted and turned it into a proper utility room, it would make life this year much smoother. Sadly, though, I had to face facts: as the practical one, I knew that this room was actually not quite big enough, so reluctantly I floated an idea on how to make it bigger. Angela loved it. We had to 'steal' part of the _cave_ by knocking through the 150-year-old stud wall and then rebuild a new wall and door. It would make the utility space bigger; it would work and wouldn't change the original flow of the house. Apart from knocking through a wall to create a larger honeymoon suite, and taking a part of the children's bedroom to make extra space for the bathroom, we have otherwise learnt to live within the old building.

Our new utility would need water, electricity and waste pipes. It was getting the waste from the sinks to the septic tank that needed a fair amount of thought. In the end, it became obvious that it would have to pass through the outside 'toilet'. To be fair, since we had removed the plank with two holes in it to sit upon, it wasn't so much a toilet as a large space with somewhere to pee. It was a matter of in for a penny in for a pound, and so we devised a plan to turn this space into two loos: one using the original outside door and the other accessed from the to-be-expanded utility room. All it needed was plumbing for two toilets and two sinks, electricity for two separate lights, a floor to be suspended above a 1.5m hole, a stud wall and a doorway made in a two-foot-thick structural wall . . . All this would provide us with a great route for the sink wastes to get out of the château and leave via the new toilet pipes.

I think I created a monster when I suggested Angela use a jack hammer to make an entrance arch in the honeymoon suite. With absolutely no encouragement she now had one in her hands and was knocking down the stud wall to enlarge the utility room. Soon the room(s) were taking shape and it was possible to see how it was all going to work.

The château is a gift that keeps giving and it's often when we least expect it that we find more little jewels. While working on the utility room we were also clearing out under the stairs that lead from the *sous-sol* up to the ground floor, and it was there I noticed a wallpaper that I had not seen before just stuck onto a piece of wood. It was a soft caramel colour, with white and red flowers on. Whilst this room was to be more utilitarian than stylish, I instantly thought that this find needed to be woven into the fabric of the space. So I set about working out how we would do it.

Firstly, we decided to remove the piece of wood to create more space under the stairs. The wood by itself was stunning and with the ancient wallpaper aged to perfection, it was actually already an artwork that could be hung as a nod to the Baglionis' history.

We had also mapped out the space, with our two sinks, our 15kg washing machine and 15kg tumble dryer (which, just for the record, were both complete game changers), our glass washer (again, I have no idea how we functioned before we had this) and the ice machine, which we had purchased second hand the previous year. In order for this area to be 'wipe-down', we decided that we would tile the counter and splashback area and now, having found the unique flower design, I came up with a plan to take snapshots of it and print it on the tiles. At this stage, I felt very happy that this room was basically designing itself. The final creative flourish is something that still makes me happy to this day.

To make the part of this room that was under the stairs which lead up to the main high-status floor more usable, the Baglionis had stuck offcuts of wallpaper to the underside of the steps to stop the dust dropping down every time someone went up or down. Obviously they had aged a lot over time, but on these stairs were decades of history. I could see the dark-green back hallway wallpaper, the caramel flower wallpaper, as well as the original wallpaper from our room. It was just amazing to see. I knew it would have to be covered up in order to keep this space wipe-clean but I was also desperate to find a way to preserve it.

It only took a night's sleep for the answer to come to me. First, I took a photo of the underneath of the stairs and had it printed onto sticky-back plastic exactly the same size as the original area. In the meantime, builder mate Steve would plasterboard over this area, covering and protecting the original paper, and stopping any more dust dropping through, and then Dick would make a piece of wood to stick the plastic onto. It all fell into place very well. The best and funniest part was Dick assisting me putting the plastic onto the wood. Memories came flooding back for us both of covering our school books with plastic, and whilst I know Dick likes to have a chunter about certain things he resents doing, he still does them with a cheeky if not defiant smile. But this roll of plastic was actually causing me real distress. I needed to be focused and concentrate, so I decided I might be better doing this task on my own.

I have to say I have never been so pleased to leave a job half done. Sticky-back plastic was invented to torture the unwary! Bubbles in the middle that don't disappear even if you pierce them, and no matter how much you squash them, bubbles that turn into creases when you move them – it is a minefield that I was happy to go around . . .

When the final cosmetics were done we had a well-designed and functioning professional kitchen area. The kitchen with its stove, fridges, stainless-steel work surfaces, freezer, access to the pantry and dumb waiter, vegetable preparation sink, cupboards and utensil racks, was a pleasure to work in. The utility room was adjacent to the kitchen and shared views back over the moat. It was easy to communicate with the kitchen and pass things through to the 'pan bash' area that was also well equipped. Apart from Angela's super-large washing machine and tumble dryer, there were two freezers, two large, deep sinks, three draining racks (one of which was over a metre long), cupboards, surfaces, a glass washer, an ice machine, a hand-washing sink and access to a loo, the *cave* and the preserves cupboard.

From the very first time we used our new facilities, I smiled. As I looked back it was hard to believe we had, for a lot of weddings, done everything in the family kitchen, with an extra sink and surfaces in the cold room. This was luxury and we felt we could now tackle anything we wanted to do. The size of the orangery limited us to eighty people seated, and time on an event day limited us to six or seven courses, but we now had the tools to make it all that little bit easier and more fun. A big wedding is still hard work but as a team, it feels like we are doing the best that can be done at the château.

With our busy season fast approaching, we were keen to be as organised as possible. The winter had been cold and brilliant. We'd had many tastings for this year's weddings alongside viewings for the future and the business felt like it really had found its rhythm. Whilst we loved every moment of the winter, we were happy when spring sprung and we saw the first delicate yellow primrose and then, shortly after, our daffodils started to shoot up. It also reminded me that now was the time to start talking about birthday celebrations with Dorothy.

It's easy to forget that our little girl is shy. In a familiar environment, Dorothy is a confident and open young lady, but take her out of her comfort zone and it's a different story. School is an example of this and for previous birthdays we have gone on trips or kept celebrations small as a close-knit family. Her adoration of various Disney princesses has normally given each celebration a theme. In 2019, Dorothy was turning five and now Arthur had a few parties under his belt, we asked her how she wanted to celebrate. We never wanted to put any pressure on her but the answer was cute. She fancied going back to the place she was born, Southend, where there was a funfair, and then when we got back to France she wanted to have a little birthday party for her school friends.

I have to be honest, Angela and I don't always agree. When you ask a nearly five-year-old how she wants to celebrate her birthday you have to be a little careful ... I have always thought the adage 'you don't ask a question you don't want the answer to' is very sound. When your little girl says what she wants to do for her birthday it is pretty difficult to say 'no', but Angela has always wanted things to be just perfect for them. Somehow, Dorothy was going back to her roots *and* having a party at the château.

As this was now a two-part birthday, I needed to get organised swiftly. The British element was easy: we would spend the early afternoon at Southend's Adventure Island and visit my childhood favourites, such as the helter-skelter, the crooked house and the big wheel, along with all the new brightly coloured rides that play loud music (yep, officially sounding old). The idea was great and actually far easier than anything we do at the château. Cousins, second cousins, friends and family gathered. Once everyone had been sufficiently thrown around on the rides, we headed to Bacchus, a favourite place of ours in Southend. It's quirky, friendly and relaxed, and also does a great cocktail. The last time we went there was when we came to say goodbye to my grandma. I had already ordered a three-tier unicorn rainbow cake and also managed to book a face painter. No one was safe and the rest was history. It was so much fun that Arthur decided this was where he would like to spend his next birthday.

Party 2.0. Arthur was to be my helper as we organised some of the activities for Dorothy's birthday party at the château. I chatted to him and he understood this was to be what Dorothy and her five-year-old friends would love, and that we would make it the best we possibly could. April is not reliable when it comes to the weather so we planned activities that could take place outside but also had games planned for inside the orangery. We could then skew the balance should we need to. The unicorn treasure hunt allowed us to explore and to find little rewards around the grounds. Arthur and I got into production, making little unicorn signposts, only about six inches tall, that were to indicate the route, and, at each change of direction, there would be little toys or sweets. I know Arthur understood that this party was rainbow and sparkles, but when he coloured one of the unicorn signposts in very un-unicorn, dark colours and said, 'This is the evil unicorn,' I thought, 'What the hell' and hoped it wouldn't scare our little princesses.

All the preparation was so worthwhile. A dozen five-year-olds can wreak more havoc than anyone expects. The weather was kind to us and, after a gentle period whilst everyone congregated and parents were given a drink or simply dropped their children and dashed off, we explained the idea of the treasure hunt and the party-goers all started searching for clues as to where to go. It seems that our roles have been decided when it comes to children's parties and I have the interesting task of organising and 'controlling' the more boisterous games. Year on year, my French vocabulary increases and helping the children with homework has given me an insight into grammar that I could have missed, but little prepares you for a briefing on unicorn signposts and searching for treasure, especially when most of your day-to-day conversations are with artisans . . . That said, I'd done some research and somehow, with Arthur's help, everyone seemed to grasp the idea and they headed off.

The diversity of characters was fascinating. Some five-year-olds just wanted to walk with someone holding their hand, whilst others were adventurous to the point of being scary and could be seen as a possible future Amelia Earhart. As a swarm, we moved around the grounds and hoovered up the goodies we had hidden, and Arthur even came to understand that he was not supposed to be leading them from sign to sign. Without a doubt, the treasure hunt was a great success, with the route taking everyone around the walled garden and through the woods across the meadows, finally reaching the orangery for the unicorn cake.

CHAPTER FIVE

Floating Dreams and Golden Nights

If we were to say, 'We went to see a man about a boat in Birmingham,' it is fair to say that was not quite the start of our story...

Chatting in bed one evening, Angela and I somehow got on to the subject of 'making more of the moat'. We had decided that we didn't want to use it for fishing. We had lots of fish but were not keen to change the well-balanced ecosystem we seemed to have. The conversation was interesting and I think we came very close to trying to buy some giant swan pedalos. Then I found a sort of boat that was actually a bathtub, so in theory you could float around the moat in your own mobile infinity pool. I loved the idea but sadly it was very ugly, and so we moved on in our thought processes.

We started searching for a boat that could double as extra, very unusual, accommodation at the château. We are only a couple of miles from the River Mayenne, which has locks to make it navigable, so we were sure there would be some sort of barges available. As a family, we have walked along the riverbank and seen some pleasure cruisers but we couldn't remember seeing anything particularly attractive. Even though France has canals, searches only turned up expensive, unattractive vessels that all appeared to be made of fibreglass. We then started widening our search and very soon we realised we were actually looking for a traditional barge, so soon we were scouring advertisements all over the UK. As with all of our projects, we did some sums and tried to see if a *bateau* at the château made any sense. The first major surprise is that older barges are a reasonable price. Then we looked at transport costs and we were happy that if we avoided being a '*convoi exceptionnel*' (that is, a load outside the width, height and/or length parameters of a conventional articulated lorry's capability) then the cost was not that scary, especially if we found a bargain less than forty feet long.

After unsuccessfully searching Google for canal boats, I turned to eBay. After the success of finding our Van du Vin there, I was secretly hoping to recreate this experience, but really I thought there was no way it could happen twice. There weren't many canal boats on eBay, but my search did pull up an adorable '30ft project narrow boat canal river boat barge liveaboard narrowboat cruiser'. The price was exactly £5,000. Yes, this was my type of boat and it was beautiful. Dick had given me instructions that it had to be under forty feet and it was. It was meant to be. As long as it floated, we could work the rest out.

When I called the owners to ask some questions, they seemed very nice and so I said, 'Great, I'll have it, please.' Sort of like how we bought the château. They were a little taken aback and said great, but insisted I came to see first. After six or seven repeat cycles of the same conversation, I said, 'OK, but it will be my

friend who comes.' Our friend and accountant John lived nearby and so by reason of geography he was chosen. He was so far out of his comfort zone it was wonderful, but nonetheless he reported back and very soon we were on our way to Birmingham to buy our very own boat for the moat.

When we first laid eyes on her, *Dolphin* was in a car park on blocks and the holes in the hull meant she was a long way from floating. In some areas, the metal was positively lacy and resembled a fine spider's web. That said, she was exactly what we were after and we'd done our research, so it wasn't very long before we were the proud owners of a thirty-foot long, approximately eight-ton traditional barge that was on the back of an articulated lorry on her way to getting some attention at a local dry dock. Common sense dictated that we should get all the main work done in Staffordshire near where she lay in the Midlands, where they know their way around barges. I made the decision very quickly to get the wonderful old Perkins engine taken out, as we would never need a powerful diesel at the château. A huge part of me wanted to keep it and play with it, but we met some local search and rescue volunteers at the work-shop so the engine found a new and much appreciated home.

A couple of months later, and *Dolphin* was completely over-plated and sporting a new paint job as she turned up at the château and was ready to be lifted off and lowered into our moat. Even with the repairs and transport, the total cost was significantly less than buying any of the leisure craft we had seen advertised locally and our boat was solid and truly gorgeous. There was a bit of work to be done if it was to be comfy as it was only a basic shell, but we weren't daunted as it was positively tiny compared to the château!

It was a glorious day when our *Dolphin* was due to arrive and as the time of delivery got closer, I was actually getting nervous,

especially after what had happened when our Vin du Van arrived and the person delivering it managed to crash it into the barns. As it came around the corner, it felt rather majestic. But there is something surreal about seeing a boat suspended in the air as it gets lifted off a lorry and onto the water. I have to say, the crane looked rather small, but Dick was confident, so I just sat back and enjoyed the spectacle. It seemed the most challenging part was attaching the straps to keep the boat horizontal. I did have a slight concern that the boat would slide out of the straps, but I decided to let Dick handle that.

I already had a vision in my mind's eye of how the space inside the boat could be used and was pleasantly surprised to see that the boat had a working shower and loo, though to use the shower the doors had to be opened up, meaning the middle section of the boat was effectively isolated and the whole kitchen area became part of the temporary bathroom. My plan was for a spacious bedroom taking up the front of the boat, with a bijou kitchenette (there was to be a large outdoor kitchen) and a comfy seating area at the back. The plan was to incorporate some sort of nautical style into the décor, but of course we also had to weave in some dolphins in honour of her name.

As normal, Dick was in charge of sorting the electrics, plumbing and heating, but first we had to decide where to put the boat. We wanted it to be lovely for anyone staying onboard, but it also had to look good when you looked at the château or out of the château windows. Dick had attached one rope to the front of the boat, which he insisted was called a 'painter' (ridiculous!), and then another to the stern, and then we proceeded to move the boat about the moat to see where it looked best. *Dolphin* may have weighed eight tons but on the water she was really quite easy to move around. I had originally thought we would put her around the back of the château, but our *Dolphin* was just too lovely to be hidden away, and you could also see the floating dome from the back, so we ended up agreeing her new home should be near the old *lavoir,* home to the laundry at the château many years earlier.

When you are busy reclaiming rooms and tending to the fabric of your home, spending time on the outside and landscaping seems a bit of a luxury. Though we all know first impressions are really important. We had laid many tons of gravel in front of the château just before our wedding to try to give the area a feeling of being loved, but I knew it was only a stopgap and that one day we would have to do something more in keeping with our beautiful home. The catalyst that spurred us into action was the fact that we were going to host Jenny and Steve's fiftieth wedding anniversary and the gravel was not the best surface for holding events.

Mum and Dad have been our unsung heroes. We tell them often and do what we can to spoil them when we can. I've grown up hearing tales of them eloping to Gretna Green to get married. By all accounts it was a very intimate affair and they always said that one day they would have a big celebration for all their family and friends as a belated wedding party, but I guess family life and work commitments always seemed to get in the way, and it just never happened. So it just seemed right as we approached their golden wedding anniversary that we should throw them this once-in-a-lifetime party to say thank you.

I popped over to Mum and Dad's to share the news. For a moment they worried that we had too many events already this year, but they quickly got over that and, gosh, they were head over heels with excitement and emotion! Mum started putting the guest list together and Dad was calling around to get people to save the date. I did say, 'Invite whoever you want, there is no upper limit,' but for some reason I didn't realise they knew so many people. Before we knew it, the guest list was well over a hundred people and we knew the orangery, which only hosts eighty people, was not going to be big enough. It was also too far away for the more elderly relatives, such as my nan in her wheelchair, so I decided it was time to have a chat with Dick about 'phase one' of landscaping.

We had seen several châteaus that had patios of magnificent flag-stones, surrounded by formal walls and gardens, so we had ideas. Though it is interesting that it's only when you get into the details you discover that your 'idea' is a lot different to your wife's! I was struck dumb when Angela shared her vision for the patio area – it wasn't a patio, it was huge! My gorgeous wife wanted flagstones around the château, in front of the château, across to the coach house and, to finish it off properly, it would be good if the paving could possibly go all the way across to the orangery . . . ! I think Angela may have thought my silence was me contemplating her idea before my formal agreement. In hindsight, she outplayed me. I explained the problems of cost and the sheer amount of work. Angela seemed to accept where I was coming from and my wife's new position was an area in front of the château big enough to host a dozen tables of guests. If she'd started with that plan I'm sure I could have reduced the size, but I was just thankful to accept her new boundaries.

Mine and Dick's recollections of this conversation are quite different. I'm pretty sure that after discussing what was needed, which he seemed to agree with, we went over what was possible. I'm sure we were talking about what would be the dream in the long term – and it's important to know this so that what you do in phase one can link to phase two, and so forth. Of course, I knew we couldn't achieve all of this straight away. What we agreed on was paving the area outside the château – although this was a minefield in itself as nothing was symmetrical. The gates, the bridge, the island, it was all wonky. But we had a plan and we also both loved the idea of adding aviaries.

As a youngster, I had kept and reared canaries and foreign finches, and as Angela and I had visited Victorian aviaries in the UK, we decided that ornate aviaries should be incorporated into the new layout.

Our patios and aviaries had to look good from the front door as well as when you approach along the driveway. But the château doesn't line up with the driveway or the gate; it's on the wonk! It just wasn't possible to do it mathematically; it had to be done by eye. So Sacha and Quentin, our château helpers, were employed to act as aviaries that were three metres high and two metres wide. Angela was on the balcony and I was on the bridge and we directed our team with their hands in the air, doing amazing impressions of inanimate objects. Somehow, we placed them so they were at the corner of a paved area that worked and exactly where the aviaries would be. Angela and I swapped, did some fine adjustment, then marked the spots where Quentin and Sacha had been. Then we became aviaries and our team did a sanity check.

Never in a million years would I have thought that my husband and I would have two of our helpers pretending to be aviaries. We still giggle about it today but there was no other way because of the wonk factor. We simply needed to judge this one by eye. It was like a comedy show: 'a foot to the left, Quentin', 'a step to the right, Sacha', 'ooh, go forward', 'no, backwards', 'please put your arms out', 'perfect . . . Don't move!'.

Now it was time for some sums and some decisions. Regular slabs or random?; what colour, what size? We knew the surface area and we went in search of what would look right. So we headed off to the internet for pictures of patios that we liked. As we knew we wanted something traditional, we looked at National Trust buildings and old château pictures. We got a feel for what we liked then started searching. Our endeavours were fruitless. We could not find anything in the local area that worked and could be delivered within the time frame – everywhere seemed to have a three-month waiting list!

I knew I wanted flagstones that were random and would look like they have always been here. By chance, I tracked down a manufacturer who made slabs for the National Trust. John at Westminster Stone was lovely and passionate about paving! We talked and he could not have been more helpful. It seemed silly buying from Shropshire in the UK but we were really struggling to get something we loved, so rather than accept a compromise we organised for a load of stone to come to us.

I hired a four-wheel-drive forklift and had it delivered in time for our slabs to arrive. I had practised to ensure I could control it, though I was slow. Thankfully, our articulated lorry driver was a forklift master. There was pallet upon pallet of mixed slabs, as we had hundreds of square metres to lay. I had them spread around the front of the château so they didn't have to be carried a long way.

We made the decision that the paved area would follow the ground that dropped away from the front of the château rather than being perfectly horizontal, as that would have created a step at the edges. The gravel that we had laid originally was on top of a solid foundation of compacted grit, so we scraped away the gravel and laid the slabs on a bed of mortar directly onto this surface. We had roped in lots of extra help for this mammoth task and soon there were people mixing mortar, setting out random patterns of slabs, laying and levelling. The pressure was on, as always, as we needed everything laid and set so the final, time-consuming job of pointing between the slabs could be done. What a difference it made.

I don't know when it was decided but Angela thought we needed some colour, so there was a requirement to put a flower bed next to the château. It meant a little less paving but it added the complication of also having to dig out an area into which we could put compost to allow us to plant . . . Luckily we didn't hit the foundations and soon got ready to plant. In went a palm tree and some ornamental shrubs, which all add a touch of colour to any photos of the front of the château.

I'm pretty sure the flower bed really came from the discussion of how we finish around the turret of the château. Dick pointed out that the slabs would need to be cut in around the edge of the château and I actually thought it would save us having to do that if we put a flowerbed in the corner. Dick's first answer to everything is no, but once it sank in that this might be easier, he agreed to give it a go, despite thinking nothing would grow there.

There was a lot happening at the château and we were just about to be back-to-back with weekend weddings, so as a break from work we decided it would be great to have a family outing. By some circuitous route, it was decided we should all take a trip to Monet's house in Giverny near Paris. I was not sure what to expect but it was a lovely day out.

Giverny is possibly the most famous garden in France and, if I'm honest, I wanted to see what the fuss was about. When looking for inspiration we take it from everywhere, but I was looking forward

to the day out with our family as much as the gardens themselves. Driving through France is always a treat with the stunning villages and flowers, but when we arrived in the commune of Giverny, the level of rustic beauty was elevated beyond what I could have imagined. Every property felt cherished, loved, groomed and unique, with carefully selected flowers and plants in their beautiful gardens. It was an explosion of colour and texture, and it felt like everyone there wanted to do Monet and the area proud. There were many visitors, lots of whom were riding traditional bicycles with baskets, but it felt bustling rather than overcrowded. We arrived early, as we were told it gets very busy and hot later in the day.

On arrival, we were all excited. Arthur and Dorothy had already been educated about Monet's life and art. We wanted them to feel excited about what they were to see and explaining the history was a good starting point. To enter the garden, there is a little windy walk, which builds up the anticipation, and then once you get through the gates your senses are overwhelmed. To the left is Monet's home, with his Clos Normand flower garden in front. It's a traditional garden, around a hectare in size, with formal alleyway upon alleyway. I love straight lines at the best of times, but the sheer number of flowers and borders and colours was mind blowing. There must have been tens of thousands of flowers. It was late spring and the tulips, irises, roses, peonies, poppies, alliums and wallflowers were all in bloom, but it's the tulips that I remember most for the sheer number of purples, blues, deep burgundies and whites. Plants, flowers, foliage – it was all loved and cared for. It was stunning. We had a lovely, leisurely stroll through the gardens and, even though lots of people were starting to arrive, it reminded me a bit of a library, as everyone spoke softly!

Next we ventured into Monet's home. From the outside, it's a striking but delicate pink, elegant country home with bright-green shutters and bright-green decking, which contrasts perfectly. In fact, it felt like it was defined by the green shutters. It was a long building with two floors and at least a dozen windows. At the entrance were two gorgeous Chinese pots. I actually cannot remember what was growing in them because I loved the pots so much. I did not take my eyes off them!

For the next part, I'm thankful that I hadn't googled anything before. I wanted to see this first with my own eyes and it more than lived up to my expectations. I immediately felt an amazing connection with it. The house was full of colour, taste, warmth and style. Monet's spirit was everywhere, from the yellow dining room bathed in sunshine, to the yellow chairs and table and other furniture. Even the incredible checked floor was yellow and brown, and every bit of wall space was filled with Japanese art. It was brave and fabulous, and glancing out of the windows at the stunning gardens took my breath away.

As I walked into the kitchen, I found Dick looking at everything in awe. Monet's collection of copper pans and fish kettles was impressive. Not to mention his cooker! Apart from the size, it was truly my dream cooker – a La Cornue in black and gold. It's what inspired the brass around the edges of our family kitchen. A cooker like this is the price of our entire kitchen and then some, but it was truly stunning and I had cooker envy. Then it got even better. Monet had a spice room, the *épicerie*. In that moment, he was added to my dream dinner party guest list, along with the late and wonderful Queen Elizabeth and Vivienne Westwood, both of whom I've always had so much love and respect for.

Dick and I found it fascinating that Arthur and Dorothy were so interested as well. They loved the history, the ambience, the flowers and the colours, and their hunger for enjoying and experiencing many different things made me feel blessed. Finally, we wandered outside, having left the best, or most certainly the most iconic bit, to last: Monet's water garden. Monet had originally bought the land from his neighbours, who were worried about the exotic plants he was planting, but unfettered he continued, and this developed into his famous Japanese-inspired water lily garden. Today it is stunning and framed with the prettiest weeping willows.

The grounds were lovely and there was so much to explore inside and out. I could see ideas for lots of bits of landscaping that we could take back to the château, but both of us were struck by the beauty of the ponds. The sound of the frogs was almost deafening. Chatting on the way home, we knew we needed to source water lilies and I could picture our bridge over the moat in a wonderful painting.

The water lilies arrived in the post with the baskets needed to weigh the roots down. The instructions were simple; the execution, however, was messy. We had chosen lots of different colours and water lilies spread and can take over a pond. If you want to keep areas clear for fishing it is not unusual to savage the plants to try and keep them under control. We were very excited about having so many flowers we'd have to chop them back, but firstly we need the plants to establish themselves and thrive. The theory involved putting the rhizomes into the mesh baskets, covering them with some form of compost, adding a weight to hold the plants down and pressing the whole package into the goo at the bottom of the pond. Obviously I was volunteered to do the planting as it was far too dangerous for the children and Angela had no desire to reach over the side of our little boat and press her arms into the pond sludge up to her elbows. Even when I told her it wasn't sludge but the 'benthic zone', she still had no overwhelming urge to do it.

Planting the lilies was messy, smelly and so much fun. I can say this because I was with the children handing Dick things. Had I been in the moat in the silt I would have been gagging because of the smell. We all had what Dorothy calls the 'giggle-pops'. And when I say we, I don't mean Dick! Although I'm certain he was smiling on the inside.

The silt layer was soft but the baskets were a bugger to push into it. On several occasions, the gravel weight wasn't enough and the baskets floated to the surface. It was smelly and everyone thought it was great fun, so I did my very best to ensure my whole family got to share some of the grey smelly yugh I had on my hands every time I was passed a new basket or plant. The whole task took a couple of hours but we'd all earned our bath and it took a lot of fragrant soap to remove the whiff!

* * *

It's a bit of country lore that when the gooseberries are ripe it's time to stop picking the rhubarb. I think it's actually sensible and something to do with oxalic acid levels in the rhubarb; however, what it does mean is that there is a point in the year when your crumble changes! Rhubarb or rhubarb and ginger have had their time – now get out there and pick the gooseberries. Gooseberry bushes do not give up their treasure easily and the thorns are to be respected. I have no doubt there is a cultivar without thorns but we are happy to be a little careful as our red and green gooseberries taste amazing. Though I have to say the red gooseberries that can be eaten straight from the bush when properly ripe are my favourite.

GOOSEBERRY CRUMBLE

Ingredients

500g gooseberries, topped and tailed
100g caster sugar for green gooseberries, 75g caster sugar for
ripe red gooseberries
200g plain flour
100g diced chilled butter
75g demerara sugar

Method

Preheat the oven to 180°C or 160°C fan.

*Put the flour, cold butter and demerara sugar into a food
processor and blitz until breadcrumb-like. Spread this onto a
baking tray and put into the oven for 10 minutes.*

*Toss the gooseberries in the sugar in a bowl a couple of times
then put them in the bottom of your pie dish. Now take the
crumble mix and 'crumble' it over the gooseberries. Don't
worry about leaving larger lumps – it's hot so be sensible!*

*Cook in the oven for 40–45 minutes until the top is golden and
the gooseberries are trying to bubble out.*

*Best enjoyed with thick cream or good vanilla ice cream that's
been out of the freezer for at least 10 minutes before scooping.
Forget the calories, think of the vitamins!*

If anyone was to make use of the *Dolphin*, it was essential that we
had power, water and ablutions. Oh, and a safe way of getting on

and off . . . It's worth noting that the moat level can vary by two or three feet between full and low water in the summer. The solution was to have a deck area big enough to use for dining but also to provide the umbilical link to the floating accommodation. There followed a significant amount of digging, and my builder mate Steve and I dug out some footings and shuttered up 'pads' that were half submerged to support our decking. I still marvel at the fact that concrete can set even if completely submerged. That allowed our foundations to be pretty formidable. With a deck built, it was finished with herbs and plants around it, but we were a long way from the château and power so, rather than a long run around the moat or even in the moat, I decided the boat was to be off-grid. A solar panel, a small wind turbine, a charge controller and some deep-cycle batteries and we had a system that would ensure enough power for lights. The heating and hot water was to be gas. Whilst we waited to sort out the *lavoir*, where we planned to eventually have decadent ablutions, we still needed to have a nice loo. We were saved when we found a cassette toilet that was porcelain and not plastic; it fitted in the boat's toilet and 'felt' substantial. Plus it was easy, and not unpleasant, to empty.

The setting for our *bateau* was gorgeous. It enjoys early-morning and late-evening sun and views across the moat to the château in one direction and then over wooded countryside in the other. When the work was finished, it would be stunning.

There had been a lot of activity inside the *Dolphin*, but it was still a work in progress when we decided to have a fishing competition. We pulled the boat aside and tied it up away from the deck, and it was competition time. To be fair, I am the only one capable of fishing so my time was taken up ensuring Angela, Arthur and Dorothy had bait on their hooks and were untangled. Dorothy didn't really get the hang of it at first but had been given a tiny Disney princess rod by our friends Johnny and Nadine.

We were all very patient for a long time. We knew there were fish in there because they kept swimming by and when Dorothy said 'Daddy', I was there in a second. Catching the first and only fish of the day was fantastic. Our little girl's face – she was over the moon. It sort of changed the mood as everyone became rather competitive, and I think the fish must have known. I loved it and was extremely busy, though the official scoreboard had Angela, Arthur and me catching *no* fish, which seemed a tad unfair . . .

It's much harder decorating a small space than a large one. It's the equivalent to having write something profound in one sentence rather than a page. Every detail has to be thought through and there is no room for errors. As the boat was on the water and already named the *Dolphin*, I felt the theme and direction had already been set. So much activity had taken place outside since the *Dolphin* arrived but the inside still needed some serious love. One morning, as the mist was rising on the moat, I sat at the front of the boat and sketched some art deco dolphins. The light was golden, even a smidge orange, and I could feel the colours that our *Dolphin* wanted to be. Blues, greens and salmony pinks, all with soft, warm undertones.

Once I knew my palette, all the individual elements were sorted rather quickly. The softwood panelling, which was once a natural wood colour, was painted with a fresh, muted salmon-pink colour; the floor was tiled with leftover light-blue tiles from the potagerie suite bathroom, and the seating area at the front was covered with art deco, scallop-shaped grey velour cushions. The current kitchen took up a third of the boat, so we replaced that with a smaller, wooden counter and hob, perfect for making a cup of tea in the morning. If it was cold, there was the cutest little wood burner, complete with a scalloped fireguard and golden grout. I'd also handmade some simple lights with abalone shells – these make anything look good and you can buy them by the kilo in craft stores – and my version of Swedish blinds.

* * *

Mum and Dad's fiftieth wedding anniversary was 4 June 2019, which fell on a Tuesday, and worked out great because we were flat out for the month of May. Running up to the party, we had hosted sixteen 'Château Under the Stars' bookings, Karen and Paul's wedding, followed by Katie and James's wedding, and then, finally, Amy and Mark's wedding. All had been incredible three-day affairs and our new professional kitchen and utility room were working out just as planned. I honestly don't know what we did before I had our 15kg washing machine and tumble dryer.

In parallel to these events, the plans for Mum and Dad's party of a lifetime were coming together beautifully. When you are responsible for every element of an event, you can find yourself jumping from hotel and accommodation questions, to cocktails, to organising balloon colours. Each and every event is made up of thousands of layers and peeling them back for the big day is half the fun!

We used our need to find aviaries as an excuse to go and look at some reclamation yards. Sadly, we didn't find much, though we did realise that we definitely wanted a round *volière* and we found an amazing copper *daubière*, which was for slow-cooking stews in a hearth, and could take coals on the lid to help by cooking from the top and the bottom. I finally found our dream aviaries in a specialised shop a couple of hours from home and – the best bit – they would be here in time. When they arrived, they were all but complete, apart from assembling and attaching the roof, and I still giggle now when I think of Angela's face as she was too short to keep a hold of it and it fell in!

With the aviaries in place, and some branches and greenery placed inside, everything was nearly complete. Angela had made some teacup water or seed feeders and I took the children out to pick the birds. We chose some zebra finches and canaries for one of the aviaries and some budgies for the second. I wasn't much older than Arthur when I started keeping foreign finches and budgies and it was like a trip down memory lane. When the birds were released into their new homes they flew around exploring and it wasn't long before they were all taking baths and chirping away.

Dick and I had already asked his son James if he would come and help with Mum and Dad's party. His passion for the kitchen was apparent and he had worked with Dick many times, so we knew they would be a great team. It was also lovely that Arthur and Dorothy got to spend some time with their big brother. With more than a hundred guests, the main reception party was going to be on the new patio in front of the château, but Mum and Dad also wanted a late-afternoon barbecue so everyone could say hello to each other when they arrived. We loved this idea and our patio would get double the use! Lots of the guests knew each other, but

not all of them, and it was lovely to see everyone catching up and getting to know each other. Our guests of honour were in their element as they saw everyone was chatting and enjoying the local drinks.

It was not to be a late night but we had to feed everyone, so our starters included platters with the following on them:

Marinated goat's cheese with pink peppercorns and fennel
Selection of charcuterie
Homemade dips
Baked local cheeses with rosemary and garlic
Sweet pickles with pink onions and turmeric cauliflower

There were obviously the obligatory fresh baguettes and local butter on the tables too!

For the main course, we rotisseried fifty chickens in my homemade roaster, which meant they were moist and smoky. These chickens were then divided and served on large boards. They were accompanied by green salad, coleslaw, potato salad – Jenny style – black garlic mayo and spicy harissa mayo, chimichurri salsa and tzatziki.

Then, to follow this, we had created a 'château mess', which was a yummy mix of fresh strawberries, vanilla ice cream, meringue, strawberry champagne jam and elderflower sugar that had desiccated elderflowers from the garden in it to provide the aromatics.

After that, everyone dispersed to get ready for the main event the following evening.

The afternoon barbecue had been a resounding success. Not all of Mum and Dad's friends had been to the château before and they loved showing it off. Mum, in particular, was on cloud nine showing people her 'Café Grandma' sign. For me, watching their

happiness and joy was the best bit. Lots of the family had found it very hard since Mum and Dad moved to France, so the chance to share their new, forever home with them all was very special. Even Dad's mum Nan was starting to warm to it.

The next day, Mum had all her sisters, Nan and Dorothy up in the honeymoon suite to get ready as they sipped champagne cocktails served in pink, sugar-rimmed teacups. It was so lovely seeing Mum surrounded by her special people. Everyone was getting ready and laughing, and it felt just like a wedding day as we were served afternoon tea with a mix of savoury cheese scones and traditional sweet scones with our own strawberry jam and clotted cream that James had brought with him from Cornwall. My dad, my brother Paul, Arthur, my uncles and Dad's friends were all chilling in the salon. It was four generations of the family everywhere you looked and, in a nutshell, that was what this party was all about: family.

The evening meal was to be 'small plates', each having some special significance for Jenny and Steve and their travels through married life. The food reminded them of holidays, eating out in the East End of London, even the meal they had after their wedding. It was a diverse menu but James, Arthur and I had a ball developing the dishes and cooking for such a special day. We had discussed the menu with Jenny and Steve, then Arthur, James and I had chatted and devised our take on what they required.

Bruschetta topped with tomatoes
Padron peppers flash fried in very hot olive oil, sprinkled with
sea salt
Asparagus wrapped in prosciutto
Arancini with black garlic mayo
Kedgeree

Homemade battered fish fingers and tartare sauce
Chicken soup with kneidel
Tandoori chicken skewers
Very rare beef served with pepper sauce (it was the meal they
had after their marriage up in Gretna Green and its perfection
has been remembered)

All this was followed by French patisseries and an evening of dancing, drinking and partying.

The party had been a huge success but it's not a grand event without a speech or two, and to my surprise my mum led the way. I've never seen Mum talk in front of so many people but she was fearless. It was a beautiful speech, celebrating Dad and the whole family. By the end, there wasn't a dry eye in the house. Once the speeches were done and the tears were wiped, it seemed to pave the way to the orangery, where everyone let their hair down and danced till their feet hurt!

CHAPTER SIX

Adventures and Happiness

Getting the right work-life balance is something we remind ourselves about almost daily. We knew we wanted to be able to spend more time exploring and having picnics; we'd even discussed camping with the children. I can't remember how it first came up, but we were chatting about having a camper van for our outings and decided we didn't want anything 'boring' (warning bells rang for me as boring often meant something that worked and was functional). I thought little of it but was looking at vintage buses thinking that could be a way forward when I spotted an Asquith wedding bus for sale in Wales. I'd come across the Asquith years ago. It looks very vintage but it's a modern vehicle based on a Ford Transit chassis and engine, so it had the look of an old vehicle but with the advantage of being relatively modern technology. We were interested so I arranged to go and see Neville, the current owner, and, cutting a long story short, I drove 'Mademoiselle Daisy' home. It was an interesting drive as I kept the top speed down to about 55mph and the high-sided vehicle was very susceptible to the wind. But she came home to the château and the whole family fell in love with this quirky vehicle.

Even though I'd just driven for several hours, there was absolutely no way we were not taking our new vehicle out for a spin. Angela threw together a picnic and soon we had the children strapped into our spacious little bus and we headed off. First, we took Mademoiselle Daisy for a jaunt around the village. Everyone who saw us smiled and waved, which was lovely. Then we headed to park up beside the River Mayenne and, once again, on our journey everyone waved. We were smiling ear to ear by the time we arrived.

We took our picnic basket, which we had hastily filled with what we had in our fridge and some crisps and chocolates. It reminded me of my adventures as a child with my mum and dad and all my brothers and sisters. We spread out the rug and shared out our goodies. We laughed and had a great time. Our adventure bus had had its first outing. It may have only been to the banks of the Mayenne, but our picnic, complete with some luminous-coloured non-alcoholic champagne, had been a great success!

During the transformation, I had joked that the bus felt very *Driving Miss Daisy*, a heart-warming, thirty-year-old film that Dick and I both loved. The name felt fitting but of course it needed a French twist. *Et voilà*: Mademoiselle Daisy was born.

Now the bus had a name, the emblem began to take shape. I wanted it to be simple and fun! For this, I went up to my *trésorie*. Inspired by her name, I set out to create a central geometric daisy motif – a playful pattern inspired by art nouveau. As the bus would be our home away from home for our travelling adventures, I wanted the colours to be rich and vibrant, so I chose a cobalt

green with touches of gold to create a warm and homely feel with a hint of decadence. Because of its simplicity, the design repeated easily and I got my trusty friend John to print it onto wallpaper so I could decorate the interior of the bus, and I also got it printed onto crushed velvet for the seat coverings and comfy cushions.

It was like a mini room renovation. First thing was to strip everything out, then we could add back in the necessary functionality. I had a wonderful couple of hours with Arthur and Dorothy passing tools, holding spanners in place and genuinely being useful as I stripped out the ivory-coloured seats and attached seat belts. I had a cunning plan. Our two front seats had to be able to rotate to face into the vehicle. The back seat needed to be able to rotate too and with some luck would convert into a bed. The search started and I found some great solutions, but they were simply too expensive and our budget didn't stretch to buying them. That said, I scoured eBay and patience is a virtue because I first found two front seats that were fully functional if a little tatty. But that was Angela's problem as I knew she'd be changing anything I bought to look in keeping with the rest of the vehicle. Just as I was beginning to think I was asking too much by wanting a rotating, sliding, folding flat-back bench, I found one. It was one of the ugliest things I'd seen but when I showed it to Angela, she loved it so we had children's seats and a double bed.

Obviously, we had to completely redesign the inside of our bus and stripping out the seats was just the first task. We needed fold-out cooking capabilities (I wasn't prepared to cook inside), then there were more beds and, vital when you have children, a loo too!

The inside of Mademoiselle Daisy looked big until Dick drew the plan out on the floor and took me through where everything was going to go. The loo was a box in the corner and I thought it best

not to ask questions. Dick knows I don't do camping so I had to trust him. After all, there would probably be a hotel nearby for Dorothy and me. The kitchen seemed to be solid boxes with lots of clever hinges that would be able to swing out the door and to the side of the bus so it wouldn't get smelly or steamy inside when we cooked. It seemed very clever and I never doubted that it would work, I just didn't really understand what he was talking about, apart from that it would go from inside to outside.

It became obvious that we would need some kind of cover for the outside. I decided we needed an awning, so I mentioned it to Dick and he told me he'd be able to put up a sort of tube above the door to attach it to. That was all the encouragement I needed and I went off in search of striped canvas that fitted our colour scheme.

The whole adventure bus project was a pleasure. The biggest challenge was getting the right bits, then it was just a matter of installing them. Once Angela confirmed the flooring, we bought it and laid it, then addressed the seats. I knew they would be coming out to get covered but taking them in and out was trivial once you had a system. It was only a matter of days before I handed over to Angela to sort out painting the wood, wallpapering the walls and covering the seats. Somehow, Angela didn't think it odd to wallpaper a vehicle, so I just remained quiet – what do I know!

The summer of 2019 will never be forgotten. It was our busiest year ever and as a team, we were bouncing and loving every moment. Our systems were getting more refined and having the new kitchen, utility, ice machine and, most recently, the roller iron, had had a positive impact on everyone's spirits. Doing things the hard way really made us all appreciate everything we now had in place.

After Mum and Dad's wedding anniversary celebration, we had

more guests to stay at the domes, more fun days, garden days and weddings. In fact, from June to the end of August, we had the honour of celebrating eight beautiful weddings: Hayley and Andy, Eilidh and Chris, Lisa and Ash, Katie and James, Michael and Sarah, Stacie and Ash, Helen and Matt, and Vicki and Mike, in chronological order. Every wedding holds a special place in my heart and it may be because we only do weddings for people we connect with, but to this day, we have only ever hosted happy and joyous events with kind couples. From our first ever wedding booking to the wedding of the beautiful teachers who worked day and night to afford their dream of getting married at the château (we could relate to them more than a little!), and the wedding party that had so many children they brought five nannies with them, to the celebration that included a speech by the youngest gentleman to date, all of these, and so many more, are cherished memories for us, and they will be with us always.

Somehow, Angela had filled most weekends but we'd found time to convert our very own adventure bus and, after all the hard work, Mademoiselle Daisy was ready to go on her first true camping trip. The big question was where should we go? We loaded up our full complement of equipment and bedding and with lots of excitement we headed off.

Arthur and Dorothy were so excited about going off in Mademoiselle Daisy that they didn't care where we were going, so off we went. We spent about half an hour passing through a number of the local villages and worked our way in a big circle until we came back to the château. It took a little time for the children to realise we'd come home, but by that time, Daddy had turned alongside the outbuildings and pulled up on the grass on the paddock behind the walled garden. We all agreed it was a

perfect location for our adventure, so we debussed and sent the children off to find firewood. Arthur is such a smarty pants that he went down to the woodstore and was going to bring back some of our pre-cut logs. But Dick was having none of it, and so Arthur and Dorothy spent ages playing with the sticks they found, and by the time they returned we had set up camp.

We built a fire pit and could easily have cooked over it but we had our travelling kitchen that had to be tested, so we cooked burgers on a griddle on the stove. As they were cooking, Angela set the 'table' – a log we had pulled up – with lots of sauces and salad, and the children and I lit the fire. Arthur and Dorothy had scavenged lots of dry kindling, moss and straw to start us off and we had built the fire well because it burst into flames. So it wasn't long before we had a wonderful set up on our campsite. By the time we had eaten our burgers and made up our beds the light was failing, so we toasted marshmallows and sat contentedly. It was then we spotted the all-but-full moon had risen, and so we all put back our heads and howled.

As we headed into our beds, it was clear that Dorothy was having none of it. Her mattress and duvet were partly under the main bed and as far as she was concerned, it just wasn't a bedroom! To make matters worse, Angela was having fits of the giggles and agreed with Dorothy. To be fair, I know what battles to fight. So, without too much complaining, we swapped 'beds'. With all the drama over we settled down and just as I was nodding off, Dorothy informed us all that she needed a pee . . . Everyone looked at me because to sit on the loo she was going to have to put her feet on my head, which is exactly what she proceeded to do.

Dick is a *little* older than me but it has never been an issue and I couldn't love him more. I know he is aware of the difference

but mostly it tends to be a joke between us rather than a serious conversation. I've heard him say many times that on his birthday he is only a day older, so don't make a fuss. But he was about to be sixty years old so that was worth a fuss. We'd discussed what we should do and how we could get the whole family involved. And rather than inviting everyone to the château, we decided it would be a great time to go and visit all Dick's old stomping grounds and see where Daddy had grown up.

I suppose being sixty is a big deal and I realised Angela wasn't going to take no for an answer, so I accepted the inevitable and was given the opportunity to take everyone back to Northern Ireland so they could understand my childhood and what made me who I am. My father often quoted 'give me the boy until he is seven and I'll show you the man'. I'm sure he knew it was Aristotle but I don't remember him saying that. It seems obvious, but where you spend your formative years is really important, so Angela and I always question if we are doing the best we can for Arthur and Dorothy and giving them the best childhood we can. To date, we know they have been our number-one priority and we are really proud of who they are becoming.

With all that in mind, we headed back to County Antrim for a gathering. With my wife, all four of my children and my three grandchildren, we filled the family home, and Mum and my sisters loved the influx and anarchy that reigned with so many little ones about. We'd hired a small 'bus' so we could all travel together. It wasn't exactly plush but our road trips reminded me of all of us children and our friends squeezing into the car and singing and chattering for miles. Thinking back, we thought nothing of Mum and Dad and one or two children being on the front bench seat (no seat belts – shock horror! Sometimes with the windows up and Mum and Dad smoking, more shocks and more horrors). My younger brother David and I would be in the boot with our large dog, Caesar, and whatever baggage or picnic we had packed, and then the remaining family plus a couple of friends would be on the middle bench seat. Our red Vauxhall Victor estate was large for the time, but ten or eleven of us and the dog was probably on the limit of what it could manage.

We visited all the homes I had lived in, in Bangor and Antrim. We stopped and had photos taken and told stories of sailing boats on the massive pond in Ward Park, which seemed to have shrunk (?), and talked about how much time I spent in detention for arguing with the obviously incorrect teachers. We went along the beautiful coast road, reminiscing about our family picnics in the 1960s and it felt as if my dad and my little sister Glenda were actually with us. When I looked across at my mum I could see that she felt it too. The whole trip was magical.

We stopped often and walked around. In Antrim, we all played football on the 'round square'. The youngsters didn't understand the prestige of owning a 'caser' (the old leather, lace-up footballs). I have to admit that I did momentarily forget my age and when I was showing my George Best dribbling skills ended up taking a tumble and going over on my ankle! I seem to remember equal amounts of concern and laughing from my audience, and a couple of 'don't be so bloody stupid' remarks being muttered. I survived and the limp went away . . .

As we all dispersed, I have to say I didn't feel older. If anything, I'd been revitalised from seeing the understanding that my family now had. We'd always shared stories but seeing the bungalow where Mum looked after six little ones when Dad went off to Libya to work put it all in context. We even considered asking if we could dig the garden to find the wooden spoons the children had all buried there . . .

I was so happy that we'd gone back to Northern Ireland for Dick's birthday. He left at the age of sixteen to go to sixth-form college before heading off to be an army officer, but still considers himself to be Northern Irish. Watching Jenny and the girls was an eye opener as they were all transported back to when they were just slightly older than Arthur and Dorothy. It was obvious that they relished being together as a family, and I knew where Dick's passion for simple fun and quality family time came from.

I loved watching our modern family connect and seeing Uncle Arthur and Indy and Auntie Dorothy and Pippin all playing together was adorable. Dick's cake this year was a walled garden cake, made by the entire family, and, whilst I'd expected the children to have a ball making fondant vegetables, it came as a surprise how much James and Holly enjoyed it too! And a cake made with love was most certainly the order of the day.

On arrival back home, we only had a few days before school started. Luckily, we were quite organised before we departed for Ireland – with so many events coming up we needed to be. It's easy for life to become too busy, and ensuring we get that balance is key to us, yet all the time we were investing every penny back into the château: our business and our home. We needed to find a way to get some extra coppers into our roof and window fund and we knew it was important not to get ahead of ourselves.

After Dick's sixtieth, we hosted the final four weddings of the year: Charlie and Jay, Liz and Ella, Connor and Beatrice, and then the very last wedding of the season was for the fabulous and laid-back couple Gemma and John. One of my favourite things about Gemma was that she had a princess-like wedding dress that billowed at the bottom and took up the width of the stairs. As she came down them, she lifted her skirt a little to reveal her trainers, which you could not see unless she wanted you to. It made my heart smile. Gemma was going to be comfy on her wedding day, as that made her a happy bride, with a very happy hubby too!

There is always a sadness at the château when the season comes to an end. And as the evening drew in on that final wedding, the team gathered together to toast all that we had achieved and share a drink and a cheers. All the weddings in 2019 had been truly wonderful. When they aren't happening we might have a bit more time but we miss the buzz, as well as the extended team that is there just for the season. Little did anyone know this would be the last toast for some time.

From the end of the wedding season to Christmas there is time to jump into some very serious renovations. Every year, we tried to make Jenny and Steve even more comfortable, so it was time to move into phase three of 'Operation Coach House'. It was time to convert the old tack room into an entrance hall, complete with a custom-built wooden staircase to give Grandma and Papi Steve access to their upstairs. Steve had a set of rickety stairs to get up to his mezzanine man cave but that was a temporary measure. Eventually, we intended to put in a lift, but our biggest criterion was to ensure that the entrance hall was spacious and had lots of storage for coats and whatever else we would like to hide away. Then, as a passing thought, it was decided it would be great to have a toilet and sink in that area. That was a bit of a challenge, but one we had to solve as we intended to place an ensuite in the bedroom that was going to be above the entrance.

Yet again, it wasn't time for a faint heart so we dug a trench all the way along the front of the coach house and laid a pipe (with the necessary 25mm per metre slope!) all the way to Jenny and Steve's septic tank. It was a pain but had to be done. The layout of the entrance decided itself but before we could start laying things out we needed to clear the room. The old tack room had a raised floor which we stripped out and under it found thousands of snail shells. It was lovely and dry but it was just an earth floor, so we had to dig down, damp-proof, insulate and lay a reinforced concrete floor. Water pipes were brought down from the attic through the room to be, as were pipes that could be used for radiators at some time in the future. The walls were insulated and studded out. We did not skimp on the insulation as Jenny and Steve like to be warm and downstream, effort now would definitely pay off.

We were nowhere near ready for Angela's creativity yet but we had to make a set of stairs and we needed to understand where in the room it would be. There followed several conversations and I mocked up some stairs so everyone could see how far they would come out into the room. The project had to be considered in three dimensions as the landing upstairs impacted on what would be the master bedroom and the guest suite. We eventually settled on a bespoke handmade staircase in the corner of the room that was gentle enough so Grandma could comfortably venture upstairs. So we made a hole in the ceiling and started to rebuild.

When the old tack room was stripped out, the entrance hall was a big room. Dick and Steve needed a decision about the floor before the stairs could be built, which made sense. Mum and I had found lovely black and white tiles that made a traditional geometric pattern and accentuated the spacious nature of the room. When I gave the green light the room suddenly took shape. I constantly talked to Mum and Dad to get their buy-in and we agreed on a set of floor-to-ceiling cupboards that were immense and would allow masses of stuff to be hidden away so the room could remain tidy and welcoming.

The new entrance hall had a lovely doorway with an ancient wisteria growing over the top of it and a couple of windows to allow light in, front and back. One wall was covered with the cupboards for storage, but with the stairs in the corner and the toilet taking up little space it was an exciting room to tackle. The windows had deep reveals and I had kept the old oak saddle posts from the tack room, which would provide me with a nod to the past, and put up hooks for some macramé plant pots that I made with Arthur and Dorothy.

My mum and dad are suckers for family photos so I used what had been a multi-panel wooden window to make a multi-frame photo display. I had a tear in my eye as I populated the display with pictures of the family over time. Beside pictures of proud grandparents with Arthur and Dorothy, there were pictures of my grandma and grandad laughing and having fun. It was just so full of memories. It's good to be reminded that there is something special about looking back when you are busy going forward and making memories. It was the perfect finish and reminder of family in this utterly striking and spacious entrance hall.

* * *

After our season was over, there was also always a lot of life admin to catch up on. Earlier in the year, Sophie, our dear agent and friend, convinced us that we should go on tour and chat in theatres about our adventures – after all, we simply could not accommodate a fraction of the inquiries we were getting. We found the idea alien but exciting. We understood why someone would want to come to visit the château, but we weren't sure if they would want to come and see just the two of us in a theatre. But Sophie convinced us there was no risk in this and the ticket price would be split between our agent, the tour company, the theatres and us. It would be a chance to have a bit of fun, relive some memories and hopefully make a contribution to our roof fund. This was our first big task that was not renovation for years and it was very exciting!

By the time December came around we were all ready for Christmas.

We had some of our nearest and dearest friends coming to visit and we wanted to completely spoil them, so we made the decision to host a fairly traditional French Christmas. We weren't exactly sure what we wanted to do but fortunately we knew a man who knew.

In order for us to understand the French ways, we decided to ask our dearest friend and château helper Quentin more about his family's traditions. It's worthwhile stating that we did not want a completely French Christmas but we wanted to know more about the French traditions so we could cherry-pick the bits we liked and start a Strawbridge Anglo-French affair. For Quentin, *Noël* starts when his family go to the Brittany coast to collect oysters. Whilst Dick and I love these little bites of the sea, we still laugh hard about Dorothy tasting them for the first time on a trip to Cancale: her face went from excited to disgusted and soon she was spitting it out and demanding something to take the horrible taste away.

Quentin would go with all the generations of the family and together they would collect buckets of oysters. He said that, as a child, Christmas Eve was their main celebration. His family would start by eating the oysters together, and there would be thirty plus of them, including all his cousins. We liked this idea a lot. This led on to the main family celebration. The big question for us was what time *Père Noël* came to deliver pressies. Apparently he came when they were awake. Well, well, well . . . I'm not sure either Dick or I felt happy about that one, but never say never. We also talked through food. Dick led with questions and I was watching them both get engrossed in the Anglo vs French Christmas feasts. No Christmas pudding? No brandy butter? A chocolate roll?! *Bûche de Noël* to be precise. Every now and again I would make them smile by reminding Dick we were just chatting to Quentin to find out more about his family traditions, we didn't have to follow suit!

We had a busy Christmas in 2019. Looking back, I don't know

how we fitted it all in, but at the time everything was manic. We were clearly in a different gear. We decided to take our château team to Rennes. It had been quite a year and we wanted to thank everyone. Rennes is the largest town in Brittany – in fact, it's the capital – and it's picturesque all year round with its mediaeval half-timbered houses and magnificent architecture. At Christmas time, this is all illuminated and in front of the Place du Parlement de Bretagne you can find a two-storey, monumental palace carousel, which is loved by children and grown-ups alike. After a couple of rounds of excitement, we all returned to our cabins to enjoy the buzz and atmosphere, and a compulsory *vin chaud*. The smell of sweet roasting hazelnuts, the Christmas carols . . . if there was anything that filled you with Christmas spirit before the big day, this was it!

Now, let me break down the 'château team': it was builder mate Steve and his lovely wife Denise; our château helpers Quentin and Sacha, and Sacha's daughter, Alisha, who we have watched grow up into a beautiful young lady; Meredith, who looks after lots of the admin as well as helping with the weddings; Sandrine and her daughter Chermaine, who only work during the wedding season but were very much part of the team, and love a party; Lydia and Craig, the husband-and-wife team who also help out during weddings and garden days, and have become life-long friends; Amanda, the brilliant artist who does unique portraits of guests at our 'Fun and Festivity' days; and Dorothy and Arthur, of course.

We all checked into our hotel and then after a couple of cocktails, we ventured out to a wonderful restaurant called Le Moon. It's a favourite of ours and Dick and I have spent a few 'date nights' there. The decor is magnificent – mainly deep colours, midnight blues and chalky blacks, but with lots of contrasting soft pinks, reds and creams. The cocktails are fantastic, the food is delicious and it was next to the lovely spa hotel where we were all staying, so everyone could have a drink and not have to worry about getting back.

The mood was merry and as the evening progressed, our camera team, Sean and Chloe, who had been with us for years, also joined the party and the evening got merrier and merrier. It must be our age but at some point Dick and I slipped off to bed with the children, but we heard that everyone got back in time for breakfast.

Back at the château, we started getting ready for a pre-Christmas Christmas, a little like the one Quentin had talked about. Mum and Dad were off to the UK to spend Christmas with my nan and brother. Nan was incredible for her age, but at ninety-six she had already done a big trip this year for Mum and Dad's fiftieth wedding anniversary, so we thought it would be best for everyone if she stayed at home. It also gave us a fantastic chance to have our pre-Christmas celebration, which seemed to be becoming a 'thing'. We have done it in the past with Dick's mum and the girls, my family, and with James, Holly and the grandchildren. When you have a large modern family like ours, you can't do everything and see everyone in one day, so having different moments like these over the festive period makes sense.

The guest list was intimate but perfect. The six of us, plus our friends Johnny and Nadine, who have bought a château thirty minutes from us, our dear friend Sophie and her daughter Rosie, and one of my oldest friends, Vicky, and her two children, Rosie and Theo. We could not wait!

I loved the idea of a boys' trip to go and collect oysters. I have a faint memory of driving around Strangford Lough in Northern Ireland with my family and stopping and collecting some oysters that we ate there and then, but I have no recollection what age I was or why we were there. It must have been pre-1976 when I left home.

Since then, I've had my share of fresh oysters, but heading off with Arthur and Papi Steve to get provisions for our Christmas party was great, and I always had a fallback of nipping into Hyper U, our local supermarket, to pick up a case! Quentin had explained exactly where his family had always gone so we headed the two-and-a-half hours to Pénestin on the south coast of Brittany. We had checked the tides so when we arrived late morning, the tide was still on its way out. It was bright and windy and we were soon wrapped up and heading over the rocks with a couple of buckets, a small pry and a couple of old chisels to help us get the oysters off the rocks.

Our first challenge was to help Arthur, who needed a pee. There was no one around so I explained to my big boy that it was important to pee downwind, which got a laugh. However, we were in hysterics as Arthur opened his coat and dropped his pants, because I think he may have set the record for long distance peeing. The wind had come from behind and carried Arthur's pee up, over the rocks and away! It was very impressive and when Arthur said he wanted a drink straight away I knew that wasn't going to be his last performance of the day, and it wasn't!

Finding oysters was not a problem – they were everywhere – but finding plump ones that were perfect took a little more effort. I set down the criteria that had to be met and from there on we were in competition mode. It was great fun and we loved splashing through the rock pools and following the tide out in search of the perfect oyster. In my pocket I had a penknife so once we had a couple of fine specimens we decided it was time to taste. You need a strong blade to slip in between the oyster shells and force them apart, so instead I used my blade to trim off a little bit of the edge of the oyster shell, until I could see the gap between the top and the bottom, and then I slipped the blade in and sliced the anchor on the flat side. It's a neat little trick that I'd been shown when I was on a wooden oyster boat in the Fal Estuary in Cornwall, so there is no excuse for not enjoying the freshest oysters. The flavour was so fresh and so full of the sea. It was amazing. My mum always said you have to chew oysters, even though people used to swallow them whole – I have to say I completely agree; each mouthful has to be savoured.

Soon we were a couple of hundred metres from the car park and we had become experts by watching the other four or five people who were also out searching for the perfect oyster over the long stretch of rocks. The wind never let up but somehow it wasn't cold as we were active, and Papi, who's well known for feeling the chill, was having too much fun to notice, even with his hat trying to fly further than Arthur could pee!

We arranged our haul in a tray in a thermal box, all organised curved side down and flat side up so they could nestle in their own liquor. We obviously had to change Arthur who had managed to soak every item of clothing he wore. As I drove home, and my passengers nodded off after all the fresh air, I thought about what a wonderful time we'd all had, and even though it was only for a couple of hours, I knew that we would be visiting the shoreline to gather our oysters every December from then onwards. A new tradition had started.

It's hard to beat a fresh oyster at the seaside but the texture had always been an issue for Dorothy (she was still young but my little girl knew what she liked and didn't like), so I decided to serve a mix of raw and grilled oysters as our starter this year. Raw was easy. We would do a selection, some with red wine vinegar and very finely chopped shallots; some with lemon juice and some 'au naturel'. The grilled oysters firm up and by adding a crunchy topping anyone can enjoy oysters, even the faint-hearted!

I arranged the oysters to be grilled on a tray in the curved shells with as much of the briny liquor as I could save. Next, I melted butter, softened a small amount of garlic in it, as we were in France, then mixed in a generous amount of fresh breadcrumbs, a squeeze of lemon and some finely chopped parsley. The mixture was good enough to eat by itself but we spread a teaspoon-ish on each oyster. Then, when we were ready for service, it was placed under a moderate grill for nearly ten minutes until the top was lovely and crispy and the oyster cooked.

For me, the preparation is as fun and important as the main event. Hearing stories of the boys having their oyster trip warmed my heart and, whilst we were suffering from FOMO, we also had a lovely time making candy cane wreaths. Surprisingly, Mum had a blast glue-gunning the red and white striped canes! As the party got nearer, we focused on the final touches.

We'd made the decision that our festive dessert was going to be a *bûche de Noël* – it's a fair cop, I'm a Christmas pudding sort of a chap, but it is the tradition in France so we were going to make our own Christmas log. Angela and I both had our own ideas about decorating and making it look good, so in no time at all it became a competition. I made the sponge and Angela made the butter icing, then we started building one log together on a large board.

BÛCHE DE NOËL

To make the sponge for one log:

Ingredients

3 eggs
60g caster sugar
30ml whole milk
60g self-raising flour, sifted
¼ teaspoon cream of tartar

Method

Preheat the oven to 200°C fan. Line a 20 × 30cm Swiss roll tin with baking paper.

Separate the egg whites from the egg yolks into two different bowls. Make sure your bowl for beating the egg whites is free from any grease or egg yolk. Combine the yolks with 30g sugar and whisk together. Add the milk, whisk again.

Sift the flour and cocoa onto the egg yolk mixture and whisk to combine, ensuring there are no lumps.

In the clean bowl of an orbital mixer, add the room-temperature egg whites. Start the mixer at low speed. Once the whites become foamy with bubbles, add in the cream of tartar. Gradually increase the speed of the mixer and slowly pour in the remaining sugar. Continue to beat the whites until fluffy and forming a 'soft peak'.

Using a spatula or metal spoon, fold about a third of the egg whites into the egg yolk batter. This can be quite vigorous and it is to help loosen up the egg yolk batter.

Add the next third of the egg white mixture, folding it gently into the egg yolk mixture. Then add the final third and gently fold until all of the egg white mixture is incorporated into the batter.

Transfer the cake mix into the baking tray. Bake for 9 or 10 minutes, until the cake surface is golden brown and springy to the touch.

Turn the cake out onto another piece of baking paper and allow it to cool.

To make the covering and filling:

Ingredients

500g softened butter
900g icing sugar
100g cocoa powder
100ml milk
1 tsp vanilla extract

Method

Cut the soft butter into cubes. Place in your mixer and beat until light and fluffy.

Sift in the icing sugar and cocoa powder, then add a third of the milk and the vanilla extract. Beat on a low speed until everything has combined.

Increase the speed to medium/high to make the butter icing soft and spreadable. If it's too thick add some more milk and continue beating.

Spread some of your chocolate butter icing over the cooled sponge and roll it up.

If you have made two rolls then you can cut one diagonally in half and then stick it to the full roll to imitate a branch on your final serving board. You can add your leftover bit to lengthen the main log or just be creative.

Cover with the rest of the butter icing and use a fork to make grooves in the bark. You can also add the grated chocolate to give your bark texture.

Decorate with holly or whatever you feel looks good!

We sort of agreed about the shape of our log then we started to see who was the best decorator . . . I made swirls to simulate the bark and thought I was doing well but somehow Angel's part looked more like a log than the part I'd done so I 'accidentally' touched her log. Angela didn't think it was funny, which was actually funny, so I did it again. Guess what, that wasn't funny either. I think boys and girls are wired differently, but I know enough that a third time sabotaging could have been messy and detrimental to my health, so I admitted that she was making a better *bûche de Noël* . . . even though her bit did look like a big turd. Just saying . . .

After all the sabotage and excitement, Dick and I sat and enjoyed a drink together. We were going to make pompoms for the children's Christmas sacks and Dick mentioned how brilliant he was at making them. It did not take long for this to turn into a 'pompom off' and whilst I'm sure Dick has made a pompom in the past successfully, he insisted on doing it his own way with a fork and failed miserably! Although, if he had set out to make half a pompom, let's say, to be stuck on a card, he would have been very successful! Watching Dick try to fluff it out, trim it and basically have a pompom meltdown gave us both the giggles.

Getting our small gang together was a delight, Vicky's daughter Rosie had not been to the château since our wedding and was incredibly excited to come back. And Sophie's daughter, also Rosie, had never been before and was loving being part of the Christmas joy. As part of the celebration, we got everyone involved in the final decorations. Armed with secateurs, we all started to collect evergreen branches, cones and rosemary from around the grounds – basically, any type of foliage that looked good. There was a massive amount of excitement and energy and this all got carried back to the château. The music was playing, everyone was having fun and the stairs had never been decorated so quickly. As they say, many hands make light work! It was adorable, and as I stood back and watched, I felt so thankful to have everyone at the château with us. Then, for the final bit of magic, the children all picked up a handful of 'snow' and sprinkled the dust over their creations.

While the party was in full swing, a very special guest appeared at the door. This moment was so incredibly beautiful, for the children and adults alike, that it felt like it happened in slow motion. First, everyone heard the bells and dashed to the entrance, then, as the door opened, Arthur sort of did a happy dance on the spot. *Père Noël* had come to see us at the château. Arthur ran and flung his arms around the man himself. At that moment, it really was the spirit of Christmas. As I looked around at our beautiful family and friends, I could see everyone felt the same. There was not a dry eye in the house.

We ended the evening with our *bûche de Noël* in the salon. It looked lovely with all the gold candles on and tasted even more fantastic.

PART TWO

CHAPTER SEVEN

Interesting (Family) Times

It was 1st January 2020 and we woke up later than normal. The evening before, true to Strawbridge tradition, the four of us had sat on our bed and looked through photos from 2019. Arthur and Dorothy were bathed and in pyjamas and we just sat and told stories, reliving memories and discussing the bits we had loved most. We often do this and it's normally a fab hour or so of fun. But as 2019 drew to a close, we spent nearly three hours walking down memory lane and (the best bit) no one lost interest. We had had a year! It felt exhausting just looking back but, whilst we had filled the year like a tin of sardines, somehow it had also felt balanced: there had been lots of work and renovations, but also holidays, birthdays, anniversaries, oodles of events, lots of new bookings and lots of promise for the future.

I remember thinking how still and calm the château felt. It often

did at the very beginning of the year. Although today we were relaxing, I could not wait to get my teeth stuck into the year ahead.

With such a successful 2019, the prospect of 2020 held no limits. We were going back to the UK on tour and the diary was full; we even had plans to go further afield with a series called *Escape from the Château*. We'd also made the decision that our life had enough balance to get a dog as a family pet. We had found a French Kerry blue breeder and had put in our request in for a bitch, and, fortuitously, one was going to be available on our return to France at the beginning of March.

When Dick says the diary was full, it was bursting. We had bookings for eighteen weddings, thirty-four 'Château Under the Stars' stays, five 'Fun and Festive Days', one garden day and a dozen 'Bateau at the Château' stays.

Dick's idea to get a dog was great but also bloody scary. I remember thinking when the children were babies that whilst it truly was a phenomenal time, every now again I just wished they could speak and let me know what they wanted. A dog was like this twenty-four-seven and I could never understand why this would not be stressful for someone. But getting our first dog was all about the family, for Dick and the children, and their happiness is what drives me.

Our little pup was born on 29th December, so at the end of January, just before we headed off on our UK tour, we drove two hours down to Saumur to say hello. Dorothy had always been scared of dogs though we couldn't understand why, so we thought meeting and having a puppy would be a gentle way for her to gain confidence and trust. When we arrived, we had a choice of the puppies and soon Dorothy was sitting on the floor surrounded by a litter of boisterous little black balls of fluff all vying for attention. Our dog was chosen, and we met the mother and father. I have to say Dorothy was a bit more wary but very happy that when we came back from our trip to the UK our family would be growing. All pedigree puppies at the kennel born in 2019 had to have a name starting with 'P', so our whole journey back was a discussion and before we got home, it was all decided: we were going to have a Kerry blue called 'Petale'.

Our trip to Saumur cured Dorothy of her fear of dogs. We had never understood what triggered her phobia but she would get so scared that she would jump up, wrap her body around us and forget to breathe. But these little bundles of fur, which Dorothy could hold in her hands, needed love and nurturing and it was a privilege to watch the fear morph into a desire to care for them.

It had been quite an emotional roller coaster and as we hit the road to head home, everyone declared they were starving, so in the spirit of trying to make the most out of every moment, we decided to head in the direction of the Château du Saumur to see if we could grab a bite to eat near the majestic four-turreted tuffeau limestone château. As we drove through the mediaeval cobbled streets, Dick told us all some of the history, and gosh did this castle have some.

Listing all the owners of a castle can be a bit dry; however, there are a couple of interesting points that I love. Firstly, Saumur was part of the county of Anjou and was once owned by the English House of Plantagenet, so it was once part of England, as was Maine, where our château is! Then, Margaret of Anjou, who married Henry VI, lived there before she got married as it was her dad's house. So the lady from Saumur became the queen of England at fifteen and she effectively ruled the country in her husband's place due to his frequent bouts of insanity. She then went on to become an important player in the War of the Roses.

Later, the château had been an opulent part of the French royal estate and the residence for the town's governors. It had been used as a prison in the eighteenth century, when it had housed a fair number of British sailors. The building was spared by the French Revolution but it was in such a poor state that it was due to be demolished. So it seems that even then, there were lots of châteaus up for restoration. The Château de Saumur was saved by being turned into a state-funded prison and in the nineteenth century it was assigned to the war ministry and used to store weapons and munitions . . . Over a hundred years ago the château was bought by the town and opened as a museum, which it still is today.

We found a charming restaurant on the hill overlooking the château and the town. It had a rustic feel with wooden benches and a chalkboard menu, which looked delicious. There was a mixture of classic French bites, such as terrines, cheeses, steak and frites. When we arrived it was empty, so we grabbed a charming table with a great view. The sun was shining and we were all on a high from meeting Petale. The children both ordered a lemonade and Dick and I shared a 2 per cent cider, which was refreshing and delicious. Within twenty minutes the place was full and it really finished off the trip beautifully.

With full bellies and the gentle purring of the car, Arthur and Dorothy only took minutes to fall asleep. They travel well and Dick and I love having the chance to chat. The main topic of conversation was our tour and how exciting it would be for the family.

I loved taking the family around the UK on tour. I have had the opportunity to travel quite widely, but as a family it was a voyage of discovery, with each area providing surprises and fun. We started in Edinburgh and worked our way down the country, travelling from Wales to East Anglia and down to the south coast. Our final venue was to be the London Palladium!

We had a few days before we were due to perform at the London Palladium so we headed back to France and continued our preparations, along with some essential laundry. When we came back to the château, the news was full of stories about a new deadly virus, and we were hearing about something called a 'pandemic'. There was a lot of uncertainty and fear. We tried to understand what was going on and, like everyone else, we scoured the news channels to try to separate the facts from the hyperbole. Surely it couldn't be as terrible as it was being made out to be?

First thing on the list of things we had to do was collect the latest member of the family, Petale. I rushed down and brought her home to a reception committee. It was lovely, and I watched as everyone fell in love with her. She was a fluffy, jet-black bundle of fun. We took her into the château for her to explore her new home and the first thing she did was pee on the floor, much to everyone's delight. Petale needed to be trained but she was simply gorgeous. Everyone was calling and stroking her and the excitement levels were very high. In addition to training our new puppy, the rest of the family would have to undergo some training too . . . I had grown up with dogs being part of the family and was really happy that Arthur and Dorothy would have similar experiences as they grew up.

Petale's arrival was a blessing and, without us knowing, the timing could not have been better. Within minutes of arriving at the château, Petale was at home, bouncing around and making everyone gooey. Even my mum, who had never owned a dog, was smitten.

Petale was settling in well, we had even developed a new routine,

but the next week was still uncertain. The final date of our tour at the Palladium was still due to be happening. That bred a certain level of anxiety because we would be hugging hundreds of people. Gathering with so many people in one space didn't seem advisable. What if one of us caught something? My mum and nan were particularly vulnerable. We had lots of questions but no one really knew the answers. It certainly kept me awake at night.

As it turned out, any decisions were taken out of our hands: France went into lockdown so we could not get to the final date of our tour which had been set for 23rd March 2020.

It was a strange feeling. One of great sadness and anxiety. The uncertainty was rife. How would we protect our family? How long would it last? Would it cause problems for the weddings booked for this year? If we moved them, when should we move them to? What about all the couples on the cusp of booking? Surely we couldn't take any more bookings until we knew how to fulfil our current commitments? I was trying to keep all our couples calm but my mind was running away with me. How would we survive financially? We had a little bit of money in the pot but not enough to continue spending at our current rates. And how would we protect and look after the team we had built? We had finally got to the position that events were running like a well-oiled machine. Everyone knew what was expected of them and everyone worked really hard. I had so many questions, so many worries, but my number one concern and priority was how we would keep my mum safe, as it appeared her medical history put her on the vulnerable list.

If anyone can isolate themselves it's a family with a moat. Angela was spending long hours organising dates for those who had to, or wished to, change their wedding plans. Some believed it would all blow over very quickly so were holding out for their already agreed date later in the year; others grasped the nettle and moved into 2021 and, as wedding dates are planned well in advance, some had to move two or three years into the future. Managing all the disappointment and staying positive took a great deal of Angela's energy, whilst I took responsibility for provisioning and protecting the six of us. We had reserves of food and supplies in our cupboards, and the *potager* did have some things growing, so we didn't actually have to venture out as a matter of urgency.

I got into a routine of shopping in the village convenience store every couple of weeks, bringing the food home and leaving it to 'decontaminate' before bringing it into circulation. We didn't know exactly what precautions were essential so we erred on the side of caution to keep everyone well. Looking back, it was the lack of factual information that fuelled our strict adherence to the isolation. It may sound macabre, but Angela and I ended up researching the 'normal' number of deaths per year and comparing the new figures that must have been influenced by the pandemic and we struggled to detect a spike or a big change due to the pandemic, but the reported number of deaths that were attributed to Covid were staggering so we took no risks.

My first call was with a wonderful couple Katie and Kiren, who were due to get married right at the start of the season on 1 May. There are many things in our business that we have no control over and so we are continuously learning on the job and troubleshooting. Every situation is different and presents unique challenges, but this was a scenario that we'd had no training for. Part of my role is to ease any worries and make sure the couple knows that there is nothing that can happen that we cannot sort out. So obviously, in this circumstance, that wasn't easy.

We talked through all sorts of different options: moving the wedding to later in the year, to next year (which at this time felt

like an eternity away), to even later, or even cancelling if they felt that was right for them. We would adapt, whatever the situation. It felt like that was the best we could offer at this point. Dick told me of a saying in the army: 'It's a decision to not make a decision'. I made sure every couple knew that Dick and I would do our best to guide them to do the right thing for them. If they wanted to cancel at any time, they could. No matter what stage we were at, we would give them a full refund. I think this helped the couples but I remember thinking, *Gosh, what happens if our weddings do not start up again?* What would we do? We would be broke. But I also knew that it was the right thing to do and at night we could look at ourselves in the mirror with pride. In fairness, calming everyone's fears and letting them know that whatever happened we would do right by them allowed us to take a pause and breathe as a family as well.

To begin with, it was like an enforced holiday for the children. However, it became apparent that their education had to continue. The school started to send lots of information and worksheets, which I gamely translated and tried to do with the children. Angela had been talking to her girlfriends with similar-aged children and there seemed to be a common guilt about not doing enough home-schooling as many were trying to work in parallel with providing full-time childcare. We decided that, lovely as the free time was, we had to restart education, so 'Daddy School' in the dining room became part of our routine.

I am a firm believer that there is so much more to education than formal academic work, but formal academic work is the bedrock that allows children to seek knowledge on their own. My big problem was there was no way I could try to teach French, or in French. It would have ruined the children forever and my struggles with the worksheets proved that. I must have spent a day working out that some dinosaur, called something French, ate ferns . . . it was a nightmare. Therefore, we concentrated on reading, writing and arithmetic, with my main acknowledgement of our living in France manifesting itself in me teaching writing, letters and numbers, as taught in France.

I felt it was important that Angela embraced this way of writing too so she joined us. We all practised the letters, aided by a French preschool textbook we had, but my problem student didn't want to do exactly what was required. We had words and, I am sorry, but even though it was day one Angela got detention. I was going to deal with her later when the children were in bed. Unbelievably, she never came back to our classroom . . . Time has proven that we did something right because when normal service restarted, the children were a little rusty at French but boy could they do sums. And, guess what? They are both top of their classes in English.

Dick is a great teacher and I enjoyed watching him teach Arthur and Dorothy the three Rs. I remember looking at him and thinking what a great team we are, because I would have been hopeless at this.

Obviously, it's not possible to spend eight hours a day hunched over a desk, so I decided that when possible, we'd have time in the garden. We have always made a point of explaining things to the children and have tried to ensure that the answer to one of their questions is never 'because I say so'. Chatting as we discovered things in the garden was easy and not like teaching. Arthur and Dorothy had their own beds to dig and play in as they wished and I'm sure there are still some Lego men and cars, and little bits of jewellery buried there under the plants. However, when we 'worked' together it had to be done Daddy's way, which, funnily enough, was Grandpa's – my dad's – and Great Grandpa's – his dad's – way. If it's not broken don't fix it.

I have a wonderful video of Arthur and Dorothy as toddlers 'helping' me in the garden, but now they understood and asked so many questions. We have some slightly less than adult-sized tools and a lot of trowels and little forks, so they could feel productive. I first prepared the ground to the point that anything that stung or pricked was removed. Then it was serious and we set about making a 'drill' with our Victorian garden line marker.

Actually, I don't even think that is a gardening term. I tried looking it up but all I got was things to make holes! From the time when I was Arthur and Dorothy's ages, with my father and grandfather, I'd make lines of raised earth, about six inches high and ten inches wide, and as long as the beds. These lines were of finer soil and had a line of string to mark the centre. When the earth is gently patted down it forms a long, neat, flat-topped ridge. Then, by slowly lifting and extracting the string you have the perfect indentation for planting seeds.

I have a memory of my dad's line marker being two pieces of batten, about ten inches long, that were worn and slightly pointed at one end with about thirty feet of string tied on and wrapped around them. It is probably still hanging on a peg in the shed back in Northern Ireland. I'll check next time I'm back there. I really hope that in fifty years' time, my two little ones have such fond, vivid memories of our time in the garden.

That summer, Arthur and Dorothy learnt to 'sow dry and plant wet'. Each drill had seeds spread along it, which was challenging for the youngsters but they did it, then the finest soil, tilth, was sprinkled on the top of the seeds, patted down and watered. So the seeds were 'sown dry' to make the sprinkling and spreading of the seeds easier and then they are watered.

As I was teaching the children, I felt I'd better go back and check my childhood lexicon was correct, so it was time for a little more research. (It reminded me of my time as a young captain in the army in the mid-1980s when I used to teach digital communications, when the subject was still in its infancy. It was imperative that I stayed at least one or two steps ahead of my students, and so it was for Arthur and Dorothy's education during lockdown!) I was surprised that the fine soil isn't actually called 'tilth', but tilth is a word that refers to the condition of the soil, meaning the soil provides good conditions for seed germination and root proliferation. I was not prepared to try to explain that to the children, so, like me, my family call the soil on top of a 'drill' the 'tilth' and long may it continue! Over the weeks, we had perfectly straight lines of radishes, peas, beans, herbs and all manner of salads.

As well as playing in the mud and planted seeds, we also planted out seedlings and young plants. Having started courgettes, haricots, tomatoes and lettuce in pots they needed to be transplanted. The children understood the principles very quickly. The ground was prepared and neat lines of holes were dug for the plants. Our young plants were soaked in water. I loved the concentration of the children when they placed their tiny hands on top of the pots with their fingers spread on either side of the stem, then turned the pot upside down and carefully squeezed, leaving the roots and the fine root hairs exposed. I explained about the hairs being in contact with the soil, allowing the moisture and nutrients to be sucked into the plant. By ensuring the seedlings were in moist soil when transplanted and giving them a healthy amount of water after they had been put into the ground and surrounded by tilth we made sure the transplanted roots were given the best start possible in the ground. Arthur and Dorothy understood and from that period on, they were capable of planting and sowing. With time in the garden, they understood where vegetables and fruits come from. It was a very satisfying time and though we may not have been able to follow the French curriculum, Angela and I were happy – as education is more than just books.

The walled garden was becoming an important part of our routine. We'd go out there and the children would help and play. It was idyllic, tiring and educational, but underlying it was also a sense of gratitude. As Dorothy's birthday approached, it became obvious that we weren't going to be able to have a typical birthday party, so we thought, let's get her an unusual present that will allow her more freedom to play . . . Our children are lucky and have a playroom of wonderful, creative toys with hobby and art resources, which makes present buying more interesting. We like to think we don't gender-stereotype the children but Arthur likes bashing things with sticks and his favourite present of all time is probably a large hammer that he calls 'mjolnir'. While Dorothy loves rainbows and sparkles, plays with dolls and is at her happiest doing Daddy's hair or nails.

Angela deciding to buy Dorothy a bell tent was inspired. We picnicked out in the garden a lot and it's a fact that children love having dens, so Dorothy's palatial tent was a great place for them to chill and to get out of the sun if necessary. The sides rolled up and revealed insect nets, so there was a through draft and Mummy didn't have to worry about the children getting bitten when they were playing in there.

Once the tent was up, we spent hours in and around it. We set up what practically resembled a holiday camp. The children had cushions and rugs in their tent; Angela and I had a table and sun umbrella and six seats so Grandma and Papi Steve could come and join us. We also had a glorified paddling pool that we could sit and play in. It was simple, wholesome family fun. When we had barbeques, Grandma would bring something out to be cooked and magically produce salad and bread. It was possible to nip out and buy what we needed but Jenny loved making bread and flatbreads, so we allowed her to experiment to her heart's content. Angela and I would often have an aperitif whilst the children had an ice cream or a soft drink. We'd made ourselves very comfortable and the tent had turned out to be a great family present that made visits to the walled garden even more appealing.

As the years move forward, our memories of 2020 will become glossed over and we may forget the everyday experiences, like the parcels we left for five days before we touched them, the routine of shopping, and the unfulfilled desires to hug or even see our relatives. But also the worry that none of us really knew what we were dealing with. There was an urge to listen to our instincts but also the fear that we didn't know enough about anything to decide what was best and, if the truth be known, that we were all so scared for our loved ones and didn't want to break any rules for fear that something terrible might happen. This was there every day, always in the back of our minds, but I knew that in having three generations of our family together we were lucky and that made it OK.

I know that in years to come, I will forget the bad feelings, and the fear and worry, but I'm sure I will always remember the 299 euros paddling pool we purchased from the hypermarket and our 4pm routine, where we would have a beer with a splash of Picon, a bitter aperitif served best with ice, and put some music on to dance the worries away. Country and western for Dick, Imagine Dragons for Arthur and Ed Sheeran for Dorothy.

It's hard to articulate what it feels like having a pause button pressed on your life. However, what we experienced in this strange, scary time is something that unites us all, so that makes it easier to understand. Many of our lives were so busy that we lost sight of what was special right in front of us. For us, our desire to create the dream family home which was financially secure for the children had taken over. Whilst we always ensured that our unit came first, we tried to fit in too much and we were permanently shagged! For all the worry and anxiety this 'pause' caused, the silver lining was that it allowed us to find the time to breathe and go back to basics.

* * *

The first wedding cancellation we received was harder than I had expected. Byronne and Scarlette were our very first dome guests. They had become engaged at the château and then booked to have their wedding here, and now they were having a baby. We were overjoyed for them and, true to our word, we immediately refunded their deposit in full. They could then be free to enjoy their dream wedding in their own time. We were content that we had done the right thing, but this moment also made it hit home that we needed to find new revenue streams to replace our wedding and events income that had allowed us to bring the château back to life.

There was a moment during this time that we felt vulnerable and, whilst it was fleeting, the memory is deeply ingrained. A few things happened in succession that changed our path. Firstly, we were receiving hundreds upon hundreds of emails from other people in lockdown who were using the time to complete projects in the garden, go through their attics, cook, sew and generally do things they probably had wanted to do for a very long time. This spurred the idea that we could help others and, after that, it wasn't long before we were in the depths of a new series called *Make Do and Mend*.

The idea of *Make do and Mend* was simple. We'd look at some of the many requests we'd had for advice. We'd film our video conferencing chat that allowed us to understand what our contributors wanted. Thereafter, it was a matter of showing them some of the DIY and craft techniques they needed for their project and being there to answer questions and support them until they succeeded.

Angela and I had an intensive training course conducted on Zoom on how to use cameras. We took lots of notes and we were there to check on each other, so it was very seldom that we forgot to turn on the microphones or cameras or . . . Soon, the whole family was involved in setting up non-synch wides, wides, close-ups, mids, and we made a point of having more shots than anyone could possibly want, so the editor was spoiled for choice.

We were busy and in contact with a lot of people, so it didn't feel like we were in isolation at all. Both Angela and I found that supporting our contributors was truly rewarding, but there was too much interaction to put it all on the telly so we had lots of fun off-camera too. (I particularly liked the call I got at 23.30hrs when a chap who will remain nameless had put two screws through his water pipe – yes, two! Frantic instructions later and we'd isolated the problem pipe and he was mopping up and feeling a bit sheepish.).

We managed to keep ourselves gainfully employed during a time when our events business produced no income and wouldn't do so until everyone got the all-clear, dates could be rescheduled and all the planning could be redone. At this stage, we had no idea when this would be, which was more than a little worrying. The final saving grace was receiving payment from our 'Dare to Do It' tour. Looking back, I can't believe how lucky we were. Firstly, that we had been able to do the tour that would financially support us through such a challenging period, but also to have done it literally on the cusp of the world going into lockdown. It sent chills down my spine thinking about it and I could not help wondering if it was luck or fate. We cried with relief.

* * *

By now, I'd spoken to all of our 2020 wedding couples and it was becoming clear that there were two camps: those who accepted the weddings weren't going to happen and had rearranged their dates – some had opted for dates in 2021, a few had gone further into 2022, and Neil and Lawrence won the trophy by moving theirs into 2025 – and the others who were not accepting defeat and instead prepared to drop everything at the drop of a hat to be at the château within hours of any restrictions being lifted. Victoria and Natasha led this gang and stayed in constant communication, weighing up facts we had to hand.

The year had not yet been written off so we decided to tackle some jobs that were difficult when our wedding business was in full swing, as we had to ensure the château and the grounds would be presentable when we could receive guests once more. It was time to make a mess. We tend to have several jobs on the go at the same time, so we decided that 'faint heart never won fair maiden' and set off on four pretty big jobs all in parallel.

Somehow, we set ourselves the challenge of sorting out the garage by the chicken house to be my new workshop; refurbishing the orangery; turning the ruin of the old wash house by where the boat was moored into spacious ablutions; and, to take the château forward, we decided it was time to tackle the library tower off the salon . . . that should keep us busy for the rest of the year. In hindsight, we were gluttons for punishment, but everyone who had worked with us at the château was up for it, so we thought, why not!

Dick had basically outgrown his old workshop in the *sous-sol*, so it was time to upsize. We'd never explored the loft above the chicken house and the garage. We'd never been in a rush to search everywhere and, with it being difficult to get up there, it was never our

priority. But now, as the rooms below were going to be restored, it was necessary to clear them both out, and I for one wanted to be part of the treasure hunt.

The chickens had been moved from their chicken house, which was a stone outbuilding, to a shed in the walled garden. We'd intended to start work on the outbuilding as it was to be my main workshop. I loved the idea as it was much more spacious and, being just off the island, would allow me to play in peace. But to clear the loft of junk we needed to do a quick repair on the only access, which was a set of very rickety stairs that went up from the garage. We popped in a couple of supports and then I went up, bouncing on every step, and tested the floor on the level above. I had to mark some areas out of bounds as they were a bit fragile, then I briefed Angela on where she and Sacha should step, and I left them to it, thinking it was a grubby, horrible job that I was sure they'd love!

Dick thinks everything that's a bit broken or tatty tends to be junk, but he knows to let me have a good rummage through before he starts getting rid of anything. The chicken house loft was full of treasure and, to be fair, very little was actually thrown away. Sacha, who has been at the château since our first paid wedding, and I put on masks and gloves and went up to investigate. It was wonderful, if a little dusty. There were lots of vintage farm tools and tins and school books, what looked like pieces of an old billiard table, a box of costume jewellery that belonged to Veronique, one of the Baglione family who still lives nearby, and a huge basket of papers that we just ran out of time to look through.

Later that evening, when everyone had gone, I showed Dick our progress. The light was low and billowing in, and as the geometric rays caught the infinite dust particles it looked magical. At first, we started looking through the air balloon-like basket together.

I was glad Dick was with me as I really do not like spiders and there was a lid to open! The magic of an old basket is priceless and we didn't have to dig far before we came across a folder full of birds painted in watercolours. They looked like plates from an old book, but the birds were tropical and the colours popped: yellow, green, orange and red. It was just my style. This was the best find so far but we kept going, and then, near the grubby and dusty bottom of the basket, we found an old ledger with details of some bills and costings. Dick and I were both delighted with this find, and so we headed back to the château to investigate further.

Once I was given an empty building, I set about turning the mud-floored, doorless garage into a modern workshop. We dug down and removed a lot of the rammed earth floor; then we made a doorway between the garage and the chicken house by inserting a concrete lintel then excavating. We marked out a level in the garage that matched the concrete floor next to it, popped in a damp-proof membrane and laid down a reinforced mesh. Then we waited for our concrete delivery. It was so much simpler than getting the ingredients and mixing it ourselves, as the room was lovely and spacious so needed a lot of concrete.

Mike, our electrician, was on standby and all we needed at this point were surface-mounted sockets and lights in the workshop. However, I'd also decided that I needed a three-phase supply, which would allow me flexibility and the ability to buy bigger machines in the future, so we dug out trenches to pass the cables through to a new distribution board for the building. Every job takes a bit of time but because the workshop had no water or waste it was pretty simple.

The day Dick's workshop got properly organised was a good day. It was just so true to Dick's aesthetic. Nothing new had been

purchased; everything was reclaimed and functional and, even though I insisted that we unify all the various woods and pallets with my favourite green paint, it was still very Dick. It all looked fabulous and neat and beautifully organised, although I wondered how long this would last in our world where everyone 'borrowed' Dick's stuff!

Our family contribution to this was minimal. There were just a few touches to remind Dick of us when he was working late at night. My contribution was a Victorian clothes hanger that I'd saved from one of the other outbuildings. I knew Dick would find some hanging space useful. But the children completely stole the show with their homemade Lego tape dispenser. It was genius and by far Dick's favourite thing in his workshop.

CHAPTER EIGHT

Finding Treasure and Pleasure

With more time at home, and no events to keep us busy, we had been using and seeing our grounds like never before. Normally at this time of year, Dad would be mowing the grass weekly and we would all be constantly weeding to ensure everything looked as lovely as possible for weddings and guests. It took some adjustment to let this go, but the truth was it really did not matter if the gravel had some weeds in it and we could put our efforts into other tasks. Once this was established, I felt lighter and it allowed us to embrace projects that we would have not been able to do otherwise.

When we first moved into the château, my mum and dad had done a great job getting the orangery ready for our wedding, and since then, we'd done very little other than add a few licks of paint and a little decoration. The outside was definitely 'faded glory' and it deserved some attention. The beautiful arched windows needed to be repainted and have extra putty added; the render also really let it down and the roof was far from sound. So we decided that, as a gift to ourselves and our wedding couples, we would use some of this time to repair and restore the orangery.

The orangery has a real art deco feel. I'm convinced it was built decades after the château. A friend of ours who owns a stud farm nearby once told us of his memories of the Baglionis serving high tea in the orangery. We really were the right custodians of this property!

The orangery was our main events space and when we had been completely locked down Papi Steve and I had dug a trench and laid an electrical cable from the outbuildings across the meadow to near the orangery to replace the rudimentary solar system that provided us with very limited electricity. We had also sourced some used slates from a Welsh refectory that were stunning. The colours in them reflected and sort of shimmered. As if that wasn't enough, we needed to revamp the render, and the lean-to service area at the back needed some love.

We'd contracted Roofer Steve to reroof the big barn, as it was on its last legs and had as many holes as slates, and we had an idea for a television series that we intended to film there. Due to the Covid rules, Steve had been 'Billy No-Mates', working with very little contact with us. Steve has been a pleasure to work with right from the first moment he turned up here. He has been a roofer since before he was allowed to be a roofer. He's a perfectionist and takes great pride in what he does.

When Steve and Angela start talking I try to separate them, as they always agree something above and beyond what I was expecting. He was genuinely excited about our Welsh slate roof and somehow, between him and Angela, some of the slates even ended up scalloped! (I didn't even know that you could shape slates to make them prettier!) Angela had come across to look at the roof and I'd guided the cherry picker up so she could chat to Steve, who was standing on a roof ladder. One moment they were chatting. The next thing I saw was Steve cutting a slate then Angela was having a go. Unbeknownst to me, they were shaping slates into semicircles to make a course of decorative slates as a feature for the roof. By the time Angela was back on the ground it was a done deal. Later, Steve continued his lesson on slate shaping and Angela and he went into production. It took a bit of time to make enough but it was definitely a feature once finished.

There's an interesting balance between doing a job quickly and efficiently (therefore cheaper) and going the extra yard to make it more beautiful/special. Once we had the basics done on the château, every decision had these considerations. The orangery is a decorative building and a little bit of investment at this stage will be visible for the next hundred years so I couldn't really complain about a day of scalloping slates. In 2120, I don't think anyone will even consider it; they will just think, 'That's pretty!'

Roofer Steve came into our world at the perfect time. I'm a bit of a believer in people coming in and out of your life when you need each other and this reinforced that sentiment for me. Steve connected with the entire family straight away. Dick loved him because he was so talented and was passionate about his trade. And I loved him because he saw beyond the functional element of everything, even if Dick tried to ban us from coming up with 'ideas' together!

To make the front of the orangery more presentable, it needed a significant amount of rendering. Château helper Sacha's husband Rob was available so he came to help us – little did he know that he was to spend most of the next couple of years working at the château and become affectionately known as 'Render Rob'. What is meant to be, is meant to be, and Rob and Roofer Steve proved such a formidable pair that they went into business together. We had such confidence in them that when it became apparent that weddings could not start properly until 2022, we made the huge decision to also tackle all the château's roof and render together. But that was a bit later. In hindsight, the orangery was simple compared to the things we asked them to do downstream!

The wood that made up the roof had been in good nick, which made the job easier. It was interesting that getting the correct gauge of lead was one of our headaches, as there seemed to be problems in lots of the supply chains for materials during the pandemic. We eventually found some, but then there was the issue of sourcing three finials. The roof would not be completed without them. The problem was that the ends of the roof ridges had lead-covered hardwood posts that needed to be finished off, and for that you require something pointy and ornamental.

I'd never had to search for finials before but I agreed with Dick that the roof needed something to finish off the lead-covered posts. I didn't want anything too elaborate as the slate on the roof was the star and I was very happy with our line of scalloped slates that Steve had put on. I told Dick we'd have to retrofit them as I hadn't found the right solution yet. When he asked what the perfect solution was I tried explaining, and ended up drawing a simple but elegant spike with rounded ball shapes and a little bit of detail. It soon became clear that Dick thought the easiest way to solve our finial problem was to make our own. Then said something about 'drilling out' and 'coaxial' and 'integrity', and he just needed a lathe. Somehow I knew he had his eye on a new tool for his workshop, so I smiled and gave him a kiss. I knew then it

wouldn't be long before we had the perfect finials.

Making an ornamental point was not going to be that difficult but I had to understand what Angela wanted – the length, thickness and just how decorative. I was in luck as Angela's vision was not overly elaborate. I initially thought it would be easy to weld up the elements and then paint it, but I thought that a hardwood post that had been turned on a lathe would last longer and need less maintenance.

In France, there is a site called 'Leboncoin' that specialises in preowned goods. As well as all the various categories of goods and services, it allows you to search by location, from our commune all the way to a whole France search. I knew there was a lot of equipment for sale on there that comes from old workshops, be it businesses closing, people downsizing or simply rationalising. As I had a three-phase electricity supply, I was shopping in a different category from the domestic 220V kit, which was great as it was possible to get some great bargains.

I searched in our *département* and was lucky to find a carpenter's workshop that was closing down, which had a perfect old lathe for sale. It was very ugly and one of the couplings would have to be replaced at some stage, but it worked and was big enough to turn wood over a metre long, so our finials could be as tall as Angela wanted!

There is something about old tools. They have a story to tell. The lathe was probably about fifty years old but the three-phase motor was sound. I cleaned everything and soon I was experimenting. I had a set of wonderful antique gouges in my green woodworking chest and I'd bought a quality skew chisel on the internet, so soon I was turning big bits of wood into shavings as I came to terms with the lathe. It was great fun. After a couple of evenings out in the workshop practising, I went for it. Angela wasn't too prescriptive, so I just had some fun and produced three finials, of which two were identical and the third was slightly larger. The wood was treated and sprayed with a metallic paint and they looked like . . . finials. I'd drilled a deep hole in the bottom so putting them up on a peg was easy. When they were up I have to say they looked good, and the thing that made me smile was that I reckoned I'd saved quite a lot by making them myself and I now had a wood lathe for my workshop.

The orangery roof was a work of art. My biggest worry when replacing anything old is that I will like it less. The old roof had character, patina and charm and I truly adored it, but deep down we knew that it needed replacing and that is why we bit the bullet. We had made the decision to have the Welsh slate and, oh my, it was better than we could have ever imagined. The slate was thick and hardy, and every piece was unique, with an exquisite patina of silvers and grey. To top it off, it was all laid with care and love by a true artisan. It looked elegant, like its best self, and literally sparkled.

Our day-to-day of life during this period was forever changing. It was as if life's natural routine no longer existed: weekends, days off and holidays no longer had the same prominence. Instead, the importance of maintaining some kind of regular routine to fuel a sense of normality took over. We all dealt with this differently.

Mum was making fresh bread every other day, so our usual trip to the bakers was replaced by a monthly visit to the wholesalers to get an industrial-sized sack of flour. She had also started to harvest everything possible from the garden and was experimenting with preserves and making cakes like never before. I remember talking to Mum before we moved to France about what retirement looked like, and she said she looked forward to the time when she could experiment in the kitchen with no deadlines. Our busy schedule pre-pandemic had affected everyone and, in Mum's own way, she was loving the simplicity of everyday life in the lockdown.

JENNY'S LEMON DRIZZLE CAKE

Ingredients

175g caster sugar
3 eggs
3 heaped tbs crème fraîche
175g butter, softened
1 tsp vanilla essence
200g self-raising flour
50g ground almonds
For the drizzle: juice of 2 lemons and 75g caster sugar

Method

Preheat the oven to 160°C fan or 180°C. Grease and put baking paper in one 20cm × 26cm tin or a 25cm round tin.

Jenny swears by this method and we all know it works, it's just a bit unusual to start with eggs and sugar rather than butter and sugar. But in Grandma's café, it's Grandma's rules!

Beat the eggs and sugar together and then add the crème fraiche. When it's all incorporated, add the butter and vanilla essence. Sift in the flour and, when mixed, add the ground almonds and combine.

Scrape the mixture into the tin and cook for 25–30 minutes, but check after 25 minutes. When a skewer comes out clean, allow the cake to cool in the tin. Then make the drizzle by whisking together the lemon juice and sugar.

Prick the warm cake all over with a skewer or fork, then pour over the drizzle – the juice will sink in and the sugar will form a lovely crisp topping.

Dad was benefiting from being guinea pig number one and was loving being the official chief taster. Every morning, I popped in to see them whilst the children were at Daddy school, and we discussed the plan for the day – who was cooking, etc. Dad often had one of Mum's culinary creations on a plate in front of him and was nearly always on the phone to either my nan or my brother. Nan was ninety-six by this time and my brother had become part of her bubble. We would have done anything to get Nan here with us but with no travel allowed and all healthcare back to basics, there was just no way. Being unable to see our frail and elderly loved ones was truly the most devastating thing about this time. We chatted every day but still it broke our hearts that Nan felt so isolated.

Every day, we continued to try to nourish the children with our time and knowledge. Often, this was as simple as going for a walk around the moat to see what had grown that week. It had been a frightfully dry summer and we had never seen the water level around the moat so low. One afternoon, we discovered the moat had sunk so low that it had created a beach-like effect at the back of the château. It was one of the places where we would regularly spot our resident herons waiting patiently for their dinner. We'd never seen this 'sandy' area before and couldn't resist going to explore. Dick was hilarious as he pretended to make the biggest jump to reach one of the raised rocks, then actually just walked through the water. Backlit by the sun, he looked like a statue. As he did a triumphant pose, we named the new discovery 'Heron Island'!

We continued our walk around the back of the château to find it was the season of sloes. Or, at least, it had been. Dick was convinced he'd seen millions there only days beforehand, but the birds must have got there first. Determined not to be beaten, Dick made a DIY sloe-picker that allowed us to reach some further up the slope. We managed to get enough to fill a bottle, which felt like an achievement, but I could see we'd be serving this year's batch of sloe gin in very small glasses!

The process of making sloe gin is simple. You take a sterilised bottle and then use a cocktail stick to make a couple of pricks into each sloe as you drop them in. When the bottle is filled, you add white sugar to around halfway up, then fill the rest up with gin. After that, you need to leave it for a couple of months to mature, but it's worth every moment – it tastes like the nectar of the gods!

* * *

Over the previous five years, the château had always been bustling with activity. If we were not renovating, we were hosting, and in between it's our family home. But in 2020, the château was our home first and foremost. Our salon had been used more in the past six months than ever before, and now with our very loved and newest member of family, Petale, that feeling of nesting really took over.

The salon had been one of the very first rooms we finished when we moved into the château. But with time not being on our side, I had made a couple of not-so-clever decisions. The first one being the paint, which I had mixed myself. It was meant to be a dusky pink, but when it went on the walls it looked lilac and just did not work. The ceiling was also painted white, again in a rush, and it also didn't cut it. Finally, I wasn't happy with the light. I had looked for ages for a suspended light, but didn't find the right one, so then I panicked a couple of weeks before our wedding and purchased an antique Napoleon III bronze French chandelier that was nice but always looked a bit stumpy to me. I had dealt with the paint by adding a lustre paint over the top, but the light was an issue that still bothered me, and with us spending more and more time in this room in lockdown, we (or maybe I) decided it was time to give this room a little refresh.

The problem with a refresh is that once you strip everything out of a room, you start to see every chip, every mark. It's like a spring clean where you keep thinking of more jobs that need doing. The need for a new light soon exposed that the ceiling rose needed some attention, which led to the ceiling needing repainting, and then the woodwork and the panelling, which was also looking tired. Before long, it was clear this was a major project and so we both said sod it, whilst everything is so messy we might as well sort out the turret, which we had wanted to make into a library from day one.

As the salon was getting a bit of a revamp it was only fair that we tackled the tower. It looked a little barren with a token bookshelf we had put in there the first year we were in the château, but a library needs lots of shelving and our tower is round so that added a complication. Though I was only to discover when I started work seriously that the tower was in fact anything but round! As always, every job involves stripping back before going forward. Once we put shelves up in the tower, it would become all but impossible to decorate around them. However, putting shelves up would undoubtedly cause some issues with the lime plaster on the walls. I decided I needed to go into serious shelf manufacturing, so I could mount them then unmount them, get the decorating done, then fix them for all time.

Then the problems started to mount up. I made a template of the first shelf on one side of the tower and it wasn't even close to the shape of the other side. I then tried the template up to the height of a big book and it wasn't a good fit! Damn! OK, the solution was simple: head to the recycling, collect every large piece of cardboard I could find and then go into template production. I'd worry about shelves later.

Whilst I was in template production, I tried sourcing wood for the shelves. I wanted oak as I was keen for the shelves to outlive us all, but to account for the curve I needed wood nearly 600mm wide and 2,000mm long to make a single shelf. Apart from the expense, that would be ridiculously wasteful, leaving a large, basically unusable, unusual-shaped offcut. In my workshop, I came up with a plan. I biscuit-jointed, glued and clamped four 200mm-wide planks together. I scribed a perfect curve for the inside of the shelf, then scribed the back to match the shape of our tower. Having cut out the first shelf, I marked the perfect curve for the inside of shelf number two and used the bespoke template to match our not-perfect wall. I then proceeded to biscuit-joint, glue and clamp another oak plank onto what I had left. Every time I attached another plank, I could mark up and cut another shelf, and so my production line continued.

I had cracked an efficient way of making the eighteen shelves I needed but the shelves had to be able to support an awful lot of weight, which was an issue too. The first shelves were easy as they were screwed into the top of the wooden panelling. I then had two distinct sets of shelves for the height of the window, after which it was possible to make a shelf that went all the way around the tower. To provide some extra support for the two sets of shelves, I used strips of oak to act as side rails at the ends of the shelves. That did two jobs: it stopped the books falling off and took some of the weight of the books and transferred it down to the bottom, very sturdy shelf.

After some quality time in my workshop, I had twenty shelves that all had perfectly curved internal edges that I'd routed to make even more lovely, and very interesting shapes against the wall. After we had attached lots of blocks to support the shelves, I stepped away and left it to Angela to do the decorating . . . After that, it was an awful lot of drilling and countersunk screws before the tower was actually a library. It was very exciting when we started collecting books from all over the château. Some had to stay in my office but the vast majority headed into the salon. They came from every floor from the attic down and there were hundreds of them. Every box was heavy and I was very happy I'd gone over the top making my shelves strong.

We decided on a sort of filing system, with the children's books at the bottom on one side and our reference books on shelves roughly by subject: gardening, cooking – in French and in English – as well as historic and modern cookery, crafts, military history, local history, poetry, engineering. . . The books that we had written even took up a good chunk of a shelf. The library is eclectic and reflects us as a family. With a comfy chair and chairs for the children, I love going in there and leafing through the books – as Walter Savage Landor said, well before the château was built, 'There is nothing pleasanter than exploring a library.'

After years of looking for the perfect salon light, I just had not found the one. I did like the classic empire chandelier shape but I always felt it was too obvious to get one of these. Then I found a version that I really liked. It was still the classic empire shape but it was made with wooden beads. I've watched these lights become quite popular over the last few years and come down in price, but at the time it was around £500 and so I thought, as I often do, I could make that! I showed Dick and he told me that we could make the beads from scraps of wood, and he had just the tool.

Well, what a joy it was being in Dick's new workshop, using his pillar drill and a ball bead blade – I can't believe that is what it's actually called but that's what Dick told me! The process was very satisfying. The drill-like tool creates half a circle out of wood; you then turn it over and do the other half. Each one needed a quick sanding, but I did not spend too much time on this as they were going to be suspended high up! For the first couple of hours, I was in heaven. I probably got around sixty done in that time, maybe more. Then I did a quick check to see how many I would need. It was around ten times that amount! I will not lie, I went straight to the internet and ordered them online instead.

I'd found a barrel band in one of the outbuildings – it was grubby but with a quick wire-brush and paint it looked just the part. When it came to threading the light it actually worked really well. The next part was very therapeutic and Dorothy actually got really involved and loved it. We threaded the beads onto some fishing line – the rougher beads I had placed at the top, giving it a nice texture and feel, then the smoother 'shop-bought' beads at the bottom, ensuring the voluptuous form of the empire light. And when it was hung, it looked absolutely magical. Seeing the reflection from the mirror gave me goosebumps.

As we continued to watch movies, play games and generally love spending time in our salon, I would guess the children didn't even notice the room had changed, but for me, these subtle changes made a huge difference and allowed me to enjoy my time there without sitting and writing a 'to do' list!

* * *

As the summer progressed, a few weddings stayed put in the diary, in an enduring and defiant 'I am not moving anywhere' way. We seemed to be working in cycles: evaluating the situation every month or so and then agreeing they weren't ready to make a decision yet. But eventually, it was time to have 'the chat' with the remaining six couples to explain that this year was just not going to happen. That was the catalyst for lots of movement: two couples moved their bookings into 2021, one went into 2022 and three decided they simply could not wait. They were rife with worry and anxiety. One had just been made redundant, one had a father who was very poorly and one was in floods of tears because she just had her heart set on a wedding this year. I made sure that everyone felt supported and knew that by the next week we would have given them the freedom to go forward with whatever was best for them, despite it hurting our bank balance.

We were enjoying looking at our château through a different, more 'home-focused' lens, but still every decision we made was with the knowledge that we would be back, and we knew that when we were, everything would be better and stronger than ever before.

Narrowboats are by their nature self-contained. But if we were to charge a reasonable price for guests to be 'glamping' on our boat we needed to improve the 'glamourous' part of the word. *Dolphin* was very comfortable and looked gorgeous, inside and out, but our boat on the moat needed a bigger bathroom. Beside the mooring, and the decking, just below the level of the moat, there was a ruined building that we had seen many times but, as the roof had fallen in and the whole area was full of brambles and nettles, we had never been inside. But it was a building and it was in the right place, so it definitely needed to be investigated.

We cleared the slope that led down to where there had been a door and then cut our way in, with me making it safe every time we moved a little forward. Down came the door lintel, which was only just balancing, and then there were precariously balanced rafters and slates. The roof was at a very shallow angle, which made it look different to all our other buildings. To top it off, there was an impressive collection of trees growing inside.

It took the best part of a day to clear the building down to what had been the floor. It was confusing to begin with but, as we dug down, we discovered what looked like a huge concrete bath. There was also a stone fireplace with a metal cauldron that was nearly three feet in diameter resting on it. We had found the washroom. The château's old *lavoir* was obviously for laundry on a massive scale. With cracks and holes in the main tub it would not hold water, but that was a minor point as the building was also missing walls and a ceiling. Apart from that it was perfect!

There were another couple of days clearing as we needed to be able to get all the way around the building. Having tackled a particularly dense patch of brambles, I pushed forward to discover there was no ground . . . The vegetation was so dense that I only went down about two feet! With a bit more care we discovered that there was a concrete culvert and when we cleared up to the moat, it became clear that we had found the route out for the water, should we ever decide to pull up the plug/sluice that could be seen just in front of *Dolphin* on the edge of the moat.

With everything cleared, it became apparent that our plans were going to change. The building was quite big and the tub was large enough to be a small swimming pool. Once Angela had had that thought there was no way the genie was going to go back in the bottle. The arguments were strong. We had the structure of a pool and it would elevate the boat on the moat to properly glam glamping.

Throughout the time we were clearing the area around the *lavoir,* there was a steady stream of barrows and trailers of debris moving backwards and forwards. Petale loves to be near us as we are her pack, so she got in the habit of sitting up near the boat watching as I went down to tackle the undergrowth, then when I took a load back she would always trot alongside, ensuring there were no problems. I pointed this out to Angela and soon we noticed just how vigilant our puppy was. Every time the children were around, she would take up her post, wanting to be near and often joining in. What made me happiest was that, despite the fact our team was around the château regularly, Petale would accept a little fussing but then ignore them as she kept an eye on us, her family!

If you look up the temperament of a Kerry blue terrier, they are, like most terriers, strong-headed and highly spirited. They have always been loyal and affectionate towards their owners and very gentle towards children, but were often considered downright mean toward other animals. They were originally bred to control vermin and over time they became a general farm working dog and a guard dog. Having been raised with Kerry blues, I value their character but it is really important to train them or they can be a handful. Petale was no exception.

I usually have a treat in my back left-hand pocket to reinforce good behaviour and she knows it! We don't have many doggy visitors and there is little need for Petale to be on a lead, so her training was all about coming when called, or if I whistle; leaving the room if there is any food about or if told to (as an aside, we have been to many restaurants in France were dogs are practically at the table being fed titbits from the plate, which makes my tummy turn); and staying downstairs, unless there is a special occasion and she gets the invite to come up with us.

Petale was actually lovely and tractable; my problems were with training the family. My gorgeous wife cares so much that I have to ensure she does not anthropomorphise the dog. I promise it doesn't hurt her feelings if she's not allowed to sit on the sofa and she definitely doesn't need doggy clothing to match the season!

The *lavoir* was a very special place. Being in there, you could not help being transported back in time to the days when everything was washed by hand. Just think of the conversations that could have been overheard here! Many of the old village *lavoirs* have been preserved and are now ornamental features to be enjoyed. Martigné has a lovely one; its tranquil setting is stunning and the edges are populated by beautiful banana plants. I'm sure there was a point in time when the local *lavoir* would be the place for friends

to meet and gossip as they washed their family clothes.

Ours was situated across the moat but the way the water flowed made that whole area very special. There was a gentle slope down to the building and what was left of the stone walls was very pretty, nestling against the side of the moat. The whole area was private and secluded. The decking by the boat was quite exposed but down here it was possible to believe you were all by yourself. I had questions. But the big one was: could it be changed into a luxurious spa-type plunge pool? And if so, how could we heat it? And what about the lighting? And the hot and cold water? The showers? I couldn't believe that, after all these years with Dick, I was actually a bit worried about the toilets and the waste. To be fair, I wasn't actually that worried; I suppose I just wanted to know if Dick was going to say it would be possible . . .

When Angela and I first discussed having better ablutions by the boat, we had chatted through what was necessary and had a sort of agreement that a sink, a spacious shower, a loo and hot and cold water were all we needed. In fact, we even talked about clearing the slope and putting a shed-like structure inside the ruins. We could even grow vines or ivy over it. How naive was I?

Soon we had our project plan sorted. From what I could see, the *lavoir* had basically been an open-fronted lean-to. That didn't work for us, so the walls had to be sorted first, then we needed some brick pillars along the side that was wall-less, which would allow us to have windows along that side and help support the roof beams. While the wall and outer shell were being sorted, we started to ensure the integrity of the tub, which now identified as a swimming pool. We addressed how we would get water to the location and explored the best solution for the loo. There are some very civilised compost toilets that have electric or battery-powered desiccators and that would save us from having to find a formal sewage solution. After much 'umming' and 'ahhing' we decided the on-board porcelain toilet solution we had on *Dolphin* would be more elegant in our ablutions and so we opted for a second porcelain, chemical cassette toilet that 'flushed'.

The progress was steady and Andy, a builder who had helped in a number of our projects, was great at laying the walls and the brickwork. Inside, we found a reasonable stone floor over all the area that was not to be our pool, and there were drainage outlets for sluicing the floor and emptying the pool. We'd actually found what could be the plug hole but there was a significant root growing out of it. If this was the original plug it needed to be tested. Checking the culvert we found what could have been the exit hole for the tub about two metres away, so it was time to try to unblock our plug . . .

It was one of those jobs that sucks your energy and you have to be bloody minded to get it done. Steve Beachill and I rodded and reamed the hole from both directions and it seemed that we were only clearing a teaspoon of soil, grit and vegetation at a time. We used metre-long masonry bits to loosen up the blockage then laid a blue, 25mm polyethylene pipe all the way across to the *lavoir*. To that, we attached a hose. We could then push the hose in and 'backwash' crap, so bit by bit we cleared our waste pipe. Both Steve and I had a massive smile on our faces when the puddle of water that had gathered in our tub suddenly gurgled and disappeared. We had a functioning waste pipe. We kept water flowing through it and when we were happy we lined it with a plastic 40mm pipe, which meant we had the start of twenty-first-century plumbing in the building!

The whole area was repointed and we built a small wall to give a degree of privacy for anyone on the loo – though we saw the room as a bathroom, should anyone need a shower or the toilet, it could be used as a small pool and social area at other times. When we had a shell that needed serious design decisions it was time for Angela to tell us what she had been planning . . .

It's hard to describe just how exciting it is to discover a beautiful old building within the grounds, work out its history and then sit down to see how we could bring it back to life. The *lavoir* started out being a simple 'outdoor' bathroom but now we had a building that was crying out to be turned into something special – in my mind, that was a spa. I was remembering the beautiful Roman spa in Bath that Dick and I had gone to early in our relationship, the contemporary spas I'd visited with Dorothy and the elaborate mosaics and gold decoration of the art deco spas and pools I'd been to. There was so much to think about. After lots of research, it was the row of windows that looked out over the rich green bushes that convinced me it should be art deco, oriental style.

I tried to make the original rustic fire and cauldron work for us, but sadly there was no way of integrating it without a chimney and quite complex plumbing, so instead we moved it outside and rather than lose the history, we preserved it as a feature at the entrance to the building.

I spoke to builder mate Steve about how we could finish the pool and we decided to go for a simple render on the inside with decorative mosaics around the edge.

There were some issues with turning the room into a spa. We had connected in mains water and we had a small amount of electricity available (for those who care we had a single 16 amp spur but the length of the cable meant a voltage drop unless we put in 100 metres of heavy, expensive cable, so the current drawn would be higher to achieve a specific power). We had solar panels and a small wind turbine to charge batteries for *Dolphin*, so our electricity was sufficient for lighting the pool room and the pool filtration and treatment system, but not for heating the water. The answer was a solar thermal system to heat water for the pool and another for the shower. We bought and set up a very rudimentary thermal panel, but it captured the sunshine and, after our capital outlay, our heating was free.

I had decided that for filtration, we would install a sand filter, so there was not an ongoing need to replace cassettes in filters, and for a treatment system we would use a saltwater pool chlorinator, which uses an electrolytic cell to sanitise your swimming pool. You add a small amount of salt to the pool water. The system monitors your chlorine levels and when necessary, converts the chloride in the salt water into chlorine (Salt is NaCl – sodium chloride – remember chemistry at school? All very useful!). Chlorine kills bacteria and other microorganisms that can cause illness. This process is much more efficient and cost-effective because the chlorine levels tend to be lower, which has the added advantage that saltwater pools are gentler on the eyes and skin. I also liked the fact that the saltwater system didn't require us to store and handle harsh chemicals and it told us when to add more salt . . .

There were a couple of key features in the *lavoir*. One was the bespoke windows Dick had created and the other was the curved mosaic edge around the pool. I'd had a vision, which always scared Dick, but I'm sure he would agree that is better than having no vision! The mosaics tiles were to be mostly white marble, grouted with black to give a monochrome art deco feel, but to break this up we had some wonderful emerald-green tiles, which would be placed in strips every metre or so along the curved edge.

Before every job, Steve and I have a little tile heart-to-heart. I always look forward to it! Together we work out the start and finish points, any unusual joins, where our main line will run from, as well as any other potential problems to be aware of. The

big challenge here was how to create the curved edge, but just like that Steve got his grinder and took the corner off the concrete, creating the perfect curve!

Angela had a very specific look she was aiming for and when she explained the oriental nature of her vision, I said the humid environment could suit some plants and wouldn't some bonsai trees look good? Her eyes lit up and there was no backing out of finding suitable bonsai trees. The slight problems were that sourcing them near us proved tricky and, quite frankly, the cost of something impressive ... OK, who hasn't seen *The Karate Kid*? I'm sure there are lots of very important moral messages to take away but one of the things I liked best was seeing Mr Miyagi growing and trimming his bonsai trees. It is something I promised myself I would do one day, so I was straight into research mode and I liked what I found out! I loved the mindset and was impressed with the simplicity of 'Bonsai is not a race, nor is it a destination. It is a never-ending journey ...' All well and good but I wanted some within a couple of months!

On discovering that any tree can be turned into a bonsai I started searching, whilst at the same time ordering a complete set of bonsai tools – neat little secateurs, scissors, wire to shape tree limbs and claws to tease out roots so they can be trimmed. In fact, the lovely little case could have been holding miniature-sized mediaeval torture weapons. I also bought bonsai compost and some bonsai pots.

Everything was of a lovely quality and since the trees grow slowly, you need to take care of them properly. It is the care that bonsai trees require that makes them expensive. Everyone said that with good care and the right tools, you can grow a bonsai tree that you can be proud of it. Research did ring some warning bells as there is a problem with keeping a bonsai tree indoors as the intensity of light is much lower than outdoors. The trees won't die immediately if they don't get enough light, but growth will decrease and weaken the plant over time. Our *lavoir* had lots of windows, including two large Velux roof lights, but we thought we could make a display at the entrance that would allow them to be outside for a significant proportion of the year and possibly protected indoors over winter.

I could happily have sneaked off to my potting shed with my tools and the collection of shrubs I'd bought (a juniper, a lovely miniature holly, a weeping fig, a little ornamental maple and a miniature pine), but Angela was as excited as I was so it was to be a competition. We'd bonsai two plants each and Arthur and Dorothy would decide which one was the loveliest. They'd seen *The Karate Kid* but somehow I think the finer points of bonsai may have slipped by them.

The night before our competition, we'd been sitting in bed side by side, each with a laptop on our knees reading up on how to train the trees and make different shapes. It was fascinating and looked so doable. We shared pictures and ideas and over the course of the evening devised the rules. We'd take it in turns to choose our plants and our pots – ladies first, as I'd bought them all – and we had the day to prepare a maximum of two bonsai each. The children would see the trees without us saying or doing anything to influence their thoughts and it was up to them to agree on the one loveliest plant before we could speak.

When we headed into the potting shed we decided where we wanted to work. Angela chose to start with the weeping fig and I took the lovely little holly and we followed some simple steps:

- Choose your bonsai tree. Done.
- Pick the right container. The containers look small, but that's the point. The trees are small but looked larger compared to the little containers
- Prune the root structure. I found this particularly interesting as all our little trees were pot bound – the pots were full of roots.

You have to be quite physical as you untangle the roots and then snip them back

- You remove the old soil from the tree's roots, then you remove some of the bonsai tree's roots. As a general rule, avoid removing more than 25 per cent of the tree's total mass of roots.
- When the roots are trimmed, gently lower the tree back into the pot
- Fill the pot to the brim with your desired potting mix.
- Work the soil into the root so that there are no air pockets remaining between the roots
- Watering the tree after repotting will help the soil to settle.
- Prune the tree. This is when you determine the shape of your bonsai. We had a selection of different thickness copper wires that you can wind around the branches of your trees and bend them into shape. The wire holds the trees there for years, if necessary, until they have followed your direction!

Time passed quickly and I ended up with the holly and the juniper, both of which I loved, and Angela had a weeping fig and a pine. I checked afterwards and reckoned we were more *moyaki* than *chokan* in our styles, though I was aiming for a bit of *han-kengai* with my holly ... though the children didn't really care about that! Both Arthur and Dorothy took their roles as judges very seriously, commenting on the pots, the use of moss on the compost, ornamental stones and even a bit about the shape of the trees, but there could only be one winner. Drum roll please ... It was my juniper! I didn't make a big speech or thank my mum. I just looked at Angela and she knew ...

This *lavoir* project was different to anything we'd done before. The architecture of the original room was special and rustic, but now with the windows and the mosaics, it was incredibly elegant,

tranquil and relaxing. I just had a few finishing touches that I wanted to make. The ceiling had to be wallpapered in my lily garden design, so when you were relaxing on your back the beauty continued. The new masonry had to be painted in the green exterior masonry paint that I had found (which I was rather chuffed with myself for finding, after believing that only white and grey existed!). Finally, I needed to add the window decorations, some lavender bags to ensure it smelt wonderful, the deck chairs, rugs, a collection of oriental pictures and, of course, the bonsai trees. We were close!

....

LAVENDER BAG

You will need

Old linen tea towel or cotton fabric
Sewing machine and cotton
Scissors
Tape measure
Lavender heads or other dried, scented petals or flowers
Ribbon or cord

Method

Step 1: Make your bag

Cut out a rectangular piece of fabric. If, for example, you want to make a 20cm × 20cm lavender bag, measure this and add 2cm onto twice the width (seam allowance) and 5cm onto the height (seam allowance and drawstring top).

Along one side, stitch a channel for the drawstring and thread the ribbon through.

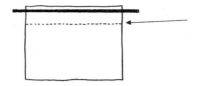

With right sides together, fold the fabric in half and with a 1cm seam allowance, sew around the sides from just under the ribbon channel to the folded edge. Snip off the corner and turn to the right side.

Step 2: Fill it with scent!

Fill with lavender or other dried scented petals/flowers of your choice and pull the ribbon to hold everything in.

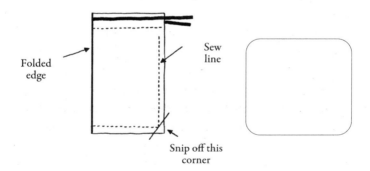

Folded edge

Sew line

Snip off this corner

Tip

- If there is anything interesting on the tea towel, cut your fabric to include this, i.e. any embroidery detail or coloured stripe etc.

Finally, the day of dressing arrived and the pool was being filled. Arthur and Dorothy were checking every ten minutes or so to see when it would be ready. We went as quickly as we could as we had promised today would be the day, but it came as no surprise to us that the pool took all day to fill up. I laid an outside rug on the charcoal tiles, hung up my collection of oriental art, which reminded me of Monet's house, popped some of the homemade lavender bags onto the lovely slatted wooden deck chairs that we have had for a number of years, and we waited. The setting really was lovely and Dick decided to grab a seat. But as he sat on the deck chair, the slats gave way and his bottom hit the ground. I'm glad he was laughing hard as it wasn't long before I joined him. As I tried to show him the problem with his chair, I took the other one and sat down, but before I knew it, the corroded tape which was held on by just one staple gave way and down I went. We both cried with laughter and wondered how we would get up!

By 7pm, the pool was finally filled. We considered postponing our first dip for a few days to give the heating system time to kick in, but the excitement for the kids was too much. Arthur was the first to jump in with his underwater Go-Pro. At first he went very quiet, and I wondered if it was too cold, but a few seconds later he was back squealing with delight. Dorothy jumped on a blow-up lilo and Dick took one for the team going in to join them. As he eased his way in, and felt the chill of the water up to his waist, he gave me an old-fashioned look . . . All I could do was smile. Someone needed to be ready holding the towels!

CHAPTER NINE

A Decade of Romance

Angela and I had been together for ten years and it was also our fifth wedding anniversary on 13th November 2020, and that was worthy of a celebration, but life was still in a bit of turmoil, so instead of us going away together for a romantic couple of days, as we would normally try to do, we decided to have a truly unusual celebration. This year's celebration was to be a full family affair! As a setting, the orangery was lovely, but to make our dining experience perfect we built an open kitchen in the orangery itself, rather than being out the back, and so we created our very own pop-up restaurant – 2020 was the year of eating in after all!

The orangery was looking better than it ever had and Dick was loving how much we were getting done. I think part of our productivity was down to the fact that there were no worries about

the mess we were creating. Normally, anytime we are doing any renovations, we are conscious that we also want the grounds to keep looking neat and tidy, so with that in mind I was delighted that I'd managed to get the front of the orangery paved with no compromises.

With our ten-year anniversary approaching, we had decided to make a pop-up restaurant at the orangery, and everyone had roles. It was a ridiculous thing to do but the skills learnt during this time were amazing . Every element that went into that event made it more fun and Mum, Dad and the children fully embraced their roles as chefs and waiters. It was a treat to see the excitement on Arthur and Dorothy's faces, and that was even before the evening started. They loved the idea of spoiling Mummy and Daddy. It was their anniversary gift to us and I loved seeing how giving our children were.

I left Dick to sort out the functional side of the kitchen whilst I took responsibility for sorting the setting. First, the staff needed a uniform, or at least something to bring them together, so I decided to go into flat cap and apron production in the *trésorerie*. I used the material I had remaining from the boys' suits for our wedding; it was a touch that tied this special occasion together.

The inside of the orangery had been split into two spaces: the kitchen to the right and the restaurant to the left. It's a big old space, especially as on this occasion there would only be one table for service, so I decided to fill the edges with bamboo and pampas grass. After I had cut the pampas grass, I hairsprayed it to keep the fluffiness there. There were many vessels of all sorts of different heights and the bamboo gave it a very distinctive twist. The place was also full of candles. It was over the top and a little bit ridiculous but I thought, why not? Dorothy was in her element lighting it all up for us, whilst Arthur was also taking his chef role very seriously.

The evening was a homage to our time together. The menu was made up of dishes we have enjoyed and shared, and represented a walk down memory lane, our menu of memories!

Amuse bouche – duck gizzards and rose jelly
Mushroom cappuccino on pureed potatoes and an egg yolk
Crispy boudin noir and pork belly with pureed apple and a celeriac mustard slaw
Hot-smoked pigeon breast with wild fungi, dauphinoise and kale
Tiramisu with personalised chocolate
Romantic cheese

Each course had a story as we had eaten something like it somewhere special, or simply together, and, in all cases, I had made up a recipe, calling upon our memories, that allowed us to recreate the dishes.

- We had served duck gizzards at our wedding as we had first eaten them on a château-searching trip when Arthur was just about a year old. It was a memorable occasion and Arthur even had some with us, though I do remember we saw his again when we went to bed in our hotel room, but that's another story . . . and I'm not sure one-year-olds should drink Beaujolais Nouveau anyway?
- We'd had a version of the mushroom cappuccino on our first trip together to France and it was on that holiday that we decided our future lay here. It was one of many courses we had in a fabulous little family restaurant in a place called Aragon, near Carcassonne
- I think I had won Angela's heart by cooking pork belly for her and pork belly with boudin noir is a marriage made in heaven, especially if served in crunchy breadcrumbs, so this was one of

her favourite versions. The celeriac slaw and the apple purée are
there to provide some of your five-a-day and to reduce the guilt
of the absolutely yummy pork!

- The first time we went out on a date was directly after I served
Angela (and another fifty people) hot-smoked pigeon breast
with wild fungi at a pop-up restaurant I catered for on 13
November 2010. If my pork belly didn't win Angela over I
know my dauphinois would have – the secret is simply too
much cream . . .
- Tiramisu is a guilty little pleasure we have been known to enjoy
and it makes us both smile
- Finally the cheese course. We know the French have a slice
before their dessert but for us, it was all about relaxing together,
grazing and having a lovely mature cheddar and digestive
biscuits, with a glass or two of a good port

THE WAY TO WIN A LADY'S HEART

For the pork:

Ingredients

A slab of belly pork approximately 12 inches long
4 boudin noir, or black pudding if you are in the UK,
approximately half the weight of the pork belly, sliced about
10mm thick and skin removed
1 egg, well beaten
3 tbs flour
4 slices of old bread, blitzed into breadcrumbs
Seasoning
Oil to fry in

Method

The day before:

Preheat the oven to 150 °C. Lay the seasoned pork belly out flat, meat side down, in a small roasting tray and cook for about 90 minutes. Leave to cool.

Line a plastic container, slightly smaller than your pork belly, with cling film, leaving enough excess film to wrap over when the container is full.

Start to assemble. You will not be using the skin. It should be possible to separate your pork belly along the fat layers. Place a layer of pork about 20mm thick at the bottom of the container, then a layer of boudin noir and press down firmly, this will get rid of air pockets and will stop the sinkers falling apart when cooked. Repeat the layering and pressing process, finishing with a layer of the belly pork.

Tightly wrap the excess cling film over the top of the meat and place a board on top and a weight to continue pressing the layers together.

Place in a fridge and leave overnight, or for at least 2–3 hours, as this allows the fat to harden

On the day:

Remove the meat from the fridge and carefully unwrap. Cut into cubes based on the depth of your layers.

Place the egg, flour and breadcrumbs in separate bowls. Coat the cubes first in the flour, then in the egg and finally roll in the breadcrumbs.

You can either deep- or shallow-fry, but make sure you cook until the breadcrumbs turn golden and crispy on all sides.

Serve with the celeriac slaw and apple purée.

For the apple purée:

Ingredients

Cooking apples, peeled and chopped
A good knob of salted butter
Sugar

Method

Gently stew the apples until softened with the butter and enough sugar to make them pleasantly tart. Pass through a sieve.

For the celeriac mustard slaw:

Ingredients

Half a celeriac, peeled and grated
2 medium carrots, grated
1 dessert apple, peeled, grated and tossed in ½ tbs lemon juice
1 tbs Calvados
3 tbs good mayonnaise
1 tsp whole grain mustard

Method

Mix the ingredients together well.

I was involved in the '*mise en place*', so the preparations were sorted in the commercial kitchen and brought forward for Grandma and Arthur to work their magic. Then our very talented front of house, Dorothy and Papi, served us. Arthur took responsibility for the plating up and it made my heart melt to see him using a squeezy bottle to carefully make small dollops of the purée and a mould to make the slaw into a perfect circle, on top of which he placed the crispy cube of meat and pudding . . .

When Dick and I arrived at the orangery, it was in style. Several weeks earlier, we'd seen a horse-drawn carriage on Leboncoin, the preloved site, and it was local and so cheap it seemed silly not to get it. Maybe when the weddings started up again it could be used to get the bride and groom from the château to the orangery? The carriage was lovely and had a bench for the coachman and lovely comfy seats under an awning for the passengers. As soon as it arrived and was wheeled off the trailer, I loved it. I did feel Dick looking at me but I felt it safer not to make eye contact, as I knew he would ask where the horses were. Arthur and Dorothy were as caught up in the excitement as I was and we all climbed aboard. Then, just as quickly, Dick stepped between the shafts and started to pull us along the track beside the moat (I guess we didn't need horses after all!). As we left the château, all dressed up and ready to head over to the orangery, there was Dad on our little tractor that had been hitched up to the carriage. I was a bit surprised at how high it was to step up to the carriage in a slinky dress, but we got in and then sat back to enjoy the trip. It was simply magical and the perfect start to our evening.

Dorothy was obviously in charge of the front of house and was really enjoying bossing my dad around! She was very efficient and soon we were seated and had placed our orders for two G&Ts. After that, the evening progressed smoothly, and was full of love and so many smiles.

Arthur was in a bright yellow chef's jacket and he and my mum were wearing their matching aprons. Arthur and Grandma were having lots of fun but it was obvious that Arthur was also taking it very seriously. He plated up like a pro and I could hear him talking to my mum about how the flavours went together. Every time a course arrived, an extra four plates were made up and our hosts would sit and enjoy the same food at the table that formed part of the bar. We were definitely the VIPs but no one wanted to miss out on this amazing evening. Dick and I were so proud of our children. They loved cooking and hosting, and seeing people happy. In that moment, my heart could have burst.

Our anniversary was the only event in the château that year and it had set the bar very high! The food was excellent, the service was excellent, the setting was excellent and the company was perfect. What a lovely evening. Angela and I were just so content by the time the cheese course was served. We kissed and thanked everyone, and then Grandma and Papi took the children home to bed.

As we sat there in the candlelight, we had a chance to reflect on the path our lives had taken . . . Ten years earlier, we had met, said hello and fallen in love. It was as simple as that. Thereafter, we had made some good decisions and fate had smiled on us: taking our first holiday together to France, deciding to live there, searching and developing the idea to see how we could live, having two beautiful children, finding the château, multi-generational living, the early days of bringing the château to life, building our business, turning things off during Covid and then diversifying . . . we knew we were indeed a lucky family.

I had to wonder if cheese could be any more romantic as Angela and I enjoyed ours in that peaceful setting. But we didn't want the evening to end, so we took our time over our digestifs – after all, we were in France, where eating and drinking is not to be taken lightly. So, as the candles burned down, we sat together appreciating what was undoubtedly our best wedding anniversary ever.

* * *

When December comes around, everyone in the family thinks about Christmas. It doesn't matter how busy we've been, we look forward to the children's holidays and the visit of *Père Noël*. This year, because Angela had found the old ledger in the loft above my new workshop, we had records of festive purchases from when the château was first built. We decided to do a bit of investigating to see what we wanted to bring from Christmases past into Christmas present. Angela and I had a chat one evening over a drink and we both agreed that the image of the perfect past Christmas was sort of Victorian; there was snow, lamplight, roasting chestnuts, mulled wine, people skating on lakes, carols ... Basically, Christmases about the time the château was built seemed to be idyllic.

As always, our Christmas tree was perfect. It was over three metres and, after the annual getting-the-tree vertical and best-side-forwards challenge, we set about decorating. Our rather special, if a little ugly (yes, I said ugly!) fairy godmother went up and the lights were organised to glitter uniformly. When the children got home from school it was time to get the decorations up as the light started to fall.

Every ornament in our house has a story or a memory attached to it and this year I made a felt Petale to join the rest of the family decorations. So Petale was immortalised as the newest decoration on our tree from this Christmas onwards.

FELT PETALE DOG

You will need
Coloured felt
Scissors
Embroidery needle and cotton
Small beads for eyes
Thin gold cord
Small amount of stuffing or cotton wool

Method
Step 1: Make your template
Find a nice silhouette image of your pet and print it out. Alternatively, if you are a good drawer, sketch one.

Cut out the image to make a template and transfer to felt in the main colour of your pet. This was easy for us as Petale is all black! Cut out two pieces.

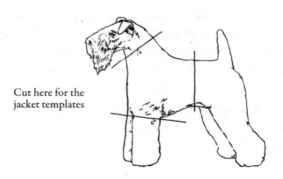

Cut here for the jacket templates

Step 2: Add the Christmas jacket
To add a Christmas jacket, take the original paper template

and cut off the head, bottom of the front legs and back end of the body: this will make a template for a jacket. Use this to cut a brightly coloured jacket from felt.

Secure the jacket piece in place on the two body pieces.

Step 3: Add the stuffing

Use blanket stitch to sew the two pieces of felt together all around the perimeter, stuffing with a little bit of cotton wool or stuffing as you go.

Step 4: Finishing touches

Add a loop of gold cord so you can hang it from your tree.

Use small pieces of felt to add ear details and tail details, and a Christmassy holly leaf on the jacket.

Add beads for eyes and berries on the holly.

Tips

- Concentrate the initial shape on the main look of your pet, i.e. its classic shape, and add details after

- For tiny details, add them later. Maybe add frills and ruffs if your pet has fluffy features, or different coloured patches if your pet's coat is more than one colour

- Adding a bit of stuffing whilst sewing thin bits, like the legs, is easier than trying to stuff after

- If you aren't confident to sew, glue everything in place using fabric glue and sew around the edge with running stitch

There is more to decorating the house than the tree and it's now a tradition for Angela, Jenny and Dorothy to go and forage for materials around the grounds. It is said you can tell what sort of a winter it will be by the quantity of berries on the holly, and from what I could see the girls had found some wonderful sprigs so it looked like winter was going to be hard. Angela decided that the front door was deserving of her attention so she made a showstopper wreath. It was massive, which is probably sensible on a château door, and it was complete with golden walnuts and dried oranges.

Looking through the ledger, I found lots of evidence about what sort of Christmas the Baglioni family would have had at the château. It was interesting to see December was the time for salmon, lots of meat, sardines and charcoal, then just before Christmas they had been out and bought foie gras and oysters, which was the level of decadence we would expect. Surprisingly, they had also purchased snails, which I'd always considered a poor man's food. Lots of chestnuts and oranges were also recorded in the ledger. It made us wonder if the French had a satsuma or a small orange in their stockings at Christmas?

We had an inside track as to what they would have eaten at the château in our old ledger, but as part of our investigation into Christmas traditions of the past, I went to the library and browsed through a collection of old cookbooks by Mrs Beeton and Queen Victoria's chef, Charles Francatelli, as well as Dorothy Hartley's *Food in England*. I loved the fact we had lots of sources to delve into.

As our menu started to take shape, I was particularly keen to explore the possibility of a savoury meat mince pie rather than the ones that are basically filled with a sugary jam. Don't get me wrong, I love the mince pies I grew up with, but I had to know about traditional, dare I say, Victorian (even though we are in France) mince pies.

If this Christmas was to be the best ever then sorting out the menu was just the tip of the iceberg. Again, inspired by Christmases of

the past, I had a vision of the family out skating on our very own rink at the front of the château. Dick's brother in Canada regularly had a rink at his house, so I knew there was a way of doing it (OK, I'll admit the temperature drops down to minus 40 degrees in their part of Canada but it could also get quite cold here at the château). Either way, I knew Dick could do it, I just wasn't sure how . . .

When we first moved in, we had found a box of old skates in the boot room and we had seen first-hand the ice on the moat being nearly thick enough to skate on, so the vision was all but there . . . When I broached the subject with Dick, he explained that making an ice rink outside would take lots of energy, especially as we didn't know what the temperatures were going to be like. I understood that if it was mild it would be difficult to keep our ice frozen, but that was only a minor problem because we didn't need cold ice to skate. I was happy for it to be artificial ice! There wasn't really an argument after that, just a lot of research and a bit of chuntering from Dick about how he wasn't built to balance on sharp edges, or wheels, or even skis. He liked boots! But, to be fair, he got over his reservations fairly quickly. I love him so much.

The plan was that the ice rink would start life in front of the château for the Christmas season and then it would be moved over to the domes so the children could continue to play on it and have fun after the festive season. I left the challenge of making an area flat and horizontal to Dick. After all, I was responsible for lanterns and fairy lights and burners to roast chestnuts . . . and let's not forget we also needed mistletoe and Advent calendars to open.

The ice rink was both a silly idea and ingenious. The artificial ice we found could be used with skates on, and rollerblades, and skateboards. So, for a couple of months of the year it was lots of Christmas cheer, then in the height of summer we could rollerblade. I said 'we' but that didn't include me. To be fair, I got some skates and I tried, but with more than sixty years under my belt it was all but impossible.

The big problem was that the patio in front of the château slopes down and away from the château. Ice rinks, by their very nature, tend to be perfectly flat and horizontal – water doesn't usually freeze at an angle! After a bit of head scratching I decided that a wooden frame, a couple of tons of sand and some tarpaulin would allow me to make the necessary flat area, and it did. The frame also proved to be essential as we needed a barrier to catch people who got out of control, and it also gave us a structure for our lanterns and fairy lights.

When the slabs of faux ice arrived they proved relatively easy to assemble and our pre-work creating a flat surface worked a treat.

One of the other traditions we now had at the château was a trip to the seaside to collect our oysters. We had established it as a job for the boys, whilst the girls collected foliage and got creative. However, the tradition was still maturing and Arthur and I decided that it would be great if Mummy and Dorothy got to experience the outing as well.

The journey to the south coast of Brittany where we knew there was an abundance of oysters to collect is just over two hours, so we wrapped up warm, packed a picnic – including some warming pumpkin soup – and off we went.

I'd never been out looking for oysters before but it was surprisingly easy. Arthur and Dick led the way and we had a bucket and some tools to pry the oysters from the rocks. After a couple of hundred metres, Dick said we were in the best place and we all splashed through rock pools and started comparing our finds.

There is nothing quite like a winter's day by the seaside and as our family headed out across the rocks, I couldn't help notice the rosy glow in everyone's cheeks. Arthur and I were more confident so we picked a couple of lovely oysters and showed the girls. It is obviously the law that the first oysters have to be tasted to see that they are OK, so I produced my oyster penknife from one pocket and proceeded to shuck the first oyster. (I just love the fact that Opinel, a French knife company, makes a folding oyster penknife!) From my other pocket I produced a lemon, as you do. The girls seemed a bit reticent, so I cut the oyster in half, squeezed a little dribble of lemon juice on it and Arthur and I tasted the first oyster of the day. It couldn't get any fresher and we both savoured our little morsels of the sea. The year before, Arthur had loved the experience but was a bit unsure of the taste and texture of oysters. This year, there were no issues whatsoever and my oyster-munching son could not have looked happier. Emboldened by our pleasure, Angela soon joined in, however Dorothy said she only liked them when they were cooked, so waited until we got home to grill them with a garlicky breadcrumb crust.

We finished our trip with the picnic, warm soup and the knowledge that going on a trip to find oysters was going to be a family tradition for years to come.

Back at the château, we had a list of jobs to get ready for Christmas. With oysters collected and safely stored in the fridge flat shell-side up, Arthur and I had the task of cooking our mince pies. So we headed to the kitchen to make mince pies from the olden days . . . Arthur is a first-class sous chef and we made the pies amidst a lot of laughing. Apparently, these pies used to be called coffin pies as they were not round but resembled little coffins. First thing to be made was the lard pastry.

SAVOURY CHRISTMAS MINCE PIES – COFFIN PIES

For the lard pastry:

Ingredients

450g plain flour
2 tsp salt
100g lard
150ml water
60ml milk

Method

Mix the flour and salt in a bowl. Bring the lard, water and milk to the boil in a small pan and then add to the flour. Beat until thoroughly mixed.

Put the mixture onto floured surface and knead until smooth – get your son to do this but wait until the pastry has slightly cooled!

Now mix the Christmas mince.

For the mincemeat:

Ingredients

700g lean beef or mutton mince
100g suet
½ tsp ground cloves
½ tsp ground black pepper
½ tsp ground mace
Pinch saffron
50g raisins
50g currants
50g stoned, chopped prunes

Good pinch of salt

Method

Mix and allow the flavours to come together whilst you roll out the pastry. Cut the pastry and put it into greased, rectangular moulds.

Fill the 'coffins' with the mincemeat and put the lids on gently, crimping the edges. Make a couple of little slits in the lids.

Our coffins took about 20 minutes at 180 °C fan, but it will depend on the size.

....

When they were cooked, we took them out of the tin and they cooled on a rack. We decided to dust ours with icing sugar, as they were mince pies after all! Sorry, but the chefs couldn't wait, so we cut open one of the pies when it had slightly cooled and it was truly delicious. The recipe worked and we knew it was going to be a great success, so yet another tradition was born . . .

Finally, it was time to party! We cracked open a bottle of our home-made sloe gin and it was so lovely that we had some more (and all agreed that this also should become an annual tradition). Next, we went through to the table to pull our homemade crackers and Arthur got his very first penknife (along with some rules about when he could open it!). I have to say I wasn't sure he was old enough, but the smile on Arthur's face told me Dick had been right.

Our meal then explored the traditions we had uncovered. For our starter, Dick had somehow sourced locally bred snails; these were poached in a flavoursome broth and were served alongside the grilled oysters. Both were a resounding success! This was followed by poached salmon (a winner!) and then a roast goose and seasonal veggies (also a winner!). We all love turkey but the goose was the biggest bird we could find, and it was so moist and rich we just couldn't say which was better for Christmas. Though we did eat the whole goose in one sitting, so we reckoned turkey was better as if you got a good-sized bird there were days of snacking that followed Christmas. By the time we finished eating, the evening was still young, so we decided we should continue the party outside.

The main reason we moved outside was to skate and enjoy some mulled wine. I was a complete failure. Everyone seemed to glide effortlessly around as I hugged the railings and wobbled my way through very slow circuits. I just accepted the fact that no matter what I did, I was a skating failure. As everyone else grew in confidence, Grandma and I sat down beside the fire pit, which contained a roaring log fire, and we roasted chestnuts as I crooned some Nat King Cole. We drank mulled wine and when they were roasted, we all ate the most delicious chestnuts collected from trees on the far side of the moat. I'm not sure if it's just our area or this goes for all of France, but there are sweet chestnut trees in abundance in the Mayenne.

Gradually, everyone came and joined us around the fire and the children had warmed 'spiced' apple juice with their chestnuts. Our final part of our meal was a platter full of the mince pies that Arthur and I had made. We said very little about what was in them and let the flavour speak for itself. It was interesting that people knew it wasn't a modern mince pie but didn't actually realise what was in it. The dried fruit and spices had melded together with the suet and meat and it tasted sweet and yummy.

We closed 2020 in our cocoon, as a family, and it was lovely being Christmassy and happy together. *Père Noël* found us yet again, and the children filled the period with innocent happiness, so we all smiled and counted our lucky stars. We were more grateful than usual for our good health after the turmoil of the pandemic, but our overall feeling was that it had been a year to remember, not just to forget.

CHAPTER TEN

The Year of the Roof

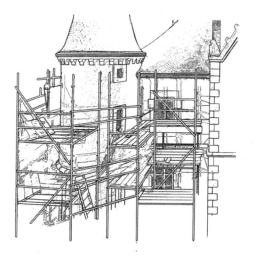

There has never been, and will never be, a day that goes by that we do not wake up with a positive mindset; it's part of the fabric of who we are. As we sat on our bed on the last day of 2020 to discuss our year, Dorothy said, 'This was the best year of my life. I got to spend so much time with you all.' Yes, she was only six, and I'm sure she cannot remember her first few years, but still, that moment was very personal and sweet to us. We had felt that 2020 had been a very unusual and, at times, very sad year, but Dorothy was right that there had been many precious family times that we would cherish always.

Our biggest challenge of 2020 was the ever-changing rules and guidelines. They never remained the same long enough for us to plan. This caused havoc with our weddings and events, and not only halted our cash flow but also put us in a position where we couldn't take on anything new as we had no idea when business would resume. Nothing was stable enough and whilst our 2020 couples knew they were in good hands, it most certainly took the magic out of the planning stage, and I wanted to make that better for everyone.

As we entered the year 2021, we shared the sense of optimism that many were feeling. This was a new year after all, and there had been a good six-week period when the world looked like it was healing. My first job was to rejig all the weddings. How on earth we would be able to recover from last year's pause was beyond me, but we had to just look forward . . .

Not being able to plan is my personal nightmare. I feel anxious if we can't make a plan for the day, let alone the year, and that's not to mention the fact that our plans affected everyone else's plans! So we made a plan, or at least enough of a plan, for me to relax and be able to let people know what we were expecting to do. Have I mentioned that I like to plan? The plan was essentially a three-month rolling plan. We would do our first pass of the rejig, then wait until March to see if it would be likely that events could happen. If there was any uncertainty, events would be paused for the three months ahead. We would use this as a rolling plan. It was simple but effective, and allowed clear communication and some comfort that all was in hand.

It was an interesting process and the biggest juggling act of my life, but getting dates in the diary again was exciting and you could literally hear the relief in the couples' voices. The magic was coming back!

Family life was good and we had our own rhythm. The children were at school, albeit with masks and play restrictions. In France, children from Dorothy's class upwards had to wear masks all day, that's from 8.35am to 4.30pm. It was brutal but children are adaptable, and we could see that they were both flourishing being back. Prior to lockdown, the children had eaten at school a couple of times a week, but restrictions meant that only those who had to stay at school were catered for, and Arthur and Dorothy really enjoyed coming home for their lunchbreak every day. We had started having lots of picnics and walks out by the River Mayenne. We were, like everyone else, finding new, simple joys in life.

Our biggest sadness, like everyone else, was not being able to see our extended family. We missed not being able to spend time with them or hug them, and every day we spent hours online catching up with everyone. Nan was incredible for her age, especially with her ninety-seventh birthday approaching. She was still active, still using her bus pass to navigate London, and was simply getting bored of waiting for this all to be over. There was no doubt about it, Nan would get a letter from the Queen for her hundredth birthday; she was just so good for her age. And at the château, we had started to work out where best to put her as soon as the restrictions were lifted.

Nan had lived a full life. For the most part, she loved living in London and really enjoyed going to the markets to get her bargains. She loved her family and would do anything for us. But having her simple joys taken away from her, she just forgot why she was living, and we saw her decline quickly on FaceTime. Even when she would chat to Arthur and Dorothy the twinkle had gone. It was as if Nan had simply got tired, and once she made that decision, she slowly slipped away. It happened before we could even get a vaccination to allow us to travel.

My brother Paul made us proud. Not only had he become part of her bubble, when Nan got bad, he sat with her for two days

simply holding her hand. He said it was clear she had wanted to go but there was something stopping her. He decided to play Nan a home movie so she could hear everyone's voices. She had not opened her eyes in days, but with this playing in the background and the feeling of family all around, she finally drifted off. My brother took a picture of her that evening and she looked peaceful, with a smile on her face even, and that gave us comfort. Never in our wildest dreams could any of us have thought we would not get the chance to hug and say goodbye to our loved ones, and that's a sadness that stays with you. That night, we all ate Nan's favourite food and told stories in her memory. As often as we can, we raise a glass to her. She would have been one hundred this year, so we hope she is up there with our late Queen having a cheeky sherry.

It is so hard seeing your loved ones feeling emotional pain and not being able to fix it, as too many factors were out of our control. Jeannette was a character and losing her left a hole in our world. However, she is categorically still with us and we talk about her often. Arthur and Dorothy's memories are so vivid they will stay with them, and photos in the château and the coach house are constant reminders that refresh the mind every time you walk past. I have a set of memories that are mine alone as I volunteered to drive Jeannette back to her east London flat after one of her visits.

Everyone said that she would probably sleep most of the way, so I should take a story tape or some music. So I did but I only actually listened to them on the way back to the château. We'd never really been alone together and previous to this our talking was the chit-chat that always takes place around the great-grandchildren and family. I knew just how sharp she was and I loved the fact that she was apparently hard of hearing but could detect a whisper across the château – not just across a room. She was frail and in her nineties, but thought nothing of hoisting Arthur onto her knee when they had a chat, and our big boy has always been substantial!

It was a standing joke that Great-Nan would ask after my older son James and had a glint in her eye when she said what a handsome young man he was. We chatted from the moment we left the château all the way back to east London. I learnt a lot about her life in London in a very different era, and we talked an awful lot about life in the army. She had served during the Second World War and I got the impression she hadn't talked much about her experiences. We laughed about how naughty she had been during the war and when she talked about the camaraderie between the girls I saw the young lass. She had a lot to say about some of the NCOs and officers she had served with, so I thought it best not to remind her I was a retired, crusty old lieutenant colonel.

Back at the château, and in our daily life, we were all getting used to there being ever-changing restrictions, and everyone seemed to accept that things were changing, but very slowly.

By late January, it looked like the world was about to open up again. What this meant in terms of our weddings we didn't yet know. But when we did, no one liked it. The maximum number of guests allowed at any event in France was thirty, which was the absolute minimum we could accept to make it work for us financially. There were also rules around compulsory masks and social distancing, including separation at the tables. Sharing platters weren't allowed, or hugging, and we simply could not work out how music or dancing would work come the evening. So the weddings that had been rescheduled for 2021 were now either moved to later in the year, or further into the future, or cancelled altogether. It was hard but, looking back, I know we did our best.

I watched Angela most evenings on the phone to brides after we had put Arthur and Dorothy to bed. She is very empathetic, so is most definitely in the right job, and my role was to support her. Things were happening but it felt like this down time needed to deliver more productivity. If our events business was going to be shut, we had to make the most of it!

Years ago, I'd had an idea that we would start our new roof in quadrants. Every year, out of season, we would tackle a quarter of the roof, and in four years our entire roof would be done. We loved the idea and it spread the load financially too. We had sourced and bought a lot of scaffolding rather than hiring it, which would have cost tens of thousands of pounds. We did our research and, surprisingly, it proved most cost efficient to buy all the scaffolding plus equipment, like winches and rubbish chutes, in the UK, go through the complicated bureaucratic task of importing it and pay the taxes. In addition to being cheaper than hiring, the big bonus was that we could sell it all after we had finished.

With the hiatus in our business came the opportunity to bite the bullet and go for this major project in one go and get all the mess out of the way. Angela loved the idea but reminded me that we still had a few weddings booked in for later in the year. We would need to be prepared to pause if our future changed. I talked to Steve and Rob and we came up with a plan to tackle the front faces of the roof first. We believed we had more than enough time to finish these before the first possible wedding; thereafter, we could hide the scaffold around the back and continue there with no one knowing about or seeing work in progress, and the front looking pretty in photos.

Having made a decision on the roof, we were always thinking about our couples and what we could do for them. They were always at the heart of our planning. The issue is that when you change the

date of any big event, you change fifty people's dates, and when you do it more than once it starts to feel like a joke. But it definitely wasn't funny. The other issue was that unvaccinated guests weren't allowed to travel, and in every party there was a mixture of both. The run-up to a wedding should be magical, and right now it was far from that. So we kept a close eye on the world, but at the château, we became focused on our biggest job to date: the roof.

The château is big. It's not a big château but it's a big building. Having bought our scaffolding, it had to be erected. We had masses but could only do just over a quarter of the château at a time. If you think about it, that's a problem, as scaffolding a face at a time was not as stable or secure as putting scaffold around the whole building and joining it all together. When we had erected scaffolding to replaster the ceiling of the main staircase, we had put scaffolding all around the walls. As it was tied together to form a square, none of it could fall in, as it was one solid construction. We just couldn't do that around the château, so we had to tie our construction to the building and put out braces to stop anything moving away from the château wall.

Roofer Steve and I chatted lots, and we had bought special bolts to drill into the walls to attach the scaffolding to the stonework. However, the proximity of the moat limited how far out the braces could go, which led us to go for a belt and braces approach. We used the anchor bolts and when the scaffolding was put up around the towers, we used the arrow slits to brace into. As we knew we had to replace the old rotten windows, we drilled a scaffold-sized hole through their frames and connected a 'T' bar on the end that was wider that the window recess, so it could be pulled against the wall and then connected to the scaffolding outside. For our scaffold to fall, we'd need a whole wall of the château to detach from the other walls, and tip with all our metalwork . . .

I loved working with Steve, who had more than forty years' experience with scaffolding and is just so methodical. He would only ever accept one way: the right way.

I'm not sure why I was surprised by how much effort went into the scaffolding, but once it was up it looked majestic and the view from the top was breathtaking! Now, apparently, it wasn't part of the original plan, but I hadn't realised that we weren't planning to replace the render this year as well. For me, a week of putting the scaffolding up and a week of taking it down, four times, was a lot of wages, so it made sense that we worked out a way of doing the two things together. Plus we had the lovely Render Rob at our disposal. And Dick understands logic and definitely doesn't like to waste money for the sake of it, so the 'year of the roof' quickly became the 'year of the roof and render'.

Angela had always said she loved the look of the château. The 'patina of the old render' and the mismatched patches, even the areas completely missing render ... Yet somehow that all changed the day the scaffolding went up. Apparently, our château was tatty and needed lots of TLC. I was surprised but actually agreed that we needed to make the most of the opportunity and go for it. Our decision-making was so much more than tidying up; it was all about ensuring that we didn't pass on a nightmare to Arthur and Dorothy. The more Angela and I sort out, the fewer problems we will saddle Arthur and Dorothy with. They will make their own decisions in life but we are able to reduce the pressures of inheriting a scary château 'to do' list!

The château exterior was really getting some love. The render colour selection had been pretty stressful and kept me awake for weeks (because, let's face it, if you make the wrong decision, it's

not like repainting a room). But after that, things started to settle down. As we were not actively involved in the work itself, we had more headspace to think about our desires for the interior and the usability of the house. Dick would check in with Rob and Steve every day to help with any problems and decision-making, but we had no urgent renovations this year and that felt very different. So we decided that we would do things for the family.

Updating our Strawbridge suite to make it work for us was at the top of the list, followed by the master bedroom in the coach house, the preserves room, the creation of a ridiculous and fabulous *l'observatoire du château*, which had sat at the top of the house for years and, unbeknownst to me, was architecturally the largest and most exciting room in the house. If we could not plan our weddings, we would plan to be busy in other ways instead.

* * *

Waking up anywhere in a winter wonderland is enough to put a smile on your face. With two young children, it's positively the best day ever and the urgency to find the correct gloves for a snowball fight was intense. If my memory serves me, Arthur had outgrown his gloves and I could only find two left hands for Dorothy, so after a couple of 'Oh Mum, hurry up' they both put on Dick's gloves and charged out to be the first one to imprint their feet in the powder. Trailing behind, I watched their cute little footprints – or in Arthur's case, not so little anymore – and, of course, after a couple of seconds, snowballs were being flung around with immense excitement. Petale was very happy being with the family in the snow and was doing her excited circle-running, which I know means she is at her happiest! The chill factor was high as the wind was bitter, which did not help with the now soggy gloves, but Arthur and Dorothy did not care for this short snowy burst and, as I turned around, they were both on the floor making snow angels, soon to joined by Petale, licking their little rosy faces.

As the excitement took place on the other side of the bridge near the meadow, Dick made a very relaxed statement that we should be getting our first goose eggs of the season soon. We knew that

we could enjoy lots of goose eggs for quite a short season, from mid-winter until mid-spring, and were looking forward to this year's bounty. So we all headed over and Dorothy, who was having a brave day, ventured inside their sleeping area to investigate. As she manoeuvred herself in behind me and looked through the straw, we found our first goose egg of 2021. We both screamed with excitement and I was naively over the moon that the stars had aligned. Then as I looked back at Dick, I saw the twinkle in his eyes. He knew, of course he did, and had ensured it was there ready and waiting for Dorothy's hunt. I was just behind the curve and rolling with the magic of it all!

Winter, before the sap starts to rise, is the time to tidy up trees. I had suffered lots of grief the first time I had pollarded our trees on the island. Angela came to understand why the trees needed to be severely cut back but that didn't stop her being unhappy with the results! Trees need to be looked after if they are to do what you want them to. I knew I would never get away with a brutal pollarding of our lime trees, so we negotiated a rolling programme whereby there was about a third of the growth cut out. You could hardly tell but there would be less stress on the old tree trunks when the branches were in full leaf and the wind blew late in the spring. That was easy compared to telling Angela her beloved eucalyptuses in the walled garden were officially unruly and needed to be savaged.

My logic was simple: new shoots were required to be harvested for bouquets and buttonholes for the weddings. Therefore, old growth or trees that were too tall to reach to harvest were simply useless . . . it was obvious really. The trees were strong and well established so we could pollard or coppice them. Angela now understood pollarding and I suggested that we could pollard about half the trees to allow us to still have shoots for the early part of this year. Then, after the new spring growth, shoots would be available on the pollarded trees. The remaining trees we would coppice as the shoots would be easy to cut.

OK, maybe I assumed that Angela knew what I meant by coppicing, I can't actually remember, but when she came and found half the trees cut off at ground level she burst into tears. And when she asked for guarantees that the trees would grow back and be bounteous, she spotted my hesitation . . . It was a fair cop; I'd never coppiced eucalyptus. At that point, my teary wife became my grumpy, teary wife. I tried to console her with the fact that we had lots of eucalyptus, but I was rapidly sinking deeper so I departed with a 'trust me'. I have to say that I was bloody well right too! We never suffered a shortage and since then, we have had more (easily accessible!) eucalyptus than you can shake a stick at – and at a euro per stalk in a florist, I am even thinking of going into the eucalyptus selling business!

As always, though, the garden had to take a back seat as there were renovations that were a higher priority.

My mum and dad were so happy in the coach house but their bedroom was still in what would, sometime in the future, be the granny flat. There had always been big plans to create a luxurious bedroom suite for them upstairs. We had drawn up plans for the building in our first six months in France and the original architect who helped us had envisaged seven bedrooms in the coach house. I suppose we were quite excited by the idea of such a big home but over time, we asked the simple question: did they need seven bedrooms?

Mum and Dad wanted room for their friends to come and stay, but six couples at a time would be highly unlikely and they could always use some of the rooms in the château if need be. So, rather than having lots of empty bedrooms, we decided to go for a separate granny flat, which was basically a spacious guest

apartment, a second comfortable guest suite and a master suite to die for. There was a lot of space so all we needed to know was what Mum and Dad wanted.

In the area that made up two thirds of the first floor, there was a window overlooking the front garden and a window overlooking the walled garden. The views were incredible but because of the size of the space it was a little lacking in natural light, so that was something for me to think about.

Our first decision was where their bedroom suite was going to start and end. Mum, Dad, Dick and I started by walking around and discussing where we should put the walls. First, we made the decision about the size of the guest room and ensuite. Then we decided on the landing area. We were left with a room that was wonderfully large. I already had the checklist from Mum and so all that was left to be decided at this stage was: how big a walk-in wardrobe did they want? I had to laugh as I saw Dick's face. The discussions went on for weeks until finally we were all on the same page.

The final plan was impressive. A walk-in wardrobe, a large airy bathroom and Jenny's very own steam room. To help bring more light into the suite we would use sun pipes to bring sunlight down into the bathroom and the walk-in wardrobe. They worked better than I could have hoped for.

The sun pipes were a revelation for me. I never knew you could take light from another place and feed it into somewhere else. They looked like little circular ceiling lights. Incredible. When the lights and the stud walling was in place, everyone suddenly got a burst of energy to get over the finish line. This had been a long, hard, grubby job. We had started with a dusty barn attic, unloved with no worthwhile features except space. Where we had got to was no mean feat, especially with the decision-making – we both love Mum and Dad to bits but it all took that little bit longer! At last the lights were in, plugs and utilities were in place and a solid oak floor had been laid. Finally, the best bit was ahead: the cosmetics.

My parents' style had been very minimalist and contemporary since they moved into the coach house. It's very much led by my Mum. When I was growing up, everything at home was filled with texture and colour, but now she likes a much simpler approach – it's as if her style has taken a complete U-turn. Her go-tos are modern white walls with clean lines, and then just one burst colour or interest in the form of a statement wall.

For their master suite, I knew they wanted it to remain modern but I felt it also needed some cosiness. So I set about taking over a statement wall with a personal design that I hoped they would love, and because it was from me, their little girl, it would be like a grown-up version of a picture I had made for them. As I started doodling the shapes, they formed what looked like peacock feathers and tadpoles. It had a nod to art deco but somehow this naive drawing looked fabulous. Mum's favourite colour combination is emerald green and ochre, so I led with these, but I also wove threads of warm pastel tones through it. My aim was to tie in these notes with the rest of the room.

Whilst I waited for the design to be made in wallpaper, I spent lots of time with my parents trying to work out what they wanted for their forever master suite. At times it felt like a 'Yes/No' game and then sometimes I would get one response from my mum and the opposite from my dad. But eventually, we got there. We found their perfect double marble sink set on oak crafted bathroom cabinets and white, black and gold marble tiles that they loved. I found a little vanity table Mum loved and two beautiful chairs to relax in. The suite seemed to flow and come together quite naturally. They say that the hard work is in the preparation and this really was the case in Mum and Dad's suite, but now I knew enough I could tie it all together for them. They even had a clear-out of their clothes. Everything in this suite had to be beautiful or practical and wanted!

It's nearly become a tradition for us that Arthur and Dorothy make something for every room we complete. They love the fact that it allows them to be part of the process and they almost always steal the show. On this occasion, we decided on a cushion for the massive master bed. I made a case for a plain linen cushion and then the children added their designs using felt. They decided to draw around their hands and to add their initials and a heart. As it was felt, the children drew the shapes, cut them out and stuck them on themselves using some high-tack fabric glue, and it looked amazing. I'm a sucker for a cushion and this one took pride of place right in the centre of the bed. The cushion moment is always the best: everything is done, clean, shiny and looking exactly how it should. And in Mum and Dad's suite with Dorothy and Arthur's homemade cushion this was never more true!

Mum and Dad's master suite looked like a room from a luxury hotel. The emerald fan wallpaper turned out better than I could have dreamt – rich in colour, playful and elegant. I used the stud wall to create the statement piece and the doors were wallpapered too, which, after pattern matching, looked like secret doors! The rest of the room was painted in an ash soft pink tone and it worked perfectly with the leather chairs and other modern furniture. It was sleek and stylish, yet still felt homely.

The bathroom was modern, Mum's new steam shower was a game changer and, last but definitely not least, their walk-in ward-robe was organised and neat and housed all of their clothes beauti-fully. We could not wait to show them and we were delighted to see how much they loved it. Mum cried and told us how clever we were, and she was right that Dick had done some very clever engineering in this room. As we all hugged and shared that special moment, the kids confirmed that the new bed was also great for bouncing on.

Jenny and Steve loved their suite and it came at a good time as it had been a hard year for them both.

I often hear people say how easy it is to take for granted what you have on your own doorstep. I'd love to think we are not guilty of that because we love our home and walking the grounds. But what we have always been focused on is driving it to be better for us and the business. And as we relaxed into a different mindset, it seemed to allow us the headspace to use the grounds differently. Last year, we found a bike frame in one of the outbuildings. I watched my husband lovingly restore it for Dorothy before I was tasked with spraying it three colours, all *ombré*. I think we did OK as Dorothy adored riding it, and since then we have all upgraded our bikes and have spent many wonderful moments going up and down the drive and around the moat with Petale chasing us. The children have to concentrate twice as hard not to bump into her. We love it!

We had the time to enjoy the grounds in a new way and all took on a spirit to make things – not just because we needed to but because we fancied it. A 'brick kite' that now lives in the attic because it never worked gave us many laughs. We experimented trying to grow avocados from pips and would have paper aeroplane competitions where we launched our creations from the château windows. Dick's competitive nature was thriving!

I have to cry 'foul' here. The brick kite was a well known, very successful box kite – I was just given shoddy materials to work with! As youngsters, we used to love making kites of all shapes and sizes. We would collect the finest bamboo or the thinnest green stakes for supporting plants in the garden, which we tied with some string, covered with material and added tail ribbons/rags and we were away. In this case, though, I reckon the struts I had were too heavy, as was the material, which was not the gossamer material I remembered from my youth. The design looked good, it was all just a bit heavy. That said, all we needed was proper winds and it could have worked!

Arthur, Dorothy and I ran up and down the track to the orangery until we were pooped; however, the kite never made it higher than three or four metres. Actually, there are no excuses that are acceptable, as I know a little about box kites having researched them in detail for the very first television series I made as a presenter for the BBC twenty years ago – that was why I chose to show the children box kites rather than the diamond shapes of *Mary Poppins*.

The box kite was invented just after the château was built by an English-born Australian, Lawrence Hargrave, as part of his attempt to develop a manned flying machine. I had heard of them when I investigated the man-lifting kites designed by Samuel Cody as a way of getting observers up to high enough to see enemy positions during the First World War (he adopted the name Cody of the much more famous showman, Buffalo Bill Cody, and dressed like him to get attention). It is possible to link several box kites together, creating sufficient lift to take a small person hundreds of metres into the air. You have to love Cody as, when he demonstrated the capability to the high-ranking staff, he sent his wife up in the air and forgot about her as he chatted away, which is a sure way to land yourself in the poop.

For the show, I successfully built a kite that took 'Douglas', our heavy, sand-filled mannequin, up 500 metres, before the kites imploded, Douglas fell and ended up a bit of a mess (as an aside, that reinforced my simple rule that I will never leave the ground in anything I have built myself. I have been happy to go underwater, as I trained as a diver many years ago, and have even driven self-built drag cars both forwards and backwards down drag tracks. But in the 1970s, when I did my French paratrooper training, I learnt that it makes no sense to take the mickey out of gravity; the ground hurts when you hit it hard!). We had a ball trying to get the brick airborne and I think Arthur and Dorothy enjoyed the brief periods when the kite went up and may have learnt some new grown-up words from Daddy. Suffice to say, our brick kite has pride of place in the attic and is a gentle reminder that we learn from our failures.

So, having taught the children the vagaries of unpowered flight it was only reasonable that I showed them what an engineer could do . . . Making water rockets out of fizzy pop bottles is easy, quick and can provide hours of fun.

....

WATER ROCKET

You will need

Empty fizzy drink bottle
Cardboard, tape, glue and paint to design and decorate your
rocket
The valve from an old tyre, cut from the inner tube leaving
about 20mm square of the innertube around it.
A cork
A bicycle pump – or, in my case, a compressor with a tyre-
blowing capability

A base to set your rocket on at least 5cm high. It can be as elaborate as you wish but it needs a hole in it.

Method

Step 1: Design your rocket

The bottle opening has to be the tail end so the nose cone has to be fitted onto the bottom of the bottle – all will become clear.

Add fins so the rocket can stand unsupported on your launching pad with the bottle opening over the hole in the launchpad.

Make it look impressive!

Step 2: Prepare for lift off!

In the background, Mummy or Daddy has to drill a hole in the cork and push the tyre valve through it. Then they have to trim off the excess inner tube so the cork can be pushed into the bottom of the pop bottle.

. . . .

We told Dorothy and Arthur the aim was to get into French air space but as they didn't understand that, we just agreed to see who could get as high as the château. When it was time to start, the children had to fuel their rockets (code for half-fill them with water); I then pushed the cork in the bottom and connected the pump's flexible hose connector to the valve. It was time for a drum roll and a countdown. This is where the bad daddy in me comes out. I reckoned counting backwards from a hundred in French was educational, but Angela was having none of it. However, he who laughs last laughs loudest, so I arranged the viewing stand suitably close to the rocket and made sure the flexible hose connector was right up against the spectators' side of the launch pad hole.

When everyone had completed the compromised countdown from twenty, I started to pressurise the bottle by pumping air into it. It only took a couple of seconds before the pressure built up and the cork could no longer stay in the neck of the bottle. The cork and water shot out, the rocket shot up and everyone got soaked, but only I was expecting it! Amidst lots of screaming and cheering our first launch went unjudged. As the children shouted for us to do it again, I did explain that launching a rocket relies on Newton's Third Law of Motion, and that the pressurised water produced thrust through action and reaction, but they were more interested in soaking Mummy.

Dick and I have always loved the preserves room. From the moment we first cast our eyes on that thin corridor, we were hooked. It was a small space, relatively speaking, but full of the château's past. Dusty, empty jam jars were lined up by the dozens, some so old they resembled one-offs, some with elegant designs that could be mistaken for vases. There was an incredibly eclectic mix of jars that would have been filled with preserves and chutneys to feed the Baglioni family and their team. The *cidre* cups were in abundance and ceramic jars for pickling were plentiful. You could not help but be transported back. The shelves were also impressive – deep and sturdy, enough to hold whatever your harvest gave you.

We had quickly made the preserves room usable when we arrived because it was so handy, so when it came to fixing it up, the biggest task was clearing it out to get ready for the renovation. There were fifty metres of the original handcrafted oak shelves still full of old preserving bottles and jars, some very old wooden ice skates and kitchenalia that was past its prime, all of which we had found in the *sous-sol*. We also had a fair number of preserves, jams, chutneys, fruits in alcohol, even honey that

we had made and stored. Very soon, the boot room had packing crates of goodies all piled up and work could then commence in earnest.

The original oak shelving was stunning, if a bit tired, so I couldn't wait to get it back to its former glory, which was simply case of sand, stain and seal. Simple! But not for fifty metres of shelves . . . Split shelves had to be pinned and glued, and Dick went in search of new oak to replace pieces that were missing and to add extra shelving to display some of our beautiful jars, presses and preserving equipment. They looked incredible. I chose the tiles for the concrete floor and decided that a duck-egg blue with brown grout would work well with the deep, rich colour and patina of the oak shelving, and the mix of jars and bottles. Dick managed to source some small brass label holders and, with a selection of little images and a mix of English and French words, we started organising the room.

I loved it as we had a wonderful mix of goodies we had made on one side and truly beautiful vintage bottles and ornamental jars on the other. We even have some shelves that hold provisions from the UK that are not easily found in France, like English mustard and creamed horseradish sauce. Putting everything in straight lines and being organised made me so happy, and being the gushy mum that I am, I also wanted the children to be involved, so we decided to add some fabric jam toppers to some of the jars we had made over the years.

I found some scraps of fabric and, using my pinking shears, cut a selection of circles each 1.5 inches larger than the jar lid they were to cover. I then raided the kids' playroom to find fabric pens and paint. Arthur and Dorothy had a ball drawing onto the toppers and did not want to stop. I like to keep the topper in place with an elastic band, as it makes it easy to tie a nice bow. But I could see the children computing that adding this small piece of material over the lid made the jars look artisan. They were loving turning plain jars into something beautiful! The highlight was seeing Dorothy's face when she found out that some of the circles had been cut out of Dick's old underpants. She thought this was the funniest thing she'd ever seen and decorated those ones with a drawing of Dick in his pants!

The principles of a preserve cupboard require it to be cool and dry. We had a little problem: the heating pipes supplying the radiators in the hallway upstairs, the family kitchen and the boot room all passed along the top shelf of the room. It all made sense five years before and even with hindsight it was the sensible idea. But we needed to ensure they were well insulated (which was a good idea anyway) and to hide them behind a false wall. The walls were all dusty French chalk plaster so it was necessary to seal them as a dusty preserves cupboard would be a monumental pain.

It was interesting watching Steve plaster in such a confined space, especially as he knew we had to protect the old oak shelving, but, as always, he smiled and just cracked on. Soon the walls were finished, the shelves sanded and repaired and the tiles laid and grouted. We put up new oak shelves as well that we hoped would last another 150 years along with the original shelving. We then filled it with some of our treasures and finally got properly organised in there. Our home-made preserves, chutneys and pickles looked very impressive all neatly lined up, although I did find it surprising that Angela had cut up my perfectly serviceable, old checked boxer shorts to make jar toppers. Moving on . . .

One of the new shelves above the door into the utility room became the home for Angela's essential oil still that I had bought her for her birthday. We had found some small but lovely old bottles that would be perfect for essential oils so we decided it was time to christen the still. There was an argument to see if we could make moonshine, but as we'd had to thin out the eucalyptus, we decided to make our own essential oil.

I was really excited about getting the chance to use my still. I had been reading up on what was possible and when we had some freshly cut eucalyptus leaves, I grabbed Dick and we headed off to the commercial kitchen.

We chopped up all the eucalyptus leaves in the Magimix and soon we had a good kilo in the still set on racking above the water that was going to be boiled and generate steam to pass through the leaves and pick up the oils. This steam rises and when it passes down the copper tubing at the top that goes through ice it condenses back into a liquid that is a mixture of essential oil and hydrosol (which is water with a weak solution of the essential oil in it). I knew that I could only expect a teaspoon of oil from this kilo, but I was very excited nonetheless. I had been reading up about its qualities and it was claimed that it could be used as an antioxidant, an astringent, an antiseptic, an anti-inflammatory, a facial toner, an aftershave facial tonic for men, a treatment for acne or blemish-prone skin, a body spray, and in facials and masks in anti-ageing skin care.

The first drip was so exciting I squealed! It was collected in a special glass tube that filled up slowly and allowed the oil to separate from the hydrosol. It held the oil but the hydrosol was transferred to a separate container. I was truly mesmerised and sat watching the drips and the oil forming on the top of the tube. I was careful not to disturb the oil floating on the top and then sucked it up with a small pipette. We ended up with a very respectable 6.5ml of château eucalyptus oil. My mind was racing – we had lavender, rosemary, mint, roses and numerous other lovely plants to go and harvest . . . I was an essential oil maker! And Dick was my essential oil maker's assistant!

It was then that we decided to hand over a section in the preserves room to essential oils. It was something we had preserved, after all. That cupboard tells a million stories as soon as you step into it and now we were preserving our own future. It felt great.

CHAPTER ELEVEN

Exploration

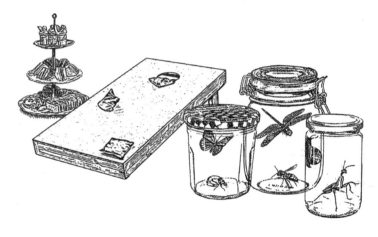

The year of 2021 was most certainly turning out not to be as expected, although in hindsight, there had been so many enforced changes by this point that we should never have been surprised! By the summer, all of our wedding couples had chosen new dates. Even Natasha and Victoria reluctantly accepted that the odds were still against them and made the decision to go for the first weekend we could offer in 2022. That was now only ten months away and would allow us to give them the wedding we had promised we would.

The year had also dealt us a number of heartbroken couples whose lives had changed so much during the past eighteen months that a wedding in France was no longer possible. Babies, dogs, redundancies and, sadly, family deaths had changed the paths of their futures. We remained supportive, as we'd promised, and, to be honest, these conversations really put life into perspective.

For the remaining couples, we started our new journey together and all the dates were rescheduled over a two-year window. It would have been too much for us and the team to squeeze everyone into one year and not fair on the couples either. So, gradually, the planning started up again and, little by little, that magical wedding excitement started to reappear. This was the turning point.

As the summer really stepped into its stride, so did the benefits of our multi-generational family. The garden was abundant in produce and we loved watching Mum getting fresh lettuce from the garden, perfecting her bread and having time in her wonderful new kitchen. She really was living her best life. The kids also loved picking fresh herbs from the garden and we even got into making our own nettle soup!

It's a fact that weeds are always the first plants to thrive every year in the garden. They just seem to burst from the earth as soon as the conditions improve in spring, and we had an abundance of lovely fresh green nettle shoots in the walled garden. I had first heard of nettle soup when I read a rather harrowing book about life in the town where I lived, Antrim, during the famine in the mid-nineteenth century. It was called *My Lady of the Chimney Corner* by Alexander Irvine. Then, the soup was a necessary supplement to a very meagre diet, but nettles are very rich in nutrients, vitamins and minerals, especially iron, which makes them a great option for vegan diets. They have been used as a natural remedy in many cultures for thousands of years to help detoxify the body, regulate hormones, act as an anti-inflammatory, improve circulation and help with allergies. I have cooked many variations over the years and, as we weren't constrained by availability of food or lifestyle decisions, my objective was to show the children that good food is available in the most unusual places.

Arthur came and helped me harvest a huge bowl of the tender tops. Angela had given me a very explicit warning about Arthur getting stung, so I proved the phrase 'grasping the nettle' by picking some with my bare hands. Funnily enough, she wasn't impressed, so my assistant Arthur wore some of my massive welding gauntlets. I know you can make soup from the non-stinging 'dead nettle' family of weeds but to be honest I've never tried it or had a desire to try it, though it would have saved Arthur from looking a tad silly.

. . . .

STINGING NETTLE VELOUTÉ SOUP

Ingredients

50g butter
50g flour
1 onion, diced
500g nettle tops
750g good chicken stock
125ml white wine
250ml cream
Salt and white pepper

Method

Soften the onion gently in the butter, without colouring, in a large pan. When it's soft, stir in the flour and cook for 2–3 minutes. Gradually add the stock and wine, stirring and heating until you have a thick sauce.

*Fold in the nettles and cook for 2–3 minutes, then blend and
return to the pan. When it comes up to temperature it is ready.*

Stir in the cream and season.

*The soup is a wonderful colour and tastes great, which was
confirmed by the empty bowls!*

....

When Arthur and Dorothy broke up from school in early July
we were excited to ramp up our family time. They are both
smart cookies (say the loving parents) and their school reports
were glowing. The six months that the children stayed home the
previous year was now firmly in the past and both had received top
marks for their French language, which we were obviously extra
proud of. Their academic year had been good, although slightly
different, but we noted loud and clear that mask wearing and social
distancing were not going to be missed this summer. And we were
all ecstatic for the seven weeks of holiday we had stretching ahead
of us. Once again, the château was completely ours and we started
making plans for how to make the most of it as a family. Paddling
pools, picnics, bow-and-arrow-making competitions and movie
nights were all on the list.

In the summer of 2021 in France, you still needed a valid
reason to leave the house. Working, school, essential shopping
and caring for loved ones were all on the list and we carried a
government-generated permit around in the car when we were out.
The gendarmes were often doing stop checks. We fully understood
the reasons for this and took it seriously. Then, one morning
early in the summer holidays, all of these restrictions were lifted.
Overnight, we were all allowed to travel within France again, so we
got straight on the internet and booked a week's holiday. It was
Dick's idea to go to Chamonix-Mont-Blanc, which is in France

but sits at the junction of Italy and Switzerland. I had heard of the ski resort but never considered it as somewhere to visit in the summer, but it was genius. The setting was stunning, it was an activity playground for all ages and just an eight-hour drive away. It delivered everything we needed.

The sense of adventure was at its best here. It was unknown France for us and we could not wait to explore. We purchased a lift pass for the week which gave us access to the mountains, including the highest summit in the Alps. Day one, we could not wait and headed up on two cable cars to the Aiguille du Midi, a 3,842-metre mountain with a Perspex box that allows you to take the photo of a lifetime magically flying over the mountains below. What we had not taken into account was how the thin the air is that high up. With the addition of face masks, which were still mandatory, it was actually hard to catch a breath. But from that amazing vantage point you felt like you were looking out at the world and it was literally breathtaking. Sadly, the queue for the Perspex box was too much for us on that occasion but we had started our mountain adventure that would be a holiday of a lifetime filled with many firsts, including Arthur and Dick's first coffee together.

Our hotel was lovely and nestled in the town itself. You could look out of our window to a stunning view of Mont Blanc; how special is that? We smiled so much. Angela loves a spa. I have to be honest, couples' massages are right up there with sticking pins in your eyes for me, so I suggested I head off with the children and give her some quality time. I don't know how the conversation went but soon Angela and Dorothy were heading down to the spa and Arthur and I had the freedom of Chamonix.

I have very fond memories of taking James, my elder son, for his first coffee, standing at a bar by the Rialto Bridge when we were off on our own in Venice. He would have been nine or ten, so I thought Arthur could join his old man for his first coffee somewhere in Chamonix. We didn't have to rush and walked around to find the perfect place. As we walked, we talked about coffee and I asked Arthur what he'd like for his first one. I assumed that a sweet cappuccino would be the easiest for him to take but he said he wanted to join me in an espresso!

By chance, we found a lovely little coffee bar that roasted its own coffee beans and had a few tables outside for guests to enjoy their coffee and watch the world go by. We took our seats, chatted to the lovely waiter and ordered two espressos. They arrived with great ceremony and I noticed additional sugar had been brought with several little coffee biscuits, which I thought was a lovely, and understated, way of making it easier for Arthur.

Arthur added sugar, we toasted and he tasted his first coffee as we looked up at the snow-capped Alps and down to all the people in the streets around us. Arthur made all the right noises and didn't hesitate when I suggested he added another sugar. It was a lovely twenty minutes and I bought him some espresso cups to keep for when he started drinking more coffee so he could remember his first. Since then, he has had several decaffeinated mochas and cappuccinos, but he's not allowed to get into the coffee culture properly until he is a lot older!

When we got back, Arthur and I told Mummy and Dorothy about our adventure and they seemed suitably impressed, though it was hard to say really, as they were both 'jellified' and totally chilled after their massages.

Our summer was very special, filled with adventure, sandcastles and family time, and whilst we knew the children had to return to school, we were going to miss all being together so much.

After another year of being pretty antisocial, and following a comment from both Arthur and Dorothy's teachers that it would

be nice to do something for their classes at the château when the restrictions allowed, we decided to celebrate being able to hug again by holding a huge garden party for all their friends and parents.

As always, we had a conversation about what we wanted to do. The idea of being able to chat and mingle again with so many people was exciting, and I think we both got carried away with the idea of vintage games, treasure hunts, a huge excavation plot, art classes, a make-your-own essential oil workshop and a British high tea with dress-up. So we divided up the tasks and started to get ready for what was probably the biggest event since our wedding.

It was hard to say how many people would be there as sometimes parents would drop off their children and return at the end of a party, and other times whole families have stayed for the duration. I'm sure it's because we don't know what is normal for the French at a party and they are not sure what is normal for us, so we do what we think the other would like . . . To save problems this time, we invited and catered for whole families, but we just didn't know how many would be in each family . . . A minor problem, so we just assumed lots and let the children invite whoever they wanted.

It was always going to be fun and the activities at the children's garden party were very definitely a mix of both Angela and my characters. The games, the art and crafts, the hospitality were all Angela. However, on my side, we had treasure hunts as well as a table full of bug- and creature-catching equipment, specimen jars and reference books to name what had been found. I was left to design and implement the treasure hunt without any adult supervision. The last thing I remember Angela saying was 'I trust you'. . .

First I sourced treasure, which arrived in the form of some exotic foreign coins, little polished shiny stones and crystals. We were to have three very different treasure hunts:

For the first, I had some of the beds in the garden that needed to be dug so I designated them as treasure zones and, using a dibber or a trowel, I seeded them with a good supply of treasure. More than enough to keep everyone interested and the children could do whatever they wished in there – I had cleared the nettles and brambles and they had gloves and trowels, so I wasn't a complete monster. Though I loved the idea of a couple of my vegetable beds being dug over by unsuspecting slave labour.

My next inspiration came from a toy Arthur had been given that was basically a plastic skeleton in some crumbly plaster that he had to bash with a pathetic little plastic hammer about four inches long to release the archaeological find. For this one, we'd provide everyone with proper hammers and cold chisels (and safety glasses – obviously!) and they could excavate their finds from a massive tray full of hardened old lime, plaster and cement. It wasn't going to be easy for them but think of the sense of achievement.

Steve Beachill and I joined a couple of old sheets of plywood together and put 4" × 2" wood on its side around the edges, giving us a very large tray, which we mounted on trestles over one of the beds in the walled garden. We set up the cement mixer and made several loads of an unusual mixture of cement, lime, sand, plaster, grout – basically anything that would harden and was past its best. We then pushed in our treasure and left it to set.

And then the final treasure hunt involved following a map and clues around the grounds and answering questions. There was a panda to find in the bamboo forest, our biggest oak tree, and the challenge of working out where the den of the coypu was. It basically took people around our boundary and into the woods.

In the workshop, Dick cut lots of pieces of wood for different games and built a large vertical rack to play Connect 4. I sorted some beanbags and dealt with the painting and decorating of all

the bits of games. There was a brilliant mix of activities for children and adults alike.

Sorting out the cream teas was like being back at my Vintage Patisserie. Dick and I smiled as we produced the sandwiches and scones that we used to make together for every hen party or event I catered. It was such fun and Arthur and Dorothy loved getting involved too. I'm glad to say we hadn't lost the knack.

The day came around all too soon but we were ready and looking forward to entertaining dozens, possibly hundreds, of guests. It was wonderful when everyone turned up. The children ran into each other's arms and the hugs were so engulfing. It was very special to watch. I started crying happy tears immediately and never really stopped! For too long we had tentatively said hello, as the traditional kissing and shaking of hands we had learnt to accept and really appreciate had been scared out of people, but somehow getting together for a party was like old times.

Watching children connect again, and adults chatting and enjoying a coffee together, was so ordinary but because it had not happened for such a long time it was appreciated in a very different way. Of course, we tried to make this a special occasion but, looking back, the most special and emotional thing was watching everyone interact and spend time together again. It was a pleasure and something we will never forget.

From the moment people arrived it was full throttle. The weather decided to play silly buggers – we had rain on and off during the afternoon but not enough to dampen spirits. We ended up with a wonderful mix of children and adults with lots of families who knew each other competing in the games of seeking treasure.

Not a single French parent batted an eyelid when their children picked up a hammer and chisel, donned safety glasses and bashed their way through our 'rock' in search of jewels. I am so glad I was not responsible for the laundry of those digging our beds. When the youngsters saw the results of digging and had coins and gems in their hands, they were all digging like little moles and filling the riddles to sift for their treasure (as were a couple of the parents!).

There were several competitions within and between families, who were raucously encouraging and jeering each other playing 'cornholing' (throwing beanbags onto a sloping board with a hole in the middle and concentric rings to score points on), Breton palets (metal discs thrown onto a board) and Mölkky (basically cylindrical skittles that you throw a cylindrical piece of wood at). Games of skill with little complexity were the order of the day.

At one time, I looked across and saw Angela had obviously been called over from the 'art and painting' and 'make your own aromatherapy mix' stand, and was the only adult anywhere near the insect table. There was a group of boys trying to share their bugs and spiders with her, and I could see she was in a 'freaking out but being calm' mode. I was laughing so hard, right up to the moment she caught my eye and gave me a look! I obviously then went over to help with the bug sorting and recognition.

The day flew by. We had to organise two sittings in the orangery to allow everyone to get through without being too crushed. We had plenty of food and everyone was chattering and laughing, so the orangery had that wonderful feeling we get when the buzz of a wedding party builds so everyone can be heard.

It was heart-warming seeing families compete against each other playing the vintage games and I had a chuckle or two at some of the dads being very competitive – it was not just Dick! And so the day was a great success. Though if we are being honest I think we could have done anything because it was the bringing together of all the children's friends and their families that was

the recipe for success. Everyone was so happy, even relieved, to be together again. You couldn't help but smile and laugh.

The annual Strawbridge family measuring tradition takes place in the playroom once a year. The children are like 'malherbe', they are shooting up. It's a lovely thing as we all know that Arthur and Daddy will try to cheat, Daddy will measure Dorothy obviously smaller than she is, Mummy will try to keep order and all the time Petale will dash around wagging her tail and loving the excitement.

This year's measurements showed just how much Arthur and Dorothy had grown, and we had the stark realisation that they were no longer our little babies. Angela and I talked that evening about this being the last year she would be taller than Arthur. Our conversations meandered the way they do, and in no time it was obvious that it was time to give the kids' room a makeover. They were too young to move out of our suite as moving to another part of the château is like taking your children and moving them to a house down the road. And they didn't want to move out. But that gave us the problem of using the space we had more wisely. We decided that since the ceilings were so high, we could install two mezzanine levels that would give Arthur and Dorothy more room and a new 'grown-up' space.

Once Dick and I had agreed on our plan we all moved out of our suite into the honeymoon suite whilst the work was done. This was a bigger task than expected. Moving 'next door' should never fool you; it still means moving everything. But I used it as an opportunity to rationalise all of our belongings, often losing myself in a bygone moment finding items from when the children were babies. Baby monitors, favourite baby toys, bottles . . . Once we were moved, I was eager to get started because this change would bring the children's needs up to date and that was important to us.

Dick and I have known for years about a hidden cavity behind the wall where our bedstead is. We discovered it when we were doing the initial restoration of our room. We'd peeked through the hole made for a Rawlplug and when we pushed a rod in it went back two feet. But at that time we had been on a deadline to finish and tidy up before a food lovers' weekend we were hosting, so we had patched the hole and cracked on. However, the unknown has been there, waiting patiently for us to explore, and my imagination has taken me to many places.

When the room was cleared, Dick attached a rubbish chute outside our bedroom window so all the rubbish didn't have to pass through the house, and we could finally see what treasure was hidden behind our wall. Though I think both Dick and I were a little worried about what we might find! As we bashed the wall with a 'lump' hammer I had to acknowledge that my husband has made me lots more technical (apparently, it's called that because it's a bit of a lump! I have no idea really but I smile for him and all is well). As I hit the wall, it was a highly charged moment – in the next ten minutes we would finally know what was inside this cavity. Was it the riches of the Baglionis? Was it hiding something sinister? Why would they put up a stud wall? It just did not make sense. But we were finally revealing its past.

When we had made a hole big enough to put our head in and shine a torch around we discovered that there was absolutely nothing in there. So a wall had been built in front of another wall to make the room smaller for some reason. Still today it makes no sense. It was only at second glance that I realised there was indeed my type of treasure in there. Right there on the wall I found the original wallpaper from our suite. It was an ethereal ivy, grey on grey. Stunning. Not our retirement fund of gold coins but treasure just the same. Of course, we saved this to be a feature in what would become our walk-in wardrobe.

Our suite was relatively simple once we had cleared out all the debris from the wall that didn't appear to do anything. Angela and I discussed how big we wanted our bedroom to be and then everything behind our bedstead became the wardrobe. We put in the stud walls and the necessary electrics for bedside tables and when it was all decorated, we still had a very large room. The wardrobe was spacious, full of hanging space and shelves and drawers for all four of us, and lit with LED panels so it could also be used as a dressing room. Dorothy particularly loves going in there to choose her outfit for the day!

Sorting the children's mezzanine was not so much complicated as time-consuming. There was no messing around as I'd sourced oak. We needed a substantial framework and newel posts, as well as handrails and balusters. The room was divided into two with the stairs going up to the mezzanine in the middle. Arthur and Dorothy had their own windows so they had lovely areas to make their own. In the end, the structure was a pleasure to make as oak is so beautiful and robust. All the screws were countersunk and when we had sanded the corners off all the pieces of wood it was so lovely that we left it au naturel without any varnish.

Updating a room is rather satisfying and feels highly productive. After the stunning oak mezzanine was in place, the changes to Arthur and Dorothy's room felt more cosmetic. I normally only get in there right at the end because of the amount of work that goes into a full renovation, but this gave me time to work out what the children needed – desks, more storage, etc. – and also allowed me to get up into the attic and bring their past into the future.

Like the Baglionis before us, we have kept lots of the children's clothes, drawings and old toys as memories. When Arthur and Dorothy grow out of their clothes, they let me know if they want them to go 'to their children' or to charity. We have bags and bags

of garments and whilst their new rooms were the epitome of who they were now (pandas and Pokémon), I'm soppy and wanted to make something nice for them to have always. The idea came when I was looking through sacks of their old clothes. Old babygrows that were handed down by our dear friends Sarah and Leroy to Arthur and also worn by Dorothy. A little sailor's outfit gifted to Arthur and then also worn by Dorothy. A gorgeous hand-sewn bib that said '*Bon Appétit*' given to Dorothy by Isobel and Jacques Baglioni, the original owners of the château. Plus some of the children's much loved, worn and stained items, such as an H&M T-shirt with a lion on it and an AC/DC T-shirt. Every article took me back to a different special moment and in the stillness of the dark and dusty attic I got lost in these memories. And that's when I had the idea to create a memory blanket for Dorothy and a memory beanbag for Arthur.

Arthur and Dorothy took part in choosing their décor for their room; after all, this was their space and we wanted them to cherish it. Dorothy's space was very pink and full of pandas and everything girly you could imagine. Whilst Arthur's was all blacks, greys and blues, with lots of Lego and Pokémon. Very Arthur! There was a clear divide between the two and they both loved their new spaces. I'm delighted to report the memory blanket and beanbag were also a big hit.

Our room was quite straightforward. Apart from a new table that we added for breakfast, everything remained the same and we did not even feel the loss of the extra space we used for the walk-in wardrobe. On the new wall we added a bamboo mural, which gave it a lovely fresh feel without doing too much. But for me, the game changer was the walk-in wardrobe – we had drawers and hanging space, and it made the world of difference to our busy lives.

As the sun started to set, our first night in our new suite was very special. Bedtime always brings us together. Even on our craziest of days, we keep our routine and bedtime is sacrosanct. So once again, we all lay together and talked about our day. Dick will often sing everyone (including himself) to sleep, and as I listened to his soothing echoes of 'The Band Played Waltzing Matilda', I looked over at our not-so-little babies and knew that we were coming into a new phase for the Strawbridge Suite.

The very top of the château is a huge room that stretches from the front to the back and is the central third of the building. As it's the very top of the building, the sloping roof sections and oak beams mean it is not an open room but a very interesting room. It was full of broken terracotta pots and slates and it was very grubby. I'd been up there quite a lot when we installed our plumbing system as it was the home for our header tank and I had kept an eye on the condition of the slates up there. Access was through a hatch from the level below and it was full of cobwebs so Angela had never been up there.

I had always seen this as the final resting place for items to be stored up in the attic. With the roof being done, it was an obvious place to stack boxes and items to be kept. Arthur and Dorothy both have things they are keeping for their children so this was the perfect place where it couldn't be disturbed. I was so naive. For some reason Angela looked through the hatch and I immediately knew it would never be a simple place to store things . . . the space was just too tempting. It wasn't long before Angela was creating a celestial-inspired 'sky bar'.

I admit it does feel odd that there was a floor in the château that I had never seen. Not just any floor but the biggest room with the most interesting architecture. But Dick had done a great job in underselling it for the past seven years. The picture he had painted was of a tiny space that was basically unusable because of the beams. Somehow I interpreted this as meaning you couldn't stand up in there and so, as the entrance was a tiny hole with a rickety ladder, I had no desire or rush to see the space. But then Rob and Steve were working on this section of the roof and told me about this incredible space. I was confused. This was definitely the moment to explore.

As I climbed the ladder, Dick kept pinching my bottom, which made my legs turn to jelly. But as I reached the top, the view took my breath away. Wow! Yes, there were a couple of beams that you had to bend down to get under but in the bigger scheme of things this was nothing. It's all about timing and now the slate had been removed the view was outstanding. I felt like I was on top of the world. You could see for miles! I knew right then that this needed to be a sky bar and after that I could think of nothing else.

The first setback was when Dick said no to an outside roof balcony but I always think it's good to set your expectations high and then negotiate back from there. We agreed on Velux windows, which was fine but no cigar. And then my trusty mate Roofer Steve said, 'Why not have Velux balcony windows?' Dick gave Steve a good old-fashioned look and said 'cheers mate!', but we all knew it was the right thing to do!

With the decision made that this room was to be used as more than attic space, it needed to have better access, so we put in a staircase that went up there from just outside Angela's *trésorie*. This meant we had a grand total of 112 steps from the *sous-sol* to the top of our château, so when we left anything in the workshop in the basement it was a 224-stair round trip. That was a great incentive to plan properly.

When the roof was done, we could insulate this section, which

osy cheeks and
osty days.

The coach house master suite.

New workshop

Keeping busy in 2020.

The garden, 2021.

Heron island.

The garden party, 2021.

L'observatoire du Chateau.

Papi Steve creating our second key.

The year of the roof, 2021.

Our roof and render heroes.

Colmar, 2021.

involved rock wool between the rafters and silver multilayer composite insulation across the rafters to give the desired high performance. We did have one lucky break because Angela came up to see how we were getting on and loved the shiny finish. That meant we didn't need to get lots of plasterboard all the way up the 112 stairs.

The shiny insulation was both a revelation and a 'get out of jail free card' for Dick and Steve, who were already worried about getting the plasterboard up the stairs. It was so different and had a sky galaxy vibe that I knew I could do something with. My first job was to spruce it up so that it looked like we did it on purpose and not simply left it unfinished, but it gave a great space vibe. After lots of playing and being rightly told by Dick that we could not punch too many holes in it, I decided to overlay a sheer sparkly linen on the bottom half. This would break up the large shiny silver blocks and bring a warmth that I felt the space needed. However, it also made me realise just how big the space is because the linen needed to be broken up further.

After deciding to use a midnight-blue paint on the chipboard floor, I had an idea to cover some 'buttons' in a matching midnight colour fabric and stick them onto the gold linen. Things always evolve and so when I found a bag of polystyrene balls that ranged in size from 1cm to 5cm, I decided to cut them in half and cover them in blue fabric. It was a happy accident but they looked like little planets and when stuck on the fabric in random places it created just the magic I was after!

The sky bar was really starting to shine. To bring a party feel, the children and I decided that we should create a disco ball solar system. It was actually a really simple process once we worked out how to do it: Fimo clay rolled out to 0.5mm cut into the desired shape by placing a paper cut-out guide on top of it. We then

covered them with gilding sheets, which stuck straight onto the clay and gave the disco ball effect.

This amazing space had gone from an unknown and unloved room into a place so different from anywhere else in the château. We named it *l'observatoire du château* and I ordered a look-a-like pink neon sign, which looked like a pink neon sign but wasn't neon, to celebrate the opening. The pink haze that reflected off the silver insulation and the disco balls was a happy accident, but it felt like you were heading up to the gods to party the night away. After the addition of two bars (for symmetrical reasons, of course) and a telescope, we were ready to have our first guests.

Having a room with three bars in it at the top of the house is an incentive to go up there.

Just to be clear, there are two bars. What Dick classifies as the third bar is actually a wooden box we had to build over the header tank. I just made it tall enough to be useful!

The first evening we spent as a family up there, Jenny and Steve joined us and both were a tad out of breath when they got to the top! It was a great evening with the children loving using the telescope with Steve to see the moon in detail and also sitting, drawing and making things at their desks, which we put at the other end of the attic we can have a guilt-free drink while the children play. Jenny and I had a little party to ourselves and I have to say I think the cocktails had medicinal properties, as neither of us noticed the number of stairs going down!

It really was an evening to remember and we now had a special space that all the generations would enjoy together.

Every year, we have a party with our staff as a thank you for being wonderful. In November, we were deciding what we should do when Angela solved our problem.

I was at home when I got a call from a rather distraught Angela. She was driving back to the château with the children when a boar had run out in front of her and she wanted to know if I could come immediately. When I discovered that everyone was OK I said 'Hold tight' and jumped in our little electric car with my survival rucksack and found her 400 metres down the road. There is very little traffic on our road and I pulled up beside them and found everything OK. Angela wasn't particularly shaken up but hadn't wanted to get out and investigate what had happened. Arthur was very excited to see the boar and Dorothy was very happy staying in the car, thank you very much. I was just grateful they had been in the Land Rover and not the little BMWi3, as the offside wing had taken a good old dunt. On investigating, I found lying at the side of the road a very reasonable-sized boar. It was a sow and it was very dead.

I checked the vehicle was still safe to drive and manoeuvred it so the tailgate was just in front of the boar. There was no way I could lift it in myself but somehow Angela, Arthur and I got it up and into the boot. It was a good 100kg and floppy so it was no easy task. We drove the couple of minutes home and I reversed up to my workshop. Angela and Dorothy had had enough excitement but Arthur was adamant he was helping me. I rigged a pulley system up to a beam and hauled our feast, forelegs first, up into the air.

Fortunately, I have gralloched, skinned and butchered a fair number of beasts, so it wasn't too long before we had several prime cuts of wild boar. The animal had been killed very quickly and there was a fair amount of damaged and therefore wasted meat, but there was still an awful lot of it. Hence our decision that, this year, our staff would dine on the finest game. We had more than enough boar but Jean Betram, who had helped us with supplies throughout the year, had also given us several haunches of venison, so we'd be dining like royalty. We prepared a wonderfully rich wild boar and forest mushroom ragout and slow-cooked the venison in white wine and aromatic vegetables.

Having lived in London for most of my driving life, I've not had much experience with boar running into the road. It happened very fast and I did not have time to swerve or stop. The damage on the car was significant but as the children told the story again and again little bits changed, and the boar got bigger and bigger. I'm sure at one point I heard Dorothy tell Roofer Steve that we could have died if we had been in the small electric car.

So it was decided: this would create the centre point of our team's feast. And then my dad revealed his surprise.

Since the day we arrived, my dad, who was a jewellery maker his entire life, had promised to make a second key to our master oak double door with ornamental grilles. The door itself was getting some TLC so now was the perfect time. It was quite emotional for me seeing Dad's workshop for the first time as I spent many years around his trade and travelling up to Hatton Gardens in London. It was amazing seeing Dad's set-up: he had his old tools out and his bench, which he has had since he was sixteen years old. He also had a silver miniature of his set-up that my mum got made for him.

I didn't see every stage of the key-making process but Dad called me down for the part he knew would be the magic – when he poured the molten silver into the mould he had cast. It set within seconds and then, when he took the mould off, there it was, a perfect key! In that moment, my dad was the clever magician my brother and I grew up with all over again, the man who could make anything with gold (or silver). It was a wonderful feeling

to remember. Just when I thought it couldn't get any better, as he handed it over that evening I saw that he had hand-carved an 'AD' at the top of the key – for Angel and Dick, and Arthur and Dorothy – this was something else for them to inherit. It was an evening to remember for many reasons!

Christmas was full of our growing traditions – choosing a tree and decorating it together as a family, letters to *Père Noël* going up the chimney, foraging for foliage and hunting for oysters were events we looked forward to. But as a family, we are always looking to experience new things and see what new traditions we should add. When we think of Christmas markets, they have always had a Germanic feel to them, and so we decided that we'd celebrate this most wonderful time of year by heading 500 miles east to the very Germanic Alsace region of France and the mediaeval town of Colmar, which is famed for its Christmas market, to enjoy local delicacies.

Our trip to Chamonix has certainly given us a taste for France and when Dick told me about Colmar we simply had to go. If there is anything the last couple of years should have taught us, it is to live life to its fullest!

It is amazing how a weekend sampling something very different can inspire you. There were two things I really wanted to get to know. Firstly the wines, which are very different to those of the Loire region – like one our family all love, the Gewürztraminer. It's aromatic and elegant, with concentrated flavours, a rich, oily texture and a lovely long finish. The nose is candied fruit, orange peel and spice. I'd talked about the German wines made after the frosts and in Alsace the wine made from overripe grapes are the *vendanges tardives*, characterised by their concentration. They are powerful and opulent, and the books say their fruity aromas 'unfold with elegance'. Basically, they are wonderful to drink by themselves as a treat, a bit like a Hungarian Tokaji wine. And secondly, and equally important, I wanted to sample the fondue where the meat and vegetables are cooked in a bouillon rather than oil. I'd had it before in Switzerland and knew it was a speciality in Alsace.

For a Christmas destination in France, Colmar was spectacular. It delivered inspiration everywhere you looked. Every shop window made you stop in your tracks and the use of foliage blew my mind. Even the excessive use of brightly coloured Christmas lights that normally I'd not like because they were too OTT won me over. As we walked through the streets, looking at the brightly coloured house decorations on stunning canals, we were not only engulfed in the spirit of Christmas but the spirit of Colmar.

When we arrived back at the château we were bursting to tell everyone of our adventures. This year, Mum and Dad had decided to visit family and friends as they had some overdue hugs and memories to make, so we took this as the perfect opportunity to share our findings from our trip.

I started off with our annual tradition of taking my mum and Dorothy on our Christmas forage. It's such a special walk for us and every year, Mum and I always talk about Dorothy and how grown up she is now! But, unbeknownst to Mum, Dorothy and I were going to make her a Christmas table wreath inspired by Alsace. Every place we went to in Alsace had wreaths either hanging or on the table and the florists were abundant with them. Though some were very expensive. Dorothy must have picked this up from us because she was the first to say 'we can make one'. And that is exactly what we did. Whilst Dorothy made Grandma one, with special homemade linen bows, I made three for our Christmas table, placing one on a silver cake stand for height, all

with candles in a glass jar. Although I was on strict instructions that we needed lots of space for the very Alsace dinner.

Dick made our Christmas 'bouillon' fondue, which was a very tasty stock and much lighter than a cheese fondue, although we love both! We set up two stations on the table so we could all reach. It was a feast. We had two plates of raw pigs-in-blankets, beef, turkey and pork, another station of raw carrots, celery, onions and Brussels sprouts (it was Christmas dinner after all), bread, buttery potatoes and a homemade white sauce. The wines that accompanied it were of course all from the Alsace and, as a huge fan of Gewürztraminer, my dad was very happy! We all sat down, eager to tell Mum and Dad about our travels and the magic of Colmar.

Fondues are a very social and interactive way of eating. You can't rush them and every mouthful feels like a job well done in managing to cook it. The whole family was loving it; we were all together and this was our Christmas meal. It did not matter what day it was! There was lots of laughing and many jokes about dropping food in the stock. As we ploughed our way through the yumminess, the stock got better and tastier, and, at the end, which was probably an hour or so later, Dick got six bowls and shared the remaining stock between us to drink like soup. To finish, Dick and Arthur had made a berawecka, a wonderfully rich and sweet fruit cake from the Alsace, which we ate with the 'Nectar of Christmas', a sweet wine made from the sweetest of dried grapes. It was a great night and the perfect send-off for Mum and Dad.

After the roller-coaster year we'd had, it was nice to slow down. Christmas was not far away but first we had another very important job: to write to *Père Noël*. Every year, we get together for Arthur and Dorothy to write their letters and then we send them up the chimney. It's always a magical evening and this year Arthur was explaining to Dorothy how the letter forms again from the smoke when it gets to the North Pole (a detail I had not given much attention to in the past!). Arthur asked for Pokémon cards, a first-edition Charizard card, something with Misty on (also Pokémon) and a surprise. Dorothy's list included a skateboard, fidget toys and something for Petale. The thought that Dorothy used one of her wishes on a gift for Petale made my heart melt. I looked over at Petale chilling by the fire and struggled to remember what these family moments were like before she arrived.

Dick always orchestrates the final part. I sat and watched Arthur and Dorothy completely mesmerised by the flames in the fire. There was complete silence and, in a puff of smoke, the children's wishes started their magical Christmas journey.

PART THREE

CHAPTER TWELVE

The Year of the Celebration

Christmas and New Year had been a special and intimate affair. Though it was just the four of us, nine months earlier, Dick had ordered a turkey from a farmer at the end of our road. We'd discovered the hard way that it was not possible to buy a big turkey in a supermarket in France. They tended to be less than 10lbs. So the one on order was a 'statement turkey', one you would expect to see for a huge family gathering, but at the time of ordering we had no idea who would be joining us. We laughed and chatted during Christmas dinner, discussing every dish imaginable we could make with the leftovers from our 20lb turkey during the coming week.

Having had a wonderful Christmas and New Year, we were looking forward to a year full of promise. We were opening up for business as weddings could happen again without the restrictive regulations. So come May, we'd have to be ready! As always, Angela and I discussed whether or not to continue making television at the château.

Every year we have this chat. We can only make the decision based on feelings and our environment at the time, and the last two years had, as I'm sure they did for many of us, given us the time to look at our lives differently and work out how we want to live. When we moved to the château, the irony was that we wanted those two-hour lunch breaks you hear about, we wanted to be able to take off the month of August to holiday with our family, but the reality was that we had bought a crumbling château that needed energy, love and cash that we had to earn.

The children were growing up and starting to understand that they were on television. The beauty of the show for us had always been the innocence of the children and we wanted to protect that. Arthur's ninth birthday was approaching and Dorothy would soon be eight, so they were nearing the time when they would move on to the next phase of childhood and would undoubtedly lose the innocence with which they tackled the world. So Angela and I concluded that, for now, it felt right for 'our' home to be just 'ours'. We made the big decision to make 2022 the final year of *Escape to the Château* and told the channel and our television production partners that series nine was to be our finale.

This year would be the end of that era; however, change is important and should be embraced, and we were excited to see what our new tomorrow looked like.

We'd been working hard for a couple of years without guests and somehow everything in the château seemed to have moved and moved again and again. With the dusty work on the roof and render, which was still in progress, we felt the need for a very deep clean. We had bought a collection of rubber mats to protect the floor and carpet of our wonderful staircase and entrance hall. This trail of mats had become a feature but it was nearly time to remove them.

Without guests, over the previous two years the château had become more of a family home than ever. At the bottom of our double revolution staircase, Arthur had created a box fort using huge flower boxes from a project that I had done with Next. It was massive and even had a sofa in it, along with many of his special toys and memories. The stunning mahogany and oak floors had not had their annual sand and varnish for years and, to make matters worse (or better, depending on who you asked), the entrance hall had become a skate park for Dorothy after Father Christmas had gifted her a skateboard.

The guest rooms were perfectly set and had been for years, but with no guests staying, including family or friends, they had just stayed as they were since our last event. The beds were made with crisp linen and cushions arranged with millimetre precision, but they were dusty. And with years of not even having the showers turned on, we thought they didn't just need a good deep clean, they needed a test run.

For two years the only guests we had had were family or friends, so we knew it was essential that we checked out all the guest suites to make sure no one would have an unpleasant surprise. We had not stayed in all the rooms but like every good tester, we decided that all aspects of the four suites needed to be checked. It's true we could have written a checklist and played with every item in the rooms, but Angela and I decided it would be lovely to spend a night in each room. Grandma and Papi were to keep the children and we'd do our research. There was no way we could leave the children in our suite and sleep in a different part of the château, as some of the rooms are quite far apart, so we would not have been able to hear them.

I felt quite excited about trial-running the rooms; essentially, it was like having four date nights whilst also being productive! I'm pretty sure Dick thought we were just having date nights because the look on his face when I unpacked my notebook was priceless.

We'd stayed in the honeymoon suite when our suite was being worked on, so we knew it was lovely and comfy and well laid out. So we went from plug to plug and appliance to appliance and tested them. One evening, I had a bath in there and Dick had a shower. We flushed the loos and used the sinks; we closed the curtains and checked the fridges for soft drinks and bubbly. It was interesting that despite it being in wonderful condition, we still had a list to make it a little bit better.

When we ventured upstairs for a night in the beautiful potagerie suite we had a slightly longer list as some of the lamp switches needed to be moved, we couldn't find any plug adaptors and, shock horror, there was no port decanter in the tower. The bathroom was so stunning but the huge tulip-shaped shower head seemed to drip after Dick's shower. We thought there was a problem but after a quick 'decalcification' it emptied much faster after it had been turned off. I loved my soak in the very deep and comfy copper bath. Dick kept talking about thermal coefficients and how quickly it would lose heat. I'd heard before that he thought a copper bath was a silly idea, but I have to say I thought it was lovely as I kept a little trickle of hot water topping it up as I lay back and chilled with a cold glass of bubbly *crémant*. It was one

of the few baths I've had where you are completely submerged to the point you float – I couldn't see what the problem was.

Our 'to do' list was a good size and the suite I'm glad we tested was the boudoir. It was so cosy but when I went into the shower the hand shower hook came off the wall. No great problem, I switched over to the chrome overhead shower. Bloody hell it hurt! Each of the holes was so fine it produced a thin jet of water that I'm sure could have been the inspiration for water jet cutters, which can cut through most things except for maybe diamonds and tempered glass. When I switched back to the hand shower, it was the same. In both cases it was time for a decalcification.

We also discovered that the pump for the booster tank, which was upstairs above the suite, was seriously noisy. We had a Challis booster which I loved, and it had a great upgraded pump on it that was very efficient; however, the vibrations came through the floor/ceiling. We greatly reduced the sound by placing the pump on an isolated panel that dampened the vibrations to the point it was barely noticeable, and all with a couple of layers of foam kneeler from the garden and some plywood.

It was a brilliant exercise. We had never had the time to do this when the rooms were initially finished because of our tight deadlines, but it was the perfect way to identify everything that was needed, from the plumbing issues that had arisen from years of non-use to the extra rugs or side counters that would make the rooms better. It really was a fascinating process. I remember sitting in a bubble bath at the end of the bed in the botanical suite with a glass of bubbly whilst Dick was writing up our notes. 'Some bloody date,' he said when he got to the fourth page. We both giggled. The exercise had created lots of work: floors that needed to be repainted, windows that needed love, items to be

replaced, baths to be re-enamelled. Little things that we would have got done gradually, but all of a sudden everything needed to be perfect, and we found ourselves the busiest we had ever been.

True to form, we started several projects in parallel. As well as attic clearing, roof and render work continuing, and repairs and renewals, we needed a home in the château for all the equipment required for weddings. That would allow us to have a destination for all the props, crockery, cutlery, glassware, linens, vases, dried flowers and flower arranging equipment . . . the list was endless. Before the first wedding, and any guests arriving, there was a lot for us to do to transform the room that was originally the cider and vinegar store and then my workshop into a dedicated wedding workshop and store room: Angela's *atelier du mariage*.

I cannot express the relief we felt to finally have firm dates in our diary that we were working to rather than just placeholders. Natasha and Victoria had moved their wedding date more than any of the other couples because they just could not wait for their big day. That first conversation we had together when the world had finally turned a corner was a real moment. We chatted about how their celebration would have a heightened sense of importance, how we would never take for granted the chance to be with friends and family again, and what a bloody journey this has been for everyone. This was big and exciting, and another reminder that we have the best job in the world.

I was a bit panicked, however, about how disorganised the château was. The outside area was full of weeds and everything was a mess. Dick always says things get worse before they get better, but boy did they get bad, with everything moving out of the attic at the same time that everything moved out of my *atelier du marriage* so the necessary work could be done in there. It was basically chaos.

With a briefing on what utilities Angela wanted in her workshop, builder mate Steve and I set to work. We had to dig out some of the rammed earth floor, damp-proof it and then lay a concrete floor. Once we knew where the lighting was going, cables were laid, the ceiling was boarded and skimmed, and all the walls sealed to stop the mortar from being dusty. Angela wanted to set herself up so that arranging the wedding flowers was easy as everything was to hand. That meant we needed a sink and some plumbing. As usual, our first port of call was the outbuildings and barns where we stored all the items we had taken out of the château and had not yet reused.

When we had first moved into the château there was a large, shallow sink in the service kitchen that we had replaced. I knew exactly where it was so we went to see if it would work for Angela. It was exactly as we remembered it and Angela declared it was perfect. As we continued to look around for shelves or storage, Angela started to get very excited about a huge trellis that has been a divider in one of the outbuildings. It stood about 3 metres tall and 1.5 metres wide so it was substantial, and apparently perfect to hang from the ceiling as a rack for dried flowers. Next thing I knew, Angela was rolling out a barrel that we had initially found in the room that we were now making over and telling me that she'd like the end cut off as a pinboard for the 'hero shots' of wedding flowers here at the château. Barrels tend to disintegrate if you saw them but that was just a minor problem . . .

Taps were proving slightly more of an issue as they needed to be surface mounted not basin/sink mounted if they were to go with our sink. I thought we would need to go and buy one (negotiations had concluded that we only needed a cold tap), but then Angela suddenly remembered that someone had once given us the most over-the-top, ornate bathroom tap set. We went back to the château and found them very quickly. I was surprised at the speed with which they were located as most things stay hidden for a long time at the château, but apparently they were in the place for ornamental, over-the-top taps (on a shelf beside the paints?). The spouts were large and were rearing, scaly, silver fish with water coming out of their mouths and scallop shell soap dishes. Again, Angela said they were perfect, so we could now crack on – if we could somehow find a way to plumb them in . . .

With all the chaos around us, I knew that once we had situated and organised everything in the new wedding room, we would be prepared for years to come. This room was the final and missing element in making our home completely and perfectly equipped for future events. I knew I needed a workbench in the centre of

the workshop that I could walk all the way around. When Dick had asked me about lighting we had agreed on the big flat LED panels that were great to work by. I loved the ones in my *trésoire* and knew that they would light up where I needed to work with no shadows.

When I saw the room with its new ceiling and lovely tiled floor, I started to get properly excited. I was also over the moon with the large trellis I'd found in the barns. But when Dick called me in to show me where he'd positioned it I was a little surprised to see it up in the air on an odd-shaped frame with wheels on it. I now know that it is a thing called a plasterboard lifter, which you can use for manoeuvring plasterboards into place before you screw them to the ceiling. It was genius and allowed us to get the trellis in exactly the right position and height before it was attached to the ceiling. Once we knew where the trellis was to be I could make a decision on the size of my central workbench. To make a robust work surface the structure was to be of strong wood with storage underneath and the top was to be tiled. To make it look tidy, the size was to be a whole number of tiles wide and a whole number of tiles long.

We had enough floor tiles left over and I loved the duck-egg blue colour, but for my work surfaces I wanted something that stood out a bit. I thought about using a variety of the floral napkins I had collected over the years, so then I just had to find a way of getting them on the tiles. Time to experiment . . . Most entrepreneurs know that every failed experiment is a step closer to success and I tried several ways of getting the napkins to bond with the tiles, but with the napkins being so thin, they tore every time I tried to smooth them out. But eventually I found a method that worked: I used PVA glue on the tiles initially and let it dry overnight, then I ironed on the paper napkin using some parchment paper over the top to ensure it didn't stick. As the heat from the iron melted the PVA glue, the napkin stuck picture-perfect onto the tile. Easy and, the best bit, it looked fantastic!

The *atelier du mariage* really came together quickly once all the utilities were in place. My suspended trellis, which would have originally been used in the Baglioni's garden decades or maybe even centuries earlier, was the *pièce de résistance*. I used this to hang a variety of dried flowers, which turned it into a spectacular floral chandelier. The rustic beauty and elegance of this looking down on the floral doily workbench was just perfect. Over on the walls, Dick's original work benches had been cut up and used as shelves, decorated with the remains of wallpaper with silhouettes of couples on them.

As I placed tools, pots and flowers onto the shelves it sent shivers up my spine. This room was always destined to be our wedding room. Nothing was wasted and everything had meaning, Dick had even cut the top off one of the original cider barrels we had found in this exact room, and this was now full of pictures of our previous weddings, buttonholes that our couples had left behind and future ideas that had been sent to me by the brides to come. The room was beautiful, organised and functional. We were well and truly ready for our first wedding of the season.

When you are out and about, the first major blooms of the year always seem to be the magnolias. There are a couple of magnificent trees on the route to the children's school and when they burst into colour you can't miss them. That was part of the reason that I'd bought Angela two bushes for her fortieth birthday. We had planted them on the island near the gateway. That was a couple of years earlier. They looked great but were not the biggest bushes I'd ever seen. I did some research and found that they liked an erica-ceous, slightly acidic soil, so I got some to top-dress the plants. When you research you tend to end up following rabbit holes like

Alice in her Wonderland ... Somehow, I was looking at recipes for magnolia flowers that, when lightly pickled, could be used as a substitute for pickled ginger when you made sushi – who knew? Well, obviously we needed to try this. Angela became our chief magnolia flower pickler.

Our family now all love sushi and in France it's really quite expensive, even in supermarkets, where the freshness/quality is not as good as it should be, so we decided it was best to make our own. It's interesting that there must be an age when children suddenly realise sushi is good. For ages, Dorothy had not been keen, even when Angela, Arthur and I would be enjoying it. She loved rice and fish and everything in a sushi roll, but the idea of eating it together or raw must have caused her an issue. Then one day, sushi dipped in soy sauce was a winner, then sashimi was amazing and before we knew it, we had a sushi monster.

I loved talking to the children when we all assembled in the family kitchen. In Japan, an apprentice may have to work hard doing dishes, cleaning and running around for three years before he or she is even allowed to touch the sushi rice. It's called '*minarau*', learning while watching, and it could be ten years before the apprentice becomes an '*itamae*', a fully trained sushi chef. Somehow, I knew my family would want results in a much shorter timescale, so we followed some of the principles without being too pedantic.

. . . .

SUSHI RICE

Ingredients

500g sushi rice
625ml cold water (it's a good rule of the thumb that the ratio

of uncooked rice to water should be 1:1.25)
20ml sushi vinegar (combine 200ml rice vinegar, 120ml
granulated sugar and ½ tsp salt in a non-aluminium
saucepan, heat until the sugar dissolves then set aside to cool)

Method

Place the rice in a bowl. Pour in some water and swill the bowl to remove any impurities, then drain the water. Pour in more water and wash the rice by stirring with your palm, then drain the water again. Repeat 3–5 times until the water remains clear. When draining for the final time, use a sieve and let the rice drain for 30 minutes.

Place the rice and 625ml of water in a saucepan with a tight-fitting lit. Bring to the boil over a medium heat. When the boiling point is reached, reduce the heat and simmer for 10 minutes.

Remove from the heat and leave for a further 10 minutes with the lid on.

Use a spatula to remove the rice from the pan and spread it into a wide, shallow container, taking care not to crush the grains. If you happen to have a traditional Japanese cypress-wood rice tub known as a handai that's nice.

Now add the sushi vinegar, pouring it as evenly as possible over the rice.

Using a spatula, make gentle cutting and folding movements to mix the vinegar thoroughly into the rice – again, take care not to crush the grains by being too rough or mashing or stirring.

As you cut and fold the vinegar through the rice, you should fan the rice with a paper fan to ensure it cools down quickly. It should take about 10 minutes for the rice to cool down and by then it should be evenly coated with vinegar.

After all that, you should be left with rice that has a beautiful lustre and does not stick together in lumps or clumps. It should ideally be used within an hour of preparation and should never be refrigerated. Therein lies the problem with supermarket sushi. This rice is so much nicer than rice that has been allowed to age in the fridge.

. . . .

We had a collection of sushi mats in our pantry for making rolls and we also had squares of dried nori seaweed. I cut tuna and salmon into sushi-sized slices/strips as professionally as I could with my Kai Shun right-handed sashimi knife that I got when I was doing *Masterchef*. I also cut strips of peeled cucumber, peppers and avocado, and very soon we all got productive.

It was interesting that the children wanted to launch into rolls, but the most common type of sushi, and generally the most expensive, is supposedly the *nigirizushi*. This is sushi where a topping, generally raw or cooked fish or shellfish, is placed on a finger of sushi rice smeared with a little wasabi paste. I love the fact that wasabi contains allyl isothiocyanate, which prevents the germination of bacteria, helping to prolong the freshness of fish. Which is probably why there is a smear on the rice. As if that isn't enough, the strong taste and smell of wasabi also stimulates the appetite, aids the digestion of food and it is an effective deodoriser, neutralising raw fish odours and replacing them with a fresh smell.

All very cunning, but in our house, we don't add the wasabi at this stage as Dorothy doesn't enjoy the heat. However, we always have a small bowl with soy sauce and a little blob of wasabi in it to dip into. I had to be strong and insist there was no tasting on the way so we had a wonderful display of sushi and sashimi before anyone was allowed to try our creation. We cut our rolls to make them beautiful and arranged them. It's interesting that a board covered in sushi doesn't seem to be that much for four people; however, we sat down ravenous and forty-five minutes later, we were tired but satiated.

We opened a tiny, ornamental jar of our pickled magnolia flowers to accompany our feast. I have to say, I love the fact that the children insist on using chopsticks to eat sushi. The ceremony is very serious and after a reminder of how to hold the sticks, they were off, with Arthur reminding us all that it's bad manners for your chopsticks to be left on the table. Obviously, etiquette is very important! The rice was wonderful and every dish was made with so much care it was impossible not to love our meal. I waited until I had eaten my first piece of sushi before trying our homemade condiment. It is impossible to accurately describe the taste, but it was slightly floral, a little bit bitter and absolutely perfect as a palate cleanser. It wasn't 'hot' in a gingery way and Dorothy, who was the hardest person to please, wasn't quite complimentary but said that she could eat it if she had to as it wasn't terrible!

You simply have to spend time in your garden as spring arrives or you will always be playing catch-up. The old saying 'March comes in like a lion and out like a lamb' is particularly fitting in our part of France. The moat can be frozen at the beginning of March and you can be working in a T-shirt as Easter approaches. The biggest challenge is to determine when the last frost will be so you can get your planting done as early as possible. Somehow, the weeds all know as they always seem to steal the march on our cultivated plants. However, our greenhouse is a game changer and I put water and electricity to it the previous autumn so now we had a frost-free environment to get things growing early. There was one task that we simply had to get right this year. Our sunflowers had to be lovely and abundant in time for Sarah and Richard's wedding later in the year.

When they had come for their tasting in 2019, I had been given a couple of bags of sunflower seeds that Sarah had from her grandfather, who was no longer with them. Sarah and her grandfather had shared quality time together in the garden and the sunflowers were really important to her, so I undertook to plant them so they would be available for their wedding in 2020, which I did. However, 2020 was the '*annus horribilis*'. We had a wonderful display of sunflowers, so we kept the second generation and planted them in 2021. Again, no weddings, so we had harvested the seeds and we just knew 2022 was the year! The third generation of Sarah's grandfather's sunflowers had to be stunning – no pressure.

Arthur and Dorothy had become old hands when it came to planting sunflowers and sweetcorn, both of which are very similar to plant. I had the task of preparing the ground, then my gorgeous children had to mark the lines, 'dib' holes and plant the seeds. I was always assured there was only one seed per hole but somehow, when they grew, there were quite a number of twins!

* * *

Angela was like a lady possessed as our first wedding of the season approached. It was all hands on deck to get the château into ship-shape condition for Natasha and Victoria's big day. In many ways, we were starting from scratch again, as the cleaning started at the very top of the château and went all the way down to the *sous-sol*. But it wasn't just inside that had to be sorted. There was an inordinate amount of weeding and tidying to do on our twelve acres of land. Everything had to be touched at least once in the build-up.

We have a small area set aside at the end of our driveway so people can pull off the main road, park up and take a look at the château. From the main road, grass was cut, branches trimmed back, fences painted, potholes filled and new gravel laid. The geese compound was strimmed to make it prettier (but, to be fair, I do that regularly anyway so it's nicer for the geese) but this time Roofer Steve added a wooden fence, as apparently Angela said the electric fence that never quite stood straight was offensive! Papi was on the ride-on a lawnmower ensuring the verges and the paths to and from the orangery looked groomed and the track around the moat and the boundary was cut using the tractor.

Then there was the weeding! We won't use chemicals but we've tried most other things to keep the gravel at the front of the château weed free. The patio slabs are great but the edges of the hardstanding were ragged and needed some attention to straighten them up, and the gravel itself had a green hue if you looked at it and allowed your eyes to go slightly out of focus . . . It is such a big area that asking one person to do it is soul destroying; it was all right for an hour or so but then you simply lost the will to live. The answer was to blitz it.

I suppose I am the driving force behind keeping the outside areas where wedding guests will go tidy. I lived in a flat in London and never had to care for a garden, so it came as a bit of a surprise just how quickly weeds take over. To get the main weeding done quickly, Dick and I decided it was best if we all joined in, so everyone at the château, including Petale, was called away from whatever they were doing and we attacked the weeds with hoes, forks, trowels and chungels (which is a mattock, but Dick's always called it a chungel), and Wilhelm, the newest and youngest member of the château team, even got to attack the weeds with a flamethrower. It was like a weed-pulling competition and, because of the party atmosphere, even Arthur and Dorothy joined in as they didn't realise it was work. I know how competitive Dick and I are, but it was interesting to see Sacha and Quentin getting competitive

as they tried to fill trugs with the weeds! Even Mum and Dad were having a bit of a competition out the front of the coach house. By the time I insisted we stopped for an ice cream, which didn't take much convincing, we had made a huge difference.

Now the island was more respectable, we needed to sort the ivy on the bridge. This was all cut and moved into my *atelier du mariage* so it could be used to decorate the stairs and wall sconces around the château. I fleetingly remembered the days when I had to buy all my flowers and greenery at Columbia Road flower market and then I spotted Arthur trying to pinch weeds from Dick's bucket to put in his own, and realised just how much I loved our country life.

The new *atelier* was already coming into use and having everything in easily accessible containers neatly under the counters was game changing. I couldn't wait for the flowers to arrive. I was especially excited as I had a new supplier in a shop called L'Atelier du Cadeau in Mayenne. Her name was Bélinda and she was very passionate about the quality of her flowers.

Victoria and Natasha both wanted all-white bouquets with some foliage and I was over the moon and giddy with excitement that finally I could pick my eucalyptus from our garden. The trees were my pride and joy as I had grown them from baby trees and being able to use foliage and flowers from our garden in the bouquets just makes them feel special. Last year, Dick and I had had a passionate discussion about cutting them back, and he did start, but when he saw the tears in my eyes he stopped and we compromised. So we now have a row of eucalyptus trees of varying heights.

The flowers in the bouquets were a variety of pure whites and included hydrangeas, one of my personal favourites, mini carnations, hypericum – which are bunches of white berries – white amaranth, three variety of white roses, dried white nigella flowers, white Persian buttercups, white lisianthus, freesias, and loads of foliage and herbs from the garden. It was like an angelic explosion of blooms in my new *atelier* and looking at all the flowers and foliage sitting pretty in the containers waiting for the magic to happen made me feel so excited for the big day.

Preparing the food for a wedding takes a lot of organisation. In France, there are five public holidays in May and, unlike in the UK, everywhere, apart from a few convenience stores which may open for a couple of hours in the morning, and of course the *boulangerie* to get your croissants and cakes, shuts for a bank holiday. You simply can't do any retail therapy. You are expected to spend time with your family and relax. Not being able to send someone out to get a last-minute item means you have to be sure you are well stocked.

We always have a 'tasting' with the couples getting married, so they are aware of options, and we fine-tune the menu to their likes or preferences. I know I will never be the person to liaise directly with our couples as Angela builds a rapport with them over many calls and emails, getting to know them well before they even turn up here. We have no desire to do a conventional three-course meal here for the wedding breakfast and, over time, we have found a structure that works. With the numbers catered for at a wedding, and the size of the orangery, it would be slow to do silver service, so we serve platters. Every table has sufficient 'stations' for everyone to be within easy reach of food and wines. The sparkling *crémant* is kept topped up by the front of house, but local red, white and rosé is self-served.

We start by providing a table of differently flavoured butters and rillettes, dips, cornichons and fresh breads, so when people arrive at the table they have something to nibble on and pass around. The guests will have started drinking sparkling red since before the celebration and through the formal photographs. We always serve a good amount of canapés but by the time everyone has moved across to eat, some need to start absorbing the alcohol!

From then on, food arrives in waves when everyone is ready for the next course. The speeches tend to be spread out over the meal between courses so there is not a big block of them at the beginning or the end. However, if there is someone who is particularly nervous about standing up and talking, the nerves can stop them enjoying the afternoon, so we encourage them to get things done quickly. Such factors have to be assessed on the day, so we pride ourselves on responding to the guests and not having a schedule to meet. That, of course, means we have to be flexible in the service, which could be a chef's nightmare! Careful selection of the menu and comprehensive preparation allows us to serve not dictate, and for that reason, the couple of days leading up to a wedding are busy.

When I was preparing for Natasha and Victoria's wedding, Arthur wanted to come into the kitchen and help me, so we scrubbed him up and he put on his chef's jacket! It's really important to Angela and me that the children feel part of what we do, and they love copying us or being intimately involved in the process. It won't be long before they are telling us to move over . . .

I thought it was time for Arthur to learn the secret of a good sorbet and allowed him to help me make the apple sorbet for the *trou Normand*, which was a palate-cleanser sorbet with a shot of cold Calvados. It's great as it refreshes the palate, and your sinuses, before the main course. As with all lessons, it's important to understand rather than just learn by rote.

There are two important points when it comes to making sorbet. Firstly, I had Arthur taste the local apple juice at room temperature. It was sweet and lovely. I then explained that if we froze the apple juice it would not taste as sweet, as it's hard for the flavours to be smelt and tasted when food is very cold. To prove that, I poured some of the juice onto a metal tray I produced from the freezer. It froze very quickly so I scraped some onto a teaspoon and let Arthur taste it. The sweetness had all but gone – case proven. So I added some icing sugar to make the juice too sweet, and this is what we put into the *gelatiere*. The second point involved using the *gelatiere* – the ice cream maker.

Before we started making the sorbet, we turned the machine on and allowed it to chill down. When it was cool, I took the bowl out and explained that the chiller below the bowl was very cold and had to make the bowl cold, but it was only able to pass the chill across efficiently where the bowl touched the chiller. To make it work much better, I poured half a teaspoon of the cheapest vodka possible then replaced the bowl. The vodka didn't freeze but made perfect contact, so chilling was more even and faster. In went the sweetened juice and we turned on the paddle. Soon we had a lovely sorbet being mixed in our bowl. When Arthur tasted it he announced it was not too sweet but absolutely lovely.

Next, we made sorbet balls with a couple of teaspoons and dropped them onto another frozen steel tray (to stop them melting before they went back into the freezer). Soon we had enough for our wedding, and I knew Arthur was now a qualified sorbet maker!

The final countdown to Natasha and Victoria's wedding was intense. In fact, it felt like it was intense multiplied by intense. As we cleaned and painted and polished and prepped and put things in place, our original lists were getting done. But with the newness of those items, other areas suddenly looked tired – so instead of the list getting shorter, it kept growing. Whilst I carry the responsibility for this, my front-of-house team – Tina, Sacha, Quentin and Jane – who also are our housekeeping team, all felt it too. They care so much and I feel so lucky to have a wonderful team that love what they do. We were all excited to have people

back at the château, especially for a wedding, and we all wanted it perfect.

As the days drew closer and the lists kept getting longer, I remember someone saying we would have to draw a line soon, otherwise the château would never be finished in time. We ended up working till late that evening. The following day, everyone was due to arrive but because we had a long few days ahead of us, I sent the team home to get some rest.

In all the chaos, Dick and I always try to keep Arthur and Dorothy to their routine, so we bathed and put them to bed as normal. When they drifted into dreamland we snuck off and carried on. Dick headed back down to the kitchens and I went back through every room in the château to finish and check everything was in the right place. I always need to go to bed knowing that we will be starting with our best foot forward when everyone arrives, even if it means I've only had a couple of hours' sleep.

As I finished in the honeymoon suite, I started crying. It was probably a mixture of emotion, exhaustion, excitement and anxiety, but I felt better for it. Every part of me wanted this to all be worth their wait. We had got through to this point after thousands of emails and chats. And now we were ready. Finally, it was happening, and the weather looked perfect.

The day of the celebration had finally arrived and for us this meant the start of a three-day event, kicking off with an intimate get-together for the guests staying at the château. At around eight in the morning, our butchers, Lorraine and Darren, delivered the meat. They have been our trusted supplier since day one and, even though we didn't have the need for the same amount of meat during Covid, we still used them. They had navigated the last two years well and adapted by doing home deliveries. It was lovely to see them again.

Not long after, the team started to arrive. First Eddie, Dick's kitchen help, then Beatrice, Quentin's soon-to-be mother-in-law, who keeps the kitchens clean and tidy, followed by our all-year-round team: Sacha, Quentin, Tina, Jane, Meredith and Wilhem. It was all hands on deck and it did not take long before the château was bustling with activity and full of wonderful aromas from the kitchen.

By early afternoon, some more of our team arrived for a special appearance: our dear friend and trusted château DJ, Leroy, and wife to my oldest school friend Aaron Dorn, and maybe the best make-up artist in the world, Emma Miles. The house was sparkling; there was not a cloud in the sky. We were ready for our guests.

When Natasha and Victoria arrived everyone literally ran into their arms. I remember Dick saying, 'I told you we would do your wedding as soon as we could hug.' In that moment, there was the purest pocket of happiness. The last two years were well and truly in the past and all that mattered was now. We got everyone some bubbles, Saumur sparkling demi-sec, and everyone cheered.

There is a moment that happens the day before every wedding. It's never photographed, never filmed, and I always shed a happy tear. The wedding rehearsal is truly one of my favourite moments. For the couple, everyone is where they need to be, either at the château or at a local hotel. This is one of the biggest anxieties and by the time you reach the rehearsal it is gone. Natasha and Victoria's wedding was happening and there was nothing else for them to organise or to worry about. They were in our hands now, and whilst they were always in our hands, in this moment I see everyone realise that. Their energy changes, their breathing. Dick explains that nothing can go wrong.

To help with positions, I put a little glass light where the bridal party will end up and we walk through everything. It's simple but benefits hugely from a run-through. It's a highly romantic moment that no one expects. It's happening, it's here. I can see that in people's eyes. We talk about all the details: the speed that everyone should walk at, when they depart, the exit, where they end up, how they leave at the end and how everyone then gets into position for the confetti moment.

Dick, on the other hand, talks about how we will direct the guests, the ceremony, the rings, the readings, and I can't tell you the joy I see watching my husband do this. He takes control and makes everyone feel at ease and safe, he gives our special couples the confidence if needed but most of all, he makes sure that they enjoy their moment.

Weddings are all in the planning and Natasha and Victoria's flowed to perfection. The smiles, the joy and the love oozed at every moment. The heightened sense of emotion from everyone being together again to share, to hug, to laugh and cry – I've never felt anything like it in my life. It was a very special moment to be part of.

CHAPTER THIRTEEN

Bringing Life to Our Folly

When the render and the roof were finally finished it was the most amazing feeling. The render on the rear of the château was the last element to be completed as Steve and Rob could work there unseen by any guests or anyone looking at the château from the front. The scaffold seemed to come down magically, as all of a sudden it had disappeared and been transported to the rear of the walled garden. We obviously thanked Steve and Rob profusely, but there wasn't the party there could have been. We had decided to save that until the end of what was proving to be an amazing year.

The roof had been subtly hanging over us since the day we first saw the château. It had never been too scary but had always been there waiting to be sorted. Angela and I, above all else, didn't want there to be any millstones passed to the children, and the costs and problems of the château's facelift had been challenging. So, as we walked around the château looking up, we got really quite emotional as we realised our children would never have to worry about the roof or the render in their lifetimes – it was a good feeling.

I shared every emotion Dick was feeling. The roof had been a mammoth task and, if I'm being totally honest, it was something we weren't sure we would complete in our lifetimes. Up until this point, every spare penny had gone into our roof fund. Dick often talks about the fact that he wants to ensure everything is in place for Arthur and Dorothy. And there are always those unsaid words, the fact that you never know what tomorrow will bring. So to have it done, and much earlier than we'd ever thought possible, was huge for both of us – and the relief I could see in my husband's eyes said it all.

If 2021 was the year of the roof and the render, we decided 2022 should be the year of the celebration. We thought it had a certain ring to it and we were already off to a good start. On the 29th of January, we kicked it off with a gigantic ninth birthday party for Arthur. Every birthday captures a moment in time and in January 2022, Arthur was into Thor, Vikings, rugby and a Pokémon character called Misty. Every time I said her name, he said '*Mummmm!*' but the first-edition Pokémon card with Misty on it that he got from Father Christmas still sits proudly on Arthur's desk.

Then it was off to the UK for the final dates of our postponed UK theatre tour, which culminated at the London Palladium, followed by a rather fabulous party with our closest friends and

family. Everyone let their hair down that night. Let's just say there were a lot of hangovers the next day! We seemed to be only back at the château for a couple of weeks before it was time for Dorothy's eighth birthday party and yes, you may have guessed it, lots more friends, lots of pandas and Disney *Descendants* things. In between all these parties, Dick and I also snuck off to Rennes to celebrate my birthday. To quote Dorothy, 'We had a lot of partying to catch up on!' So we were burning the candles at both ends and loving it.

And the same theme continued at the château as more of our beautiful couples returned to celebrate their love with friends and family. After Natasha and Victoria's wedding, we celebrated Hayley and Tom's wedding, followed by Liana and Patrick's (oh, what a party that was!). We caught up on our long-awaited Fun and Festivity Days and the Château Under the Stars was also back open. The whole place was buzzing and it was tonic for the soul. It felt great.

With the arrival of summer, when we got a moment we turned our attention to the walled garden. With Sarah and Richard's wedding approaching, Angela had been checking the sunflowers regularly. The sunflower plants had grown strong and tall and looked magnificent, but the long-awaited flower heads seemed reticent to form. The sunflowers just got taller. I was beginning to get a bit worried but eventually it looked like some flower heads were starting to form. Sadly we had no sunflowers in the garden as the wedding approached. Some of the sunflowers were ten feet tall but everywhere was green.

The day Sarah arrived, I took her into the garden with some of her family. When we got to the sunflowers we discovered the first of the flowers had opened and were beautiful bursts of sunshine amongst the green. It was very special and I left Sarah and her family there to share the moment. I have to say I was happy and not a little relieved . . .

That sunflower head had definitely not been open in the morning – I knew because I had checked! It truly felt that Sarah's grandfather was with us through them, but we did not hang around to share this moment. Emotions were high, so we left Sarah and her family to be together in the walled garden.

On the north-facing wall, hidden beneath the ivy, is a rather special nineteenth-century folly that was definitely in need of some TLC. Obviously, when it was built 150 years ago, the folly was designed for fun and to delight visitors to the garden, so we decided to return it to its original purpose.

The *potager* is a big garden and in its heyday there would have been a team of gardeners looking after it. For us, working in the garden is a joyous activity but we don't need every square inch under cultivation. We'd built Jenny and Steve's patio doors joining the coach house to the garden and their patio area so they could enjoy the benefits of looking over the garden and they love it. We wanted an area to entertain and chill out in the privacy of our garden as well, so a great starting point was the folly.

Since we'd moved to the château, the folly had been a store for garden equipment, a pigsty when we had pigs to clear the garden and then a store again. The roof has never been waterproof and it's always been a project for way downstream. Well, we'd now navigated our way downstream.

Roofer mate Steve and Render Rob had done the most amazing job on the château render and roof, and we had told them we had work for them for months ahead, so it was matter of deciding what to do next. The piggery needed a roof to save the ruins, we wanted the roof put back over the side gate to the walled garden – it had been partly there the first day we had seen the château but by our second visit it had been pulled down 'for safety reasons' – and we had the folly to restore. It was unanimous we'd do the folly first. It was an exciting project and we had enough of the stunning Welsh slate left over from the orangery to complete it, which was a real bonus.

It was only when the scaffolding went up and we could see the skeleton of the roof through the ivy that I started to get excited about what lay beneath. Dick and I joined the boys as we all started to cut the ivy off. There was tons of it – but, bit by bit, we could see the rafters and the surprisingly well-preserved oak. I kept telling Rob and Steve to save the slates. We don't have a use for them right now and they are a bit tired looking, but they are also part of our history, so I hated the idea of them just falling to the floor and breaking.

As the ivy got stripped off, the scaffolding was built up higher and eventually, we only had the very top bit to cut away. To everyone's surprise, it came off in one piece and revealed an ornamental zinc spike with what looked like round leaves on it to indicate which way the wind blew. I immediately headed off to the tower of curiosities and added it to our collection of things discovered during our restoration. In hindsight, this find must have been the thing that made me think we needed a weathervane on the folly, but that was a way off as we only really saw the building properly for the first time when it was all stripped back.

It's not often you have a project that transforms a building that looks like a tree into somewhere romantic that doubles as a place to spend time with the family. The folly isn't very big, maybe ten feet by ten feet, but as soon as we were inside I could see two distinct areas. There was more than enough space for a couple of

comfy chairs and a table for us grown-ups and a separate space for the children up a ladder in the loft. I can't help myself; I always want to make something special for the children. They are only young for such a short time, so I want all their memories to be wonderful. I thought the folly loft would be the perfect place for them to play and spy on the wildlife outside whilst we had a drink down below.

To put up the scaffolding to get around the folly we had to cut back the bamboo. Boy, was it tough! Having first cut down a swathe of the green bamboo and put it aside for later, I used the dozer blade on the front of our little Kioti tractor to try to scrape up the roots. I tried to imagine the first bamboo clump or two that had been planted all those decades ago and wondered if anyone had imagined the way it would spread. Now we had a triffid to be tamed. The backhoe on our tractor was not powerful enough to dig up the roots that hadn't gone very deep; they were a serious tangled mass of fibrous, intertwined roots. So I called in reinforcements in the shape of Roofer Steve's father-in-law Bob, with his beloved little digger Doris.

I know Bob was surprised by just how challenging the job was but he continued along the 'path' I had cut between the forest and the *potager* wall and cleared all vegetation out of the way, including everything resembling a bamboo root. From that time on, this track separating the bamboo and the wall has been on my route when I have the flail mower on the back of the tractor – we won't let it come back in the same way.

I think fixing the folly was the first project we'd done that wasn't for purely practical reasons. It had been built as a statement to decadence, so we felt it had to be restored with that in mind. It was going to be somewhere that gave us pleasure, so when Steve suggested that the rafters that needed to be replaced should be in oak to stay in keeping with the original build, the answer had to be 'yes', especially as they were going to be visible from inside the building.

I love talking to Steve about roofs. He has such a passion for them and always wants them to be as lovely as possible. We all agreed the Welsh slate was going to twinkle and I was planning what could be done inside and out the front. There was a small slit window on each of the walls but that wasn't really enough to light the area above the beams. At first, Steve and I discussed roof lights but we both agreed they weren't attractive enough. And then Steve suggested 'eyelid windows'. I loved the sound of these immediately and when Steve described dormer windows with curved tops that made them like eyelids, it was a resounding yes from me. I had the romantic notion that the folly was looking over the château like a guardian, so it all made perfect sense.

Steve Pierson has a lot to answer for! I made all the complaining noises expected of me, quoting time, cost, etc., but I knew it was a done deal and, to be fair, people looking at the folly a hundred years after I'm gone will still get pleasure from our decision, so I smiled and nodded . . . And anyway, I had another problem to sort. We had always talked about having a secret door between the walled garden and the magical world of the bamboo and forest behind it. It was now time to make that happen. Since we had to do work on the folly walls, why not pop in a lintel and make a small doorway, then we could hide it behind a curtain or tapestry or some such thing.

With a solution decided it was actually lovely and straightforward, and soon we had a hole in the wall with a piece of plywood leaning against it to stop Petale escaping and heading off to explore. It was only when we had dug out the earth floor, laid a reinforced concrete floor, and laid the flooring that beautifying the hole could be addressed.

While all the work was going on and Mum was cooking us dinner, I snuck out to have a moment of thinking time in the walled garden. I'd really grown to love the privacy of this space. The paved area out the front of the château is wonderful and, at some point, we would like to complete phase two of the landscaping there, but I've never felt anywhere out the front was the right place to have a paddling or a swimming pool. It would be a bit like being in your front garden in your swimwear. The walled garden is more like our private back garden and, after much debate, we had decided the southern section, tucked away behind the flower beds and overlooking the château, would be the perfect place for our pool that was always part of our bigger master plan.

As I stood there in the walled garden in the beautiful late afternoon, I realised we needed to find a way to tie together the folly and the area surrounding it. Left on my own, I would probably have got carried away, but before I went too far, I spoke to John at Westminster Stone, the brilliant company that had supplied the paving for the patio at the front of the château. We had lots of fun looking at the different styles together and then I got really excited when I realised we could make quite sophisticated patterns with some of the slabs. From that point, I started to think of the folly differently – I began to see it for the magical place it would become, rather than the rustic space that used to house our pigs, so I made a list of everything that was needed to bring my vision to life. Top of the list was a weathervane.

My dad loves making things in his workshop, be it a bird table for the garden or a ramp for Arthur's Hot Wheels cars. After decades working in the jewellery trade to support his family, he now had time to spend on projects he couldn't have imagined in his wildest dreams – like the beautiful silver key for the château door. All my attempts to source a weathervane that was worthy of being placed on top of our folly had been fruitless – as much as I like a cockerel,

I wanted our weathervane to have more meaning. And what could be better than a Steve Newman original? I knew he would be great at working in copper, so we started the design process.

I loved the simplicity and complexity of making a weathervane, and when Steve and I started talking it was never about the imagery, it was about where the 'centre of gravity' was, ensuring the 'centre of pressure' was nearer the 'tail' and 'bearings' to make sure it followed the wind freely. I loved seeing him smile when it all made perfect sense. When we'd managed to source a good variety of copper sheeting, he headed off to his workshop to be creative.

Seeing the elements of our folly come together was beautiful. Rob and Steve had done an incredible job with the roof and the eyelid windows, in particular, was better than I could have ever imagined. The Welsh slates on the curved ledge glistened beautifully. The inside stonework had all been pointed, the rustic walls had been restored to look stunning and the oak floor was a token of quality that showed our commitment to the folly's longevity.

The secret door to the bamboo forest was Dick's genius idea and added a lovely touch of playfulness. I smiled at the idea of our children's children finding this secret connection to the great outdoors. To finish the main floor, we had hand-made charcoal encaustic cement tiles. Initially, I'd wanted traditional black and white Victorian floor tiles, which Dick said weren't right for an outdoor space. But then we met Matt, a master paver at Westminster Stone, and he told me about some beautiful terracotta lozenges they had that were inspired by antique Provence tiles. They were perfect for creating a pattern with the square charcoal tiles, and as soon as I saw the two together I knew this was right and felt giddy with excitement. This was the statement floor design that the folly deserved.

With the ornate floor laid and a wooden door covering the hole into the walled garden (that was bolted from within), the recess looked like it needed shelves to finish it off. That thought must have caused some of my synapses to fire because I was soon in the workshop building a wooden bookcase, on castors, that fitted exactly in the door gap and disguised the secret exit from the folly into the world behind.

Access to the loft was by an old ladder and I had to board it out with oak planks and build a banister to make sure no one could inadvertently fall the three metres down to the stone floor. With the eyelid windows and ventilation slits, the loft was an amazing vantage point to look out behind the *potager* and into an area we knew was visited by lots of birds, wild boar, badger and deer. The loft was simply the ultimate hide, so we moved a telescope and some binoculars up there to encourage spotting the fauna.

I'm not really into themes as such but having some direction when creating a space is essential. This one was easy because of the surroundings. The walled garden and the views of it from the eyelid windows are the epitome of flora and fauna. It would be rude not to celebrate that! Animals, pollinators and everything that makes up the flora have always been my passion. From the very early days of the Vintage Patisserie, where I had light-up rabbits and squirrels, to the vast anthology of pollinator pictures and designs I have pencilled here at the château, I have always been surrounded by my surroundings.

The idea was to keep the downstairs rustic and minimal, and to make the upstairs comfy, playful and magical, with a little bit of education. The downstairs was simple: we picked up two chairs for forty euros each and re-covered the first in my flora fabric and the other in my fauna fabric, added a couple of small wooden tables and some books to Dick's shelves. It felt weird not putting a rug down, but the floor was exquisite and looked like it had been

there forever, so I didn't want to cover it up. And, to be honest, I more than made up for it upstairs, where I put so many rugs and cushions and soft things, including the simplest hand-made beanbags.

. . . .

FLORA AND FAUNA BEANBAGS

You will need

Flora and/or fauna fabric for the outer bag
Fabric for inner bag
Beanbag filling (polystyrene balls or similar)
Scissors
Tape measure
Zip
Sewing machine and cotton
Pattern

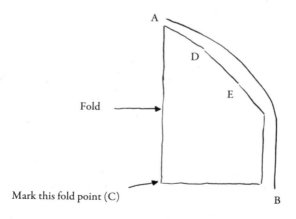

Method

Step 1: Make the inner bag

Cut out the fabric as per the pattern. Note the fold. The material is twice this shape.

With the right sides of the fabric together, sew the longest side from point A to point B.

When you hold the open end BC upward, it will form a bag. Put this sewn seam at point B on the centre fold mark (C) and sew up the open end from end to end, leaving a gap.

Turn through. Fill with beans and close the hole.

Step 2: Make the outer bag

Cut the fabric as per the same pattern.

With right sides together, sew the longest edge from point A to point B, leaving the gap D to E for the zip. This is the back of the beanbag, so the back seam. Fit the zip.

As with the lining, put the back seam at B onto the centre point (C) but this time sew from end to end without a gap.

Step 3: Put it all together

Turn through and stuff with the inner bag!

. . . .

With the beanbags and soft furnishings in place, I even managed to convince Dick the upstairs needed a swing on the apex beams. It looked magical. Now we were just waiting for its crowning glory.

The whole family gathered to see Papi Steve christen the new folly with his weathervane. I took the cherry picker around the back of the walled garden and positioned it so Steve and I could swing it up to the top of the folly, attach the weathervane and ensure the cardinal points were correctly aligned. The roof was stunning from up there and the lead-covered oak post had a spike attached ready for Steve's creation. It couldn't have gone smoother and, as we pulled the cage back, a little bit of wind swung the vane to orientate into the wind – the copper image could easily be identified as Angela, Arthur, Dorothy and me, even from ground level. As it was constructed in copper it would weather, but not degrade, over the coming decades, so it was perfectly in keeping with the rest of the folly.

We all squealed with excitement when we saw the finished weathervane – and the pride I saw in Dad's eyes in that moment will stay with me forever. It was beautiful, a perfectly cut-out silhouette of the four of us, the Strawbridges of 2022, forever preserving in time the moment when both Arthur and Dorothy were shorter than Dick and me.

We all moved through into the walled garden and soon the children were in the loft as the grown-ups toasted the weathervane, the folly, the family . . . in fact, we were so enjoying my homemade rhubarb and cardamom liqueur we found lots of things to celebrate and toast. The folly was back.

. . . .

RHUBARB LIQUEUR

I had made my rhubarb liqueur earlier in the year and it couldn't have been easier to make. I'd made several litres in the time it took to wash and slice up some rhubarb.

Method

Take a wide-necked litre glass bottle, the sort you get passata in, and cram it full of thinly sliced rhubarb (less than 10mm is perfect) with about half a dozen cardamom pods spread out amongst the rhubarb, then add 250g of sugar. Allow it to shake down then fill the bottle with the vodka, or if you are in France use the alcohol that is specially for fruit liqueurs. Screw on the lid and rotate the bottle several times; the sugar will soon dissolve. Over the next couple of days, rotate the bottle to ensure everything is well mixed.

It's ready to drink after a couple of weeks and you can stew the rhubarb to make a lovely cardamom-infused crumble or syllabub. We force our early rhubarb by keeping it out of the light as the new year's shoots come up from the crowns that we heavily manured when we put them to bed in late autumn. The lack of sunlight produces the vibrant pink stems that are so associated with the first rhubarb of the year. We think these stalks are much sweeter than the greener stalks that grow in sunlight.

When the summer holiday began the enormous potential of the folly and the area around it was soon obvious and the project just kept on growing. Angela had bought some feature paving that allowed us to make a semi-circular step in front of the entrance to the folly, and so it was sensible to extend our paved area to provide us with a bespoke al fresco food preparation and dining area. One day, we intended for it to be a poolside summer kitchen, a *cuisine d'été*.

This area overlooks the château and we were creating a new

Arthur turns ten.

Atelier du mariage, 2022.

The folly.

Up to his elbows,
saving the fish.

Quentin and Alexi's wedding day, 2022.

Christmas extravaganza, 2022.

Our forever home.

outdoor entertaining area that was sheltered, totally private and a place of tranquillity and calm, where friends and family could relax all year round. It was everything we could have dreamt of.

We had spent time in the garden during previous summers so we knew it could get very, very hot. Shade was important to us, so we knew we needed a reasonable roof for at least part of our area. I got Steve and Rob together and we counted all the remaining Welsh slates with care. We could slate a reasonably sized area but we had to work out exactly where. That decision proved not to be too difficult as the wall of the garden was not perfectly vertical. That rings warning bells, doesn't it?!

The wall looked like it was leaning inwards. There were two abutments already on that section of wall but the longest expanse left would need another one in the middle of it to ensure the wall stopped moving. It had undoubtedly been built with only a fairly rudimentary foundation. The abutments were basically supporting walls that were tied into the original garden wall and divided the area into four sections. We decided that we had to leave the wall nearest the folly free of any construction so as not to detract from its beauty; the next section would have a slate roof and be a shaded kitchenette; the third section would be a light and airy pergola for dining and the final section in the corner would be planted up with things allowed to grow up against the wall.

We had a plan, and our new abutments would support and preserve the original stone wall well into the future. But then I had an idea to incorporate a barbecue pit and a chimney inside the stonework of the abutment, so we killed two birds with one stone. Rob confirmed it was definitely doable, so I set about sourcing the grill and a flue liner to become our chimney.

Our kitchen ended up being approximately 6m by 3m, with a gently sloping slate room, and the gazebo area was about 6.5m by 5.5m. We made the decision to put a clear roof on the gazebo so it would remain bright but also protect us from the vagaries of the weather. There is something special about having an al fresco capability that works in the rain too. The set-up was definitely big enough to socialise under.

The year had been the hottest on record for the Mayenne. The meadow was scorched, the moat's water level was at the lowest we had ever seen it and the garden that was a suntrap at the best of times felt like the south of France. Our retreat at 5pm was the bright-blue paddling pool in the walled garden. With the temperature at 40 degrees most days, the water in the pool often felt like a bath but still it brought us so much joy. After two hours of splashing around and creating paddling pool tornadoes, Dick would send the children on a hunt to harvest something for the barbecue.

Meanwhile, this area was literally transforming in front of us. With the help of our trusted team of Steves, Rob and special helper master paver Matt, we were able to continue work in the garden when the wedding season began. Up until now, most of our work had been at the château, so every time we had an event, work had to stop and we would have to spend days clearing up. But with this project hidden in the growths of our walled garden it was a different situation. It was a new approach for us but I liked it a lot.

CHAPTER FOURTEEN

Family, Friends and Celebrations

It felt great seeing the château back to its old self again. It was buzzing and filled with happiness and appreciation from our guests and from our team too. After two years of masks, tests, always ensuring you weren't too close to someone and certainly no hugging, we were all just eager to get stuck in. It felt like everyone had had their enforced 'rest' and now we were ready to give our all to every project, every event and every hug. It was a joy to watch and be part of. Obviously Covid hadn't gone completely – we were still testing regularly and we had several difficult moments when key members of our team were out for weeks at a time after testing positive. It caused worry and concern in the run-up to every wedding, but thankfully Dick and I escaped any positive tests.

It was also a welcome surprise to see how much Arthur and Dorothy loved their home being back open again for events. They had been very vocal about how much they had enjoyed our special family time over the last two years, so we worried they might not like having to share the château again, but they were loving it. We always try to ensure that every twist and turn we make is right for them and as I watched them welcome guests and visitors back into our home, I was overjoyed to see two kind and caring children enjoying life. The comments and compliments about Arthur and Dorothy came thick and fast and we were so proud of who they were becoming.

At Sarah and Richard's wedding, I watched with pride as Dorothy chatted with the guests and hung out with the younger crew. And if anyone ever needed a toddler looking after for a moment, she was your girl!

Arthur also started to shine like a star. Dick often says, 'Show me the boy and I'll show you the man.' And Arthur was becoming a true gentleman. He may not appreciate me telling this story but as a parent, isn't it your duty to be proud and gushy, even if that sometimes means embarrassing your child? So, sorry Arthur, I'll begin. . .

Lynwen and Geraint had been patiently waiting to get married at the château ever since their first enquiry on 9 April 2018. They were an older couple, both second-timers and grandparents, and the wedding was a proper family affair. They were also both big jokers. The party started from the moment their coach delivered them to the château. They wanted to chat and hug, and actually loved having us with them as part of the celebration. It was very special and Arthur was in the thick of it chatting to everyone. On the day of the actual wedding, I came into the dining room at cake o'clock and found Arthur holding the attention of a huge group of ladies. Sitting at the table was Geraint's daughter Laura, and next to her Laura's daughter Rosie (Geraint's granddaughter), along with many others. Three generations of the family all chatting together and Arthur at the centre of it. He was talking about food and school and any answering questions that came his way. It was remarkable to see.

Dorothy had become good friends with one of Laura's other daughters, Florence, as they were the same age and liked lots of the same things. Rosie was more shy but a lovely girl too, and I noticed that she was listening intently to Arthur. The next day, Arthur came up to me and said, 'Mum, I need an email address.' 'Well, you don't have one yet,' I replied. 'But I need one,' he insisted, 'Rosie wants to stay in touch.' So, off I went. The coffees could wait for a moment; this was important business. And one year later, their friendship has stayed alive. In fact, we are planning a reunion as I write these words!

Becky and Jean-Francois's wedding followed next. This was the biggest of the year and we were excited to have Jean-Francois's Canadian contingency at the château. The hugs were especially tight as everyone arrived for this wedding, as, being so far apart, many of the family hadn't seen each other for years. Even for me as an onlooker, it was emotional. I remember thinking how blessed we are to be doing what we do.

Over the years, we have only ever had good people through our doors. I'm not sure if it's something we do to choose the couples, or something about the couples that choose us, but they have all been kind and respectful souls, people who feed off each other's good energy. It might sound strange but I feel like the château has some kind of protective bubble around it – anything negative or unhappy gets rejected very quickly!

We never have just one project at a time! Amongst the many things to juggle, Arthur and I had been given the task of perfecting and making 'bitterballen' for Louise and Mikael's wedding, which was definitely going to have a Dutch feel to it. I had never been exposed to bitterballen but that didn't stop me saying, 'Of course we'll have them as one of the canapés.' We started weeks in advance doing research and when I was happy with the principles, I then set about developing my own recipe that I felt would give the best château bitterballen possible.

BITTERBALLEN – CRUNCHY SOFT BEEF CROQUETTES

The basis of this recipe is slow-cooked, melt-in-the-mouth beef, mixed into a thick bechamel that is then made into croquettes and deep fried in crispy breadcrumbs.

Ingredients

500g shin or brisket, trimmed of most of its fat but not all
125g butter
2 carrots, roughly chopped
1 onion, roughly diced
1 bay leaf
500ml stock (beef is best but any kind will do)
250ml red wine
Seasoning
75g plain flour
2 eggs, beaten
Plain flour
Breadcrumbs

Method

I used our pressure cooker to make sure the beef was cooked until soft. I dried the beef and browned it in 50g butter, added the onions to soften, then added in the carrots, the bay, the wine and the stock, brought it to the boil and put it into the pressure cooker for 30 minutes.

When it had cooled, I strained off the rich liquor and set it to one side, then 'pulled' the beef into small pieces.

Having melted the remaining 75g butter and cooked the flour gently for 2 or 3 minutes, I removed it from the heat and stirred in approximately 500ml of the reserved beef stock, mixed it to ensure there were no lumps, put it back on the heat and continued stirring until the sauce thickened. Then it was removed from the heat and I stirred in the beef, seasoned it and left it to cool before popping in the fridge to chill properly.

When cool you can make your bitterballen. Roll the thick mix into balls about the size of a walnut, roll in the flour, then the egg and finally the breadcrumbs. Deep fry in batches at 170°C until golden. It has to be served with a bowl of mustard mayonnaise to dip the ballen into. I know we are in France but Arthur and I both agreed that a mix of English mustard and mayo was better than Dijon or wholegrain.

. . . .

When it came time to testing time, Arthur and I both did a little happy dance in the kitchen. The bitterballen were fabulous. We allowed everyone in the château to taste them. It was like a rehearsal for the wedding as Arthur, the proud chef, went all over the place finding people and insisting they taste our creation, as he explained how they were made. I watched my big boy and was very proud of how openly he shared his passion, insisting that everyone try the canapés, with and without the dip, for feedback. I have to say it was unanimously favourable. The next batch we would make was to be for the wedding and then five times as much.

Our latest canapé, as produced by Dick and Arthur Strawbridge, really was a total revelation. They were perfectly crispy on the outside and soft on the inside, oozing with meaty unctuousness. Generally, we have an FHB (family holdback) principle when it comes to our events. But this time, as Arthur wandered around the château sharing his plate of 'ballen', I shamelessly played the 'I'm your mummy card' to get an extra one. I could have eaten a bucket of them!

Mikael, the groom, and his best man had chatted to us many moons ago about how they would like to arrive on a tandem bike. We love a challenge, and I'm sure they mentioned it was a Dutch tradition, so we did everything we could to accommodate this request. Dick actually owned an old touring tandem bicycle, so that part was relatively easy. Dorothy and I took on the task of decorating it to give it a glamorous Dutch feel suitable for the occasion. Dorothy was having a blast as we decked it out with a rainbow of ribbons and greenery, and sunflowers and other large orange blooms. By the time we were done it looked like a Dutch-themed moving bush. It was great fun and the groom was over the moon when he saw it! In fact, he was so pleased, he decided he wanted the whole groom party to cycle down the drive to the château. What could possibly go wrong?

As they rode down the bumpy drive, Mikael and his best man on the tandem, and the rest of the party on other bikes, everyone was cheering and clapping, but I just kept saying things like, 'slowly does it', 'careful, not too fast', 'mind the bumps'. It was a nerve-wracking couple of minutes but once they dismounted in their finery, I allowed myself to breathe again. The groom was in

one piece and the wedding could start! What an entrance!

Louise and Mikael's wedding celebration was joyous. As they headed down the aisle amongst lines of their friends showering them in confetti rose petals, I nipped inside, took off my jacket and slipped on an apron. This time, instead of meeting Eddie, our French-Tunisian sous-chef, as I entered the kitchen, I was greeted by Eddie and a beaming Arthur in his bright-yellow chef's jacket with his sleeves rolled up. There was no way he was missing this canapé service.

We divided the work, with Arthur plating up for us as Eddie and I turned out gazpacho and chilli shots, with chive flowers, goat's cheese and red onion crostini, and our bitterballen. We had had two fryers on the go during the morning prior to me heading for my duties upstairs, so we popped our pre-fried bitterballen into the oven and very soon were able to get them on the pass ready to go for service.

Arthur briefed the front of house like a pro and made sure they could tell everyone that these were traditional Dutch bitterballen served with an English mustard mayo. As the empty plates started coming back into the kitchen, we asked how they were going down and the answer was everyone, particularly the Dutch contingent, loved them. I could see Arthur was itching to see for himself, so I suggested he take a plate out and see what people thought. That was the end of Arthur's service as he immediately became front of house and mingled with the guests, explaining how they were made, the cooking of the beef, the thickness of the sauce and the need for English mustard to make the mayo sing out . . .

The 2022 wedding season was special for so many reasons, and as it was drawing to a close, I was engulfed in comfort that we were on exactly the right path. I have always believed that

when things are hard, or it feels like nothing is working in your favour, it's important to recognise those moments. Sometimes, it's because you have taken a wrong turn and a simple pivot or sidestep can get you back on track. On the flip side, I've always thought when things are so bloody perfect that you want to scream it from the rooftop, then you need to celebrate those moments.

Opening the château back up had been the tonic we needed after two years of lockdowns and disruptions, and the wedding season was the icing on the cake. It had been absolutely faultless, pure magic, and so special to watch our couples, and their family and friends, get stuck into the celebrations. And also to see our team and family, who we love to bits, back together, working their socks off and growing every day.

Dick and I took it as a huge compliment when one of our much-loved and key members of the team, our darling Quentin, asked if he and long-time boyfriend Alexis could have their wedding reception at the château. It was an honour to be asked and we were of course delighted to say yes!

In four short years, Quentin had become such a big part of our château family. Our relationship with him is precious. At a snap of your fingers, he can go from working in the garden to being the perfect host, sharing stories about his childhood in France to being Uncle Quentin and doing homework with the children. He is amazing with Arthur and Dorothy. Over the years, we have watched him grow and develop his skills to become such a valuable member of our team. In return, we have learnt so much from Quentin about France and its cultures and traditions.

The morning of Quentin and Alexis's wedding was busy, even busier than normal. Now, weddings at the château are always busy but obviously on this occasion we were also down several helpers, as most of the team were guests at Quentin's big day!

On the day of the wedding, I'd been up since around 5am making the buttonholes.

Earlier in the year, Quentin had seen some yellow and white buttonholes I made for another wedding and asked me to make the exact same for his. Two months on, the flowers and foliage available were slightly different, but the key to this design was that it resembled a micro bouquet in its form. The night before, I had foraged fennel and garlic seed heads, plus another greeny/yellow seed head – I wasn't sure what it was but it looked great. I mixed these with dried gypsophila, a single white craspedia and a bright-yellow burst of sanfordii. They looked lovely and as I carefully wrapped the stems in jute and placed the buttonholes in a hand-carved wooden box that I had bought just for the occasion, I was overcome with emotion. Our dearest Quentin was getting married!

But, like I said, there was a lot to do. So I quickly bounced into the kitchen to help Dick. He was making 250 scones for the cream tea. He was making great progress but as we wanted to keep service to a minimum, I made a suggestion it might be a good idea to add the cream and the jam now, so that later it would just be a matter of putting them out for people to enjoy. Great idea. But sticky! It was time to get the family team organised: Dad was in charge cutting the scones, then Mum added the clotted cream and Arthur added the jam. Dorothy was moving them from station to station and I was in charge of making sure they were all up to standard. Meanwhile, Dick was still churning out more scones. It was good old-fashioned mayhem!

Quentin and Alexis were married at the *mairie* in Laval. There is something very special about seeing your local *mairie* marry a couple and officially welcome them to the town with a *livre du mariage*. It was the one element of their wedding that I had not given much thought to in advance, but it was just beautiful. We loved watching Quentin and Alexis softly share their vows before giving each other a ring. It was stunning. After the ceremony at the town hall, we returned to the château for some serious scone-eating, but first they wanted all of their guests to sign their van – it was the most incredible 'guest book' I've ever seen.

* * *

Work continued in the walled garden during our wedding season and we soon had a fully functioning *cuisine d'ete*. Our first family lunch under the pergola tasted glorious; it was so tasty and simple. The boys cooked a shoulder of lamb over charcoal on the grill. We had gorgeous new potatoes with too much butter and scallions, salad from the garden and, to accompany the lamb, Grandma (and Dorothy and Arthur's) homemade chilli tomato jam. It was such a pleasure being there as a family. The facilities worked, the setting was gorgeous and, to top it all off, the view of the château was magnificent. It worked so well we knew we were going to have many more intimate meals there in the future.

The first function to test our family space was for a very important fiftieth birthday party for our dear friend Sophie, the lady who had introduced Dick and me. It was her birthday gift to host a party for her family and friends, but like everything else, this had been postponed! As she was fifty, it felt rude not to theme the event 'gold' and we were going all out to make it a proper celebration. We'd asked Dick's eldest son, James, to come across from England to help cater; he was also a friend of Sophie's and was with Dick the first night we met! We had a strong team of Strawbridge men on hand and I had a cupboard of edible gold in every guise!

We had made a plan for Sophie's party. Angela sorted the flow and timings and James, Arthur and I created a menu for an al fresco

French/British fusion feast. As always, we would be led by the ingredients available.

Arthur joined James and me in the kitchen, and when we stepped through the menu he asked if he could create his own canapé. James and I were more than happy to assist, and Arthur came up with a recipe for 'Little Lingot'. Lingot is a rectangular, strong, soft cheese, a bit like a flavoursome Camembert, and it's made just down the road from us. Arthur wanted to panne and deep-fry them. But what to accompany them was the question. So we had a chat and threw some ideas around.

The canapés we served were coronation crab and ikura vol au vents with the ubiquitous gold leaf, Arthur's little Lingot with honey chilli, and smoked duck breast crostini.

I could not stop giggling at the dynamics in the kitchen. My stash of edible gold was being used to finish everything. I loved it, and whilst this was driven by James, Arthur was completely into the bling too. Dick spent lots of time rolling his eyes but I had to say, 'You created two sons who love the gold, you need to take some credit for that!'

Somehow, James and I even managed to create possibly the best cocktail in the world: the 'château shimmer'. It had 'gunfire' as a base, which Dick had told me was traditionally served to soldiers on Christmas morning by their officers, so Dick used to be up bright and early to serve this tea and rum mix to his troops in Germany.

In our cellar, some forty-three years later, Angela and James got pickled mixing combinations of rum, tea, Aperol, dry vermouth and some pear juice. Funnily enough, the variation with more rum was their favourite and it looked impressive with the gold dust added. The 'château shimmer' was born: one part gunfire, one part Aperol, one part dry vermouth, ice, pear syrup and a twist of orange peel.

The gold dust shimmered like the nectar of the gods! James and I had had so much fun testing combinations, but all for research purposes of course, that the following day we both had hangovers! Now the cocktail was locked in we were ready for our guests.

Sophie, her husband Will, their two children Rosie and Fred, and friends and family started to arrive. Everyone had made such an effort and the gold factor was high alongside everyone's spirits.

Whilst the boys had been in the kitchen, I had been quietly beavering away in the folly. Because of its location overlooking the bamboo forest, that was part of the decor that I had woven through. I made napkin ring holders from pieces of bamboo and the napkins were simply some of my ochre bamboo fabric with each person's names sewn on. With forty people, we needed to ensure the seating plan was correct! Dorothy helped dress the table and pick the foliage from our walled garden, which she sprayed gold (of course!). I have to say, the setting was gorgeous.

The evening started at the château with our birthday cocktail. Everyone loved it before they even tasted it, which I guess was the plan! They were quite potent too, I may add. After the canapés, we started our walk over to the walled garden. It had started to rain but that made it all the more exciting. It was the journey into the unknown and I could see Sophie leading the procession of people who were walking two by two! It was a wonderful sight. Sophie knows the château inside and out, but this area was a complete surprise to her! I was at the end of the line but could hear the squeals of excitement and joy as people found their place and settled for the feast.

For the starter platters, preparation was the key. We had char-grilled vegetables with heritage tomatoes all drizzled with a good extra-virgin olive oil and sprinkled with *fleur de sel*. A lovely selection of local charcuterie, and *poisson crudo* (thinly sliced raw fish with slices of segmented oranges and lemon oil) served with fennel and sweety drop peppers. This was followed by queen scallops with a garlic herb butter cooked in their shells on the charcoal grill.

And then for mains we had savoury faggots of slow-cooked ox cheek served in a cabbage leaf, slow-cooked fillet of beef and butternut squash fondant (discs of squash poached in butter then roasted).

Finally, for dessert, each guest had their own individual stewed plum and orange polenta birthday cake with a candle on the top to make up for all the birthdays we missed. We all sang 'Happy Birthday' to each other and then we all blew out our candles.

The atmosphere was golden that evening, and we had finally got to gift Sophie the celebration we promised.

CHAPTER FIFTEEN

A Festive Extravaganza

Clearing out the attic had been a huge and grubby task, but we had managed to make a head start before the wedding season started. We had to ensure that the mess associated with taking old furniture and rubbish down a hundred steps was completed and cleaned up so it didn't interfere with the events. A large corner of the attic had not been explored at all as it was extremely dirty and full of wood, dust, slate, cardboard, metalwork and broken furniture. We rigged up some bright lights and put on dust masks, and Angela and I went to sort the rubbish from the rubbish. I'd found an old musket up in that area of the attic but now what was left looked like it was for the bin or bonfire. However, we did find old packing cases and labels going back to before the Second World War, trinkets, old letters and books, even bits of a very old mechanical train set.

With the children growing up fast, we had decided to turn this area of the attic into a games room for them. They had all but grown out of the playroom near the salon, though it had a plethora of art and craft kits and they still played in there, and so looking forward, we knew our little ones would soon want some space to be with their friends . . . We weren't quite ready for them to be up there by themselves yet, but that time was approaching.

The wooden beams in the attic were just so beautiful. Dick had pointed out the marks that showed where they had been assembled on the ground prior to being carried up there over 150 years ago and some showed signs of having been reused from the earlier château that had been on the site. I loved the idea that the history here could go back to the very earliest fortifications that were build more than 800 years ago. It makes us very aware that we are looking after the château for future generations and that's a big responsibility.

With many of our big jobs done, we were eager to get the games room sorted quickly and not to make too much of a mess for a long period. So everyone was up there at one stage, with Rob and Roofer Steve insulating and plaster-boarding, Steve Beachill skimming and Dick doing electrics, whilst the rest of us helped to carry things up and down, and sort everything that had been moved.

The games room was a big room and it naturally split into three areas. The area immediately to the left at the top of the stairs was partly separated from the rest of the room by an amazing and huge brick chimney stack. Then there was the rest of the room, with a cathedral-like space above it. And finally, on the other side, there was the tower. The entrance to the tower was a door that was so small you had to go on your hands and knees to get through it, and when you got in there it wasn't possible to stand up easily, as the structure that made up the pointy roof of the tower was like spokes of a huge oak wheel. I could see why Dick was so excited to discover it. As Dorothy was the only one who would be comfortable in such a small space, we decided the tower would be her area.

We were also very excited by the idea of fitting carpet in the largest section of the room. This may sound silly but it was to be the first fitted carpet in the château and it would completely change the feel of the place. When Dick and I went carpet shopping we were after something comfortable but hard wearing, and with enough left on the roll to cover the large loft area.

Carpets are heavy. That's stating the obvious but when you have a five-metre-wide roll to get up a hundred stairs you know it won't be fun! Steve, Rob and I headed up with the carpet. You get lulled into a false sense of security at the château, as getting up to the front door and then up the main staircase is relatively easy as it's all very spacious. But from outside my office to the attic is a monumental pain as the stairs are narrower and steeper, so longer objects have to be carried vertically. We paused briefly at the bottom of the last two flights to get our breath back and then it was up and away. Three very sweaty men deposited the carpet up in the attic. It was there and was staying there.

The area immediately at the top of the stairs was not going to be carpeted and became a 'making and doing' space. Instead of carrying the doors from an old wardrobe all the way down, we used them as the children's worktops. As a homage to Angela's dad's background in the jewellery trade, we made the desks a similar shape and design to the ones Steve had used since his apprenticeship. Complete with a chamois leather skirt to catch any filings or shavings.

This area made me very happy and worried Angela a lot. The children's workbenches had tools on them that could cut them, burn them and stab them, but if they were at all sensible they didn't have to find out the hard way ... I can probably be classed as a bad dad, as Arthur did manage to bleed a little with a small saw, and Dorothy got a little burnt with her glue gun, both within the first excited ten minutes. I got that look from Angela, but guess what? They haven't hurt themselves since. Dorothy worked out how not to burn herself and Arthur decided he didn't want to leak, so lessons were learnt and experiences gained.

The carpeted side of the attic was full of lots of games and toys for the children to grow into. Arthur, Dorothy and I have started playing chess and an old games table we had bought for the room had a chess board on it. There was table hockey and even a wonderful old train set that Will, Sophie's husband, had found for us as a thank you for hosting Sophie's birthday party.

This is where I have to admit to not having had a train set growing up, so I was probably the most excited about this. The children helped Mummy make all the scenery around the tracks that we set up, complete with points and a turntable. I explained all about how the central rail and the tracks formed two sides of the circuit and how we had to get the track joined properly so the electricity could flow. We went to their work benches and soon they were wiring up batteries to motors with switches and making cars and things with propellers, all of which had proper electrical circuits. Daddy was very happy and maybe one day, when the children are much older, they'll be allowed to play with the train set. Maybe.

Even though our new games room was rather high up, it's in a great location for the family. My workshop is next door and the *l'observatoire du château* is above. Over time, I knew this part of the château would get more and more attention.

When all the grubby work was complete, it was my time to add my mark. All the beams had twinkly lights carefully wrapped about

them and the cupboard was painted midnight blue, to match the *l'observatoire*. I had made a Newton's cradle out of footballs and also taken many of the original items we had found in this space, including a side-saddle, to ensure we did not lose its history. The children's benches were full of new and slightly grown-up items that excited me and scared me, and the entire place was packed with games. It was a child's dream.

For me and Dick, the star was the train set. We knew that the Baglionis had one too because we'd found a piece when we were clearing out. But for Arthur and Dorothy, the highlight was their work benches and the endless possibilities that they can make and repair anything. This was probably a good thing, as Dick definitely had a 'this is my train set' vibe, but I'm confident in years to come they will all play together nicely! What we did know was that our children are growing up. They are nearly too big for the helter-skelter in the playroom and it feels like we only built it yesterday.

* * *

For years, I joked that the château would soon need an extension due to all our trips to *brocantes* and Emmaus, my favourite charity shop. But after several conversations over the summer, it became apparent that we would actually be turning this dream into a reality . . .

Back when we were first château shopping, we made a list of all the facilities and features that we would love to have. For example, I knew I wanted symmetrical towers, so that was on the list. After seeing an orangery for the first time, I knew if our château was to be our forever home, we *needed* an orangery. Dick was not as demanding when it came to his wishes. He wanted a walled garden, if possible, and said that if we were going for the ultimate home then a moat would be great, but he'd also settle for a lovely lake or water feature. As we searched, the list got longer and less likely to be fulfilled, but we knew that.

One of the châteaus we viewed a couple of days before we found Château de la Motte Husson had an amazing winter garden. It was the most beautiful inside space that gave you the feeling of being outside during the winter months but much more comfortable. We both loved it and so Dick added 'winter garden or Victorian cast-iron conservatory' to our wish list. Why not? We could but dream.

We were visiting a château we were interested in but we knew it wasn't exactly perfect when the details for Château de la Motte Husson came up via email and it basically had everything really important from our list. We were so excited we didn't even think about the winter garden for years. Later, when we were planning our projects, we thought about a Victorian-style conservatory but we just couldn't make it work as it would be wrong out the front of the château and access from the sides and the back were all through the *sous-sol*, which are the work rooms, not the reception rooms. We even considered a two-storey conservatory with spiral stairs going down to it, but it was all a bit on the expensive side. All that changed when we were on tour and Angela and I were walking to the Guildhall in Portsmouth for our performance, and I noticed the Theatre Royal ... There was an amazing cast-iron conservatory on stilts over the street. I took several pictures and the idea started to form.

The views out the back of the château are stunning but there is nowhere to enjoy them unless you go outside and sit behind the château. However, if you were to build yourself a conservatory on stilts it would be possible to access the area from the ground floor behind the main staircase. It all made sense. We knew it was going to be reasonably expensive; however, when I contacted a local conservatory company, I think the length of our drive caused him to misplace his decimal point!

We explained what we wanted. I was going to do all the necessary structural metalwork with the company just down the road from us. We basically wanted a lean-to ornamental conservatory. We to'd and fro'd getting the size right and I just couldn't get a price or a delivery date from him. It was so frustrating that I restarted my research and just as well, as when he finally put a price in writing there was a five-month delay and it was about half of the price of buying the bloody château. I told him what I thought and he immediately said that was only the starting price, but the damage was done so we walked away.

It is funny how things work out because my research led me to a lovely company called Villadorica in Italy that seemed to have truly beautiful products. We emailed, we talked. Luca understood what we wanted and loved the project, and very soon we had paid the deposit and had a delivery date to work to, all at a very reasonable price!

Rob and Steve had all the skills needed to change a large window into a doorway on the reception level, approximately 3.5 metres up in the air at the back of the château. When it was finished, the stone surrounding the doorway looked like it could have been there since the château was built, but actually half of it was brand new and fabricated by Rob. I had found a set of double-glazed glass doors with wooden frames and they were up there waiting for our floor, and thereafter the arrival of the conservatory

Robin, the metal expert, and I did the sums and soon he was fabricating a ring beam, the pillars and wall fixings to act as the base for our conservatory. I'd gone to the mayor's office to check on the regulations and as we did not intend to build a concrete base, apart from the three 1m-square and 1.5m-deep bases for the three supporting pillars, they were very chilled, so there were to be no delays in us moving forward.

Having built our ring beam and pre-assembled it all at his workshop to see that it fitted together, it was taken apart and we arranged for Robin and his team to come and put up our metal balcony.

I had asked how the 6m by 4m metal work was going to get to us but Robin just smiled and said it was included in the price, don't worry! The day arrived and I was coming back from dropping the children at the school in the village. As I approached the château, I was held up by a little traffic jam of a metalworker's van with four-ways on, a very large forklift with an impressive load of metal girders sticking out and another pickup truck with four-ways on in the middle of the road . . .

It was half a day's work for four of them to put up my metalwork and it was safely done, if a bit unorthodoxly. I asked at every stage what was to happen next, was told and then it happened. No fuss.

Dick was in his element with Dorothy's schoolfriend Janelle's dad Robin, and his team. I had a quick peek at what was happening, and there was a fair amount of hand waving and using power tools, but as Dick was smiling, I knew it wouldn't be long before our platform would be up. By lunchtime, it was bolted to the granite of the wall and the new, very slightly ornate pillars were holding up the other side. It looked bigger than I thought it would be, which was great.

As the vehicles all headed away down the driveway, the floor joists and the panels to hold the tiled flooring and insulation were already going up. Apparently, all the wood was already cut so it wasn't long before you could walk out through our new double doors onto a lovely deck area. The setting was beautiful.

That evening, Dick and I grabbed a couple of chairs and sat out there to absorb the tranquillity. It was so peaceful, and we just sat and looked out over the moat and neighbouring countryside not saying much at all. I knew this was going to be a very special part of the château when it was done.

Luca was giving us regular updates on when our beautiful, green, ornamental, glazed, built-to-order winter garden would arrive to be connected to the floor and the château, and I was busy sourcing furnishings, lights and the tiles. I'd decided on very traditional black and white Victorian square tiles laid on the diagonal. It was lovely having everything ready when we had our delivery. It had all happened so quickly and now we were just days away from completion and being able to enjoy a tea or coffee as the rising sun bathed the room and the mist rolled in over the moat.

When the numerous pallets of the conservatory arrived, Jean Betram came to our rescue with his all-terrain telehandler and helped us organise them all. The instructions made me pause for a moment – it was a book, not even a booklet! I'd seen it as an email attachment so had printed it off and assembled all the necessary tools. I shouldn't have been surprised but there was an awful lot of glass, though thankfully everything had arrived intact, which was a result.

I'd rather stick a pin in my eye than assemble an IKEA cupboard, and this was so much more. Roofer Steve and Render Rob thought it was funny when I showed them the instructions before it all arrived, but they stopped laughing when they realised there was a reason I was showing them the instructions . . . 'He who laughs last laughs loudest!'

Our biggest concern was that everything was square, and square to the château wall, which was hopefully vertical . . . Assembling the room was quite straightforward – however, it was intended to be done at ground level, on a concrete foundation, so you could walk around and sort out your fixings. Thank goodness for our cherry picker. It was like mobile scaffolding, and when we couldn't reach through to fix anything we swung the basket into place. Thankfully, the instructions were very clear and we just had to be methodical.

During the course of the week, I cleared the building suppliers in Mayenne out of clear silicone adhesive as we were taking no chances that there would be a leak.

I smiled a lot; the conservatory was, and is, gorgeous. Builder mate Steve came in and tiled, I mounted a panel heater on the wall, we added the light fittings and a couple of sockets, and the room was handed over to Angela. We had set out to find our dream home and, as far as I was concerned, this was the final piece.

The *jardin d'hiver* is a room to relax in and has the advantage of receiving the first morning sun; it is wonderfully light and airy. When you are up there you feel like you are floating over the moat. We moved Dick's treasured copper and brass coffee machine in there and set up a coffee station with his grinder and other accoutrements. We also needed somewhere to sit, and I'd found a couple of completely over-the-top peacock chairs that Dick said reminded him of the late 1970s, a couple of complementary cane chairs and a small table. We had always intended to have some greenery in there, so I added some lovely hanging spider plants, and we decided this was also the best home for Arthur's avocado plant, 'Angus', which he had lovingly grown from a pip. We had watched Angus grow and now he was four-feet tall and very bushy, so he needed his own corner, and what better place.

We were in the midst of deciding how best to christen our new room when Arthur and Dorothy took the decision out of our hands – they wanted to cook us breakfast to be served there.

It was interesting: was our new room a *jardin d'hiver*, a conservatory or a morning room, or a breakfast room? I suppose it didn't matter as it is all of those. I loved the idea of the children making us breakfast but Mummy got a bit twitchy . . . The children help us in the kitchen all the time but to be given total responsibility is something very different. We asked regularly if everything was all right and I have to admit to watching through the service kitchen door to ensure all safety rules were adhered to. I needn't have worried as they both rose to the challenge and what made me proudest was how they looked after each other.

I was in charge of the coffee for Angela and me, and by the time I made that, our breakfast of coddled eggs with truffle dust, buttered toast and, of course, Arthur's famous guacamole had arrived. The children were so pleased with themselves, and rightly so as it tasted extremely good. Our extension had been christened.

* * *

Planning for our Christmas party in 2022 had started months before. It was to be our eighth Christmas in our forever home and when Angela and I sat down to do our planning it was late summer, but we ended up reminiscing about our journey to get to where we were and we made the decision to throw a full-blooded Christmas extravaganza to thank all those who have helped us along the way. We even started discussing fireworks to mark the end of an era the best way we could. 'Save the dates' went out immediately. We contacted a lovely coach company based in South Wales that had been used by one of our wedding guests, and we organised for collection and drop points near Ashford in Kent. We then set about agreeing the best way to party in December with over a hundred guests.

It was an interesting challenge as we wanted all our staff to party with us too! After all, our team have been wonderful and supportive right from our first year in France. Way back in 2015, Tina was the first to come to work for us and to join our team, followed by builder mate Steve a couple of weeks later. Sacha had come to help at our first paid wedding and had not been allowed to leave as she was the only person who knew where she had hidden things. Then came Quentin. We always think of Quentin as a late arrival but, on thinking about it, he's been with us five years now. Meredith and Jane help with admin and have also lent a hand doing everything from turning around rooms to ironing my underpants (which actually came as a shock to me). We were also going to be joined by Roofer Steve and Render Rob. Then there was Wilhelm who is game for anything, and Beatrice who helps keep me in order in the kitchen and cleans anything that doesn't move – these two had only recently joined us when the weddings restarted. And of course my big boy James was coming to help and, as he would be partying, he arranged for Chef Glynn, a mate of his who I'd worked with in the past, to be on hand to look after both of us if we got a bit messy. What we needed was a plan that allowed everyone to have a ball with lots of dancing and lots to eat and drink. . .

My dream was a party to truly celebrate our journey since arriving in France. I had the image of lots of twinkling lights, fireworks and people dancing, but a marquee would block the view of the château and dominate the island. When I first saw a see-through marquee I knew there was something in it. Our guests could party but see the château at the same time, and if we did manage to organise fireworks, they could all dance and watch the magic

from the warmth of the tent! However, they were all a little ugly and my dream was to find a clear marquee in an elegant sailcloth shape. It appeared after nine months of hunting that this was not really a thing, so I started to work out what plan B looked like. While deep in discussion of what were not really good plan Bs, I found what I was looking for. I hadn't given up hope and then there it was, the exact marquee I had dreamt of. There followed that terrible period when we find what we are after and you try to get confirmation that it's in stock, or available, and not just a hook to get you on their website. It took a number of days to find out that it was actually a crystal sailcloth marquee, albeit located in Belgium. But it was available, and it was the only one in Europe that was big enough to seat 120 guests! We booked it and paid a deposit as quickly as we could

As the party got closer, we realised that there was a lot to pull together and quickly! Mum and Dad had not had their family over since their fiftieth wedding anniversary, so they also wanted their house to feel warm and Chritsmassy! This year, they even asked us to get them a Christmas tree, which is a first. Mum also wanted to ensure every part of their house was sprinkled with Christmas sparkle, and so when Mum, Dorothy and I went foraging in the grounds for foliage to decorate the château and the coach house, we really meant business! In addition, we also had the small matter of a massive marquee to decorate, but I knew I'd come back out for a round two.

As we walked around, cutting holly and mistletoe, we couldn't help thinking about the changes in our lives. Dorothy was toddling on our first Christmas forage; now she was a beautiful, confident young girl who knew her mind and was full of fun and a little mischief. I smiled at her and my eyes misted up.

Before everyone turned up for our Christmas festivities, we had managed to start a project that appeared to be even more expensive than the roof and the render. Unbelievably, the quote for new windows came in at not far off the price we had paid for the château. It made our eyes water. We had asked for quotes for new double-glazed oak windows that reused our original metalwork, and that were pressure painted so would last twenty-five to forty years before they would need to be repainted. There were not a lot of people doing this work but we had found a Paris-based company whose boss was a wooden window guru. We'd made the decision that we would get the four main windows downstairs at the front of the house done and the window at the front of the botanical suite. That way, the front of the château would look lovely and all the windows would work.

After lots of toing and froing, it was the very end of November when we had confirmation that the team were coming to install our windows. We were over the moon as the château would be looking its best for the Christmas season.

I had started to get my head around the fact that the windows may not arrive in time, so when Dick gave me the news, I was elated. It meant that they were arriving the week of the party and, as it was a very grubby job, that was not ideal. But it also meant that we had started the final big job we had to do. Our friends and family have cheered us on and supported us all the way. We could not wait to show them a roofed and rendered château, now with new windows as well! It was also a subject that Dick and I had talked about for hours, as at times we did not know if we would ever be able to afford it.

An installation team of six appeared and started taking out the old and putting in the new. It happened very quickly but it felt brutal, and I have to say I couldn't watch. What the eyes do not see, the heart does not feel . . . So instead, I snuck upstairs to continue with Christmas prep.

Later that same day, they were done, and with the old window furniture put back in, they looked like replicas of the originals (with the added benefit of being double glazed). This was a very special moment, and Dick and I savoured it together.

Somehow, the diaries aligned for our annual trip to collect oysters, and Arthur, Papi Steve and I were joined by James as we headed to the beaches of Brittany. I should have known James would come prepared. I had bought him an oyster penknife to use in Cornwall, but when we hit the beach, all wrapped up to keep warm, he produced from his pockets all sorts of accompaniments. The next thing I knew, Arthur was shouting out that Strawbridge and Sons' Oyster Shack was open. Between the four of us, we must have eaten thirty oysters. Some plain, some with lemon, some with raspberry vinegar with finely diced shallots and some with a very spicy salsa, which was the surprise hit of the morning!

When the boys got back from collecting oysters they were high as kites. It was beautiful to see our multi-generational and modern family all together. James's relationship with our children is precious, and seeing my dad be part of that too was wonderful. Everyone was talking over each other, fast and loud, but we worked it out: they'd collected lots of oysters, eaten a lot of oysters and, on the way home, also stopped in a salt museum. Of course they did!

As a family, we had chosen our Christmas tree, my mum and dad's Christmas tree and three trees for the marquee, which I had planned to decorate with pictures of the special moments we had shared with family friends. Putting up the château tree is always a joyous family moment. Dick gets a Christmas playlist ready and some treats for the family; we argue a little while getting the tree straight and the lights even, and then we all enjoy dressing it. For us, it's the real start of Christmas and whilst there was a lot happening this year, we ensured this moment was cherished. When the Christmas tree is up, we sit on the floor, turn the house lights off and look at the twinkles of the decorations. Petale seems to know what's happening as she always jumps on our laps for the big reveal.

With the arrival of the marquee everything stepped up a gear. It was exactly what we needed: it was spacious, there were heaters and you could see in and out. It wasn't long before everyone was in decorating mode as we brought the tables and chairs from the orangery and augmented them with the outdoor tables and chairs for our hog roasts. Then we festooned it with lights, and Christmas decorations and garlands were added everywhere.

There was a lot to do to decorate the marquee and ensure everything was ready for service. Our team are wonderful and I think we all get on so well as we strive for perfection. My darling friend Hazel, who is a florist, came a little in advance, as did Dick's friend Johnny, so we had some extra manpower to get this done. But never put a bunch of creatives together, because instead of getting things on the list done, Hazel and Johnny came up with a new idea to create some eight-feet-tall angel wings. All of a sudden, they were off to create this wonderful thing of beauty, which would make a great photo opportunity for the party . . . I was actually very excited too!

I knew it was going to be manic in the build-up, so I made sure that there was enough time ahead of that to make our homemade Christmas crackers. After all, it was Christmas, and for me that always has to be marked with something personal or handmade. The children also helped this year, making each family member a stocking of goodies. They loved the opportunity to use their new workspace.

HOMEMADE CHRISTMAS CRACKERS

You will need

Fabric
Sewing machine and cotton
Scissors
Tape measure
Cardboard roll
Embroidery needle and cotton
'Goodies' to put inside the crackers, including a joke
Water-soluble embroidery pen
Jute string, fancy cord or ribbon

Method

Step 1: Make your napkin

Cut out a rectangle of fabric, the size of the napkin you want. Mine were 30cm wide. Using a contrast thread, sew two lines down each edge of the napkin.

Step 2: Make it personal

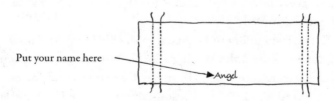

Put your name here → Angel

Use the water-soluble pen to write the name of the recipient on the napkin and embroider with a stem stitch or chain stitch. When you have finished, dab with a damp cloth to remove the ink.

Step 3: Construct your crackers

Roll the napkin around your cardboard tube, tie one end, fill with goodies and tie the remaining end.

Tips

- I ripped the fabric into the napkin-sized piece to give them a handmade feel

- If you want to add a snap, it is best to buy a box of them, then put one inside the cracker so it can be snapped once the cracker is open. It's the only way if you wish to use fabric!

....

As our guests started to arrive, the party had already begun. It was the night before and the house was heaving, but it was full of people prepared to get stuck in. We had Dick's brother David and his wife Jayne and daughters Alice and Sarah; Jon and Miguel; Hazel and Andrew; Johnny; Lian; Paul; my goddaughter Stella and her sister Iris; Amanda and Ester; Jimmi and David; my brother Paul and our family friend Pat, all either staying at the château or helping out with preparing for the party. It was the best kind of bonkers you could wish for. There were no orders but things were getting done, and you know that 'many hands' saying . . . Finally, everything was sorted and the party animals from the group carried on the pre-party till the early hours of the morning!

The beauty of our guest list was that everyone was friends or family, which meant there was no standing on ceremony. Everyone just jumped in and helped. At one stage, there were about fifteen people working in the family kitchen, all preparing vegetables, chatting, joking and having a drink. James and Glynn were sending out plates of food to keep everyone happy. The ages ranged from three to sixty-three and it reminded me of our wedding, during our first year at the château, when my mum and sisters were supposedly sous chefs of Alan, our chef friend. He never stood a chance as Strawbridge ladies are not known for taking orders, but there were lots of laughs and the food was yummy.

Sadly, my mum had been unwell and hadn't fully recovered yet, so simply wasn't up to travelling to France. My sisters were back in Northern Ireland looking after her but we knew they were with us in spirit. I made sure to phone on several occasions so they knew what was going on and I also called to get cooking advice from Mum . . .

The next morning, I woke up at 4am and slipped into our crystal marquee. It was an exceptionally cold weekend but I needed a couple of hours by myself to finish dressing the tables and ensuring all the final details were perfect. My brother came to see me first; we had a hug and he left. Next was Jon. We had a hug and he left, and so it went on. It was like a big family get-together. This was the biggest Christmas dinner we will probably ever host or go to in our lives. I was feeling nostalgic and my emotions were raw. I kept welling up! But these were happy tears and, as I finished the last little bits and placed the last stocking down, I felt really excited for the party.

When the coach arrived, it was one of the many moments we will never forget during this celebration. Everyone who had been on our journey was there. Family, friends old and new, work colleagues who had become friends. Many we had not seen in a long time and they were in awe of how far the château had come. Maybe they knew it, maybe not, but all of their love and belief in us was what had kept us going throughout our journey, and so this party was our thank you to them.

We had decided that we would use the eagerness of everyone wanting to help to our advantage. Our team looked after drinks and canapés on arrival, but once we were seated there were two aprons per table and the wearers of the aprons were the workers for that course. Then the aprons were to be passed around, so course by course there were always two people per table providing service. It sounded so easy until it started, then we realised our family and friends were all anarchists at heart, and soon there was chaos in the kitchen and in the marquee. But it was organised chaos, so everyone loved being involved. We did not know it at the time but by doing this, not only did it allow our team to be guests, it actually resembled a real Christmas dinner, just on a larger scale!

Our meal was:

Sparkling red and white wines from the Loire with oysters and canapés to start

Local baked cheese with cranberries and fresh baguettes

Prawn cocktails done three ways served in vintage teacups

Beef fillet and capons cooked in our roaster served with seasonal vegetables and roast potatoes, bread sauce and gravy

Christmas pudding with flaming brandy and white sauce (and cream for the uninitiated)

One of my calls to my mum was with James and Arthur so we could get the recipe for the white sauce that we were to make to have with the Christmas puddings – this goes back to the war and has been a family favourite in our house since I was a child.

WHITE SAUCE FOR CHRISTMAS PUDDING

Ingredients

50g margarine – definitely not butter
50g plain flour
300ml milk
2 tbs sugar

Method

Lightly cook the margarine and flour together then add the milk. Keep stirring and when it starts to thicken, stir in two tablespoons of sugar. It's not supposed to be too sweet as it goes with a rich and sweet Christmas pudding. It is so simple but perfect with Christmas pudding.

Glynn was amazing in the kitchen and the service couldn't really have gone smoother. Angela and I debated whether or not it was safe for our guests to carve their own capons and beef at the table, but I won the argument with the simple logic that on each table there was bound to be someone half competent and half sober!

By the time the Christmas pudding was served I was, however, having second thoughts about people carrying flaming puddings around the marquee. I surreptitiously moved a fire blanket into the entrance of the tent and took up station there. I only poured the flaming brandy on the puddings when they were in the marquee and I had assessed my servers and could see they had a reasonable chance of making it to their table from there!

When the meal ended, Dick, Arthur, Dorothy and I stood up and thanked everyone for coming on our journey. As we concluded, Dick gave the signal and across the moat, our fireworks display erupted into life and the château was lit up with starbursts of different colours. Every guest was staring up and we slipped outside together to look out across the water and experience this moment as just the four of us. Our hearts simply melted as our big boy was in floods of tears saying it was the best day of his life. Being surrounded by so many people that you love is a wonderful experience and as a family we could not have been happier. We had done this as a team.

The château was magnificently illuminated by the explosions of the fireworks ahead of us. Then, as we looked back to the marquee, all we could see were our loved ones smiling, and so we rejoined them for the party of a lifetime and danced the night away.

* * *

Saying goodbye to everyone was hard but to say 'goodbye' you had to say 'hello' and be together. We were so thankful to have shared those couple of days with so many people who mean so much to us. Some barely knew each other when they arrived but by the end of the party, connections had been made and everyone understood how much they meant to us.

Within a couple of days, we were completely tidy and everything was where it should be again. We'd had a very busy year. Our business had been restarted, we had concluded *Escape to the Château* and our home had never been more comfortable. Christmas was a time to relax and enjoy being together as a family. *Père Noël* spoiled us all. We walked our boundaries on Christmas day between breakfast and lunch and then we spent New Year's Eve looking through our year in the photographs we had taken. Life at the château had a rhythm and we were comfortable with

our home and our life. We headed into 2023 rested and looking forward with excitement.

I love Christmas and I have particularly loved every Christmas at the château. It is so magical with the children and withdrawing from the rest of our manic world for family time, being busy just doing nothing. We still have a routine, as every day we go out with Petale first thing in the morning and last thing at night, plus chickens and geese have to be let out and locked away, ice has to be broken on the animals' water, they have to be fed, compost to the worms, eggs collected . . . It's lots of simple but necessary little tasks. Over Christmas, we sometimes do our early morning chores in our jimjams or in our slippers with a big coat on. It is the same but different. A bit more relaxed. No school to go to, no deadlines. And to top it all off, we chill out in the salon with the log fire lit and surrounded by 'set-ups' of the children's presents, as they are allowed to live there for days after they have been opened . . . it is Christmas after all.

A New Era

My dad was always full of quotes and words of wisdom, and lots of them have stuck with me. He often quoted Omar Khayyám, a polymath who lived in Persia in the second half of eleventh and first half of the twelfth century, and these words still ring very true:

> *The Moving Finger writes; and, having writ,*
> *Moves on: nor all thy Piety nor Wit*
> *Shall lure it back to cancel half a Line,*
> *Nor all thy Tears wash out a Word of it.*

We find ourselves blessed and where we are now because of all the decisions we have made in the past. Now we must look forward. Angela and I are very lucky people, we know that. We found each other and realised we were meant to be together. As we sit in our home, with the children playing outside the window, we are very aware that time continues to march on and that we have to savour every moment. It is just so lovely spending family time together, and Arthur and Dorothy have always been our motivation to find the balance and the ideal lifestyle and way of life. What is really important is to look forward and to know that anything is possible ... Angela and I were born decades and continents apart, but we are living with our bright and beautiful children in a château in France. If that doesn't tell you that anything is possible, I'm not sure what will.

Having a new life canvas to draw on is exciting. Change may be scary but when embraced it's full of endless possibilities. This year was already written in the stars to be busy. As a multi-generational family, we travelled to Australia and had an adventure that we will cherish forever. Dorothy is now looking into her future where she will have a kangaroo sanctuary in the garden. We can only dream that both our children will find their 'thing' that gives them happiness and, more than ever before, we feel that we have given them the best start in life we could.

On arrival home, we slipped straight into wedding preparation. Last year had made a huge difference, but the floors needed their annual sand and varnish, walls needed to be repainted and the entire château spring cleaned. It's still hard to believe that this year's weddings were all booked pre-Covid. With every wedding, we still pinch ourselves that we have the best job in the world. And for the first time ever, since the completion of my *atelier du mariage*, we have an entire working system in place to host events.

Our team is loving it and going from strength to strength. It's not just us who are evolving – our château family is. Builder mate Steve has gone down to three days a week; Quentin is in the process of buying a farm and Sacha now has a tiny bit of time on her hands to find all the things she has hidden in the past! But not too much because while we have slowed down on our project work and we have nothing urgent that needs to be done, Dick is still keeping busy, and so are Steve and Rob.

We have just reclaimed the pigsty that was a complete ruin. Last year, it had substantial trees growing in it, there was no roof and sadly not all the walls were there. However, as I write this, I've just moved all my art equipment in there and, as it's got large garage size doors (as well as five other smaller ones!) Bordeaux Rose, our 60-year-old Renault car, has moved in there with her tools and spares. I don't have to justify why I have a car in my studio, but she does look like an art installation and we get pleasure from her.

We're waiting for the final clearance so work can commence on our swimming pool in the walled garden. Roofer Steve and Render Rob are due back soon to work on the roofing on the outbuildings that was removed just before we signed for the château. The walled garden is evolving and this year will undoubtedly be our most prolific in terms of fruit and vegetables. And after two years of nudging it along, we finally have a new three-phase power supply in the outbuildings, so we have enough power to finally start our secret projects . . .

And on our 'to do' list is:

- Biomass heating system
- Solar thermal on the château and the coach house
- Solar Photo Voltaic on the coach house roof

Oh, and let's not forget we want to have time to chill out in the *jardin d'hiver*, the *observatoire du château*, the *cuisine d'été* and to take a moment or two for Angela and I to just sit on the warm steps in front of the château after a sunny day when the children are in bed and have a drink and smile together . . .

Dick and I had tears in our eyes as we chatted about where we were and where we are going, and yet again I wanted time to stand still so we could bottle the lovely feelings and savour the life we are living. Though I know time can never stop and I have actually come to understand that I don't really want it to. The children are growing and becoming more wonderful. We continue to find more challenges and as life changes, it somehow keeps getting better and better.

Our family is still a story that is mostly unwritten, but what we have managed to do is find ourselves a forever home . . .

Acknowledgements

Thank you

For the love and support you have given to our family over the years. We may not have met you, you may have sent a letter, a gift, or an e-mail of kindness and support. We may have seen you in the street and exchanged a little chat, even a hug. We read every piece of correspondence and, when life allows, take pride in replying. We see it as part of our history and one day, when Arthur & Dorothy are a little older, we will show them all the lovely words of support. This year especially, your support has meant even more to us. Thank you.

Our Family:

Our Mums, the two Jennys, and the reason that we are who we are. You are completely biased, loving, and have lived every step with us. Thank you.

Our Dads – Papi Steve, for being the biggest kid, and best granddad . . . never grow up. George, who has always been present, looking down, shaking his head and smiling.

James & Charlotte – for being part of our 'modern family', for helping out, and for the gorgeous photos.

Siblings, dear friends and family – you cheered us on from the start while we worked at creating the life we dreamt of, and your continued love and support kept us going – you are the people that have been with us throughout. When the Chinese whispers started, we said to you 'let it go . . . lovers will love, haters will not be converted, but you guys know the truth.' We love you!

The people that look after us:

Orion books – Vicky, it's been a complete pleasure working with you on *Forever Home*. Your hard work, kindness and complete attention to detail is remarkable. It is so lovely that your team at Orion completely 'get us'. Thank you.

Team Chateau – Tina, Steve & Denise, Sacha, Rob, Ellie and Alisha, Quentin, Meredith & Imogen, Jane, Chermaine, Lydia & Craig, Steve P, Beatrice & Wilhem. We have grown the perfect team – Thank you for your hard work and happy spirit. We love you all very much.

www.TheChateau.tv – Once upon a time a gentleman called Paul and his amazing wife Emma came to an event at The Chateau. We formed a partnership that is still thriving years later through hard work, care and dedication. We are quite a team now! Thank you to Ella for looking after us all and thank you to everyone for continuing to make the ideas and dreams we had right back at the start of our journey come true. Thank you for being honest, lots of fun, generous, kind and hard working.

Escape to the Chateau on the ground TV crew – Sean, Miles, Tom, Jonathan, Ash and Chloe – For the love and laughs we have shared and for always being there for the family. Thank You.

ACKNOWLEDGEMENTS

Bella – Thank you for being with us from the start and caring so much. It's been some year and we cannot imagine anyone else looking after us with so much love, and somehow on the side you manage to continually fill our press folder with lovely articles that capture moments in history for Arthur & Dorothy.

Sam Steer – The friend and artist who has brought so many visions to life, our work and friendship goes from strength to strength. Sophie and Lyra – thank you for sharing!

Ian Wallace & Lou – For capturing moments so wonderfully and being so much fun to work with!

Alex Fane – For being great at what you do, for opening up Australia & America for us, and our family, and just being there for us. You and your team are epic.

Will at Kontour Productions – Thank you for making us feel safe in your hands on so many levels!

Mega Mikki – Looking forward to you being the gate-keeper at The Chateau's Kangaroo sanctuary in years to come. It's in writing now!

Ian Holmes – Thank you for your beautiful images of Eloise & Matt.

The Soho Agency:

Sophie – Our TV mum and the reason we are together; what a year! We don't need to say much more – 2023 will not be forgotten.

Cliff – It probably would not be legal to write what we would sometimes like to write, thank you looking after us.

Julian – Thank you for being by our side through this process – your calmness and wonderful knowledge of our industry is always so soothing – you have been amazing.

Megan – You are Mega!